Lincoln in Marble and Bronze

Lincoln *in Marble and Bronze*

BY F. LAURISTON BULLARD

A Publication of

THE ABRAHAM LINCOLN ASSOCIATION

Springfield, Illinois

Rutgers University Press

New Brunswick, New Jersey

MANUFACTURED IN THE UNITED STATES OF AMERICA

THIS BOOK IS DEDICATED
WITH MANY FOND MEMORIES
TO THE LINCOLN GROUP
OF BOSTON

Contents

List of Illustrations

Lincoln in Marble and Bronze

"A Portrait of Lincoln is a challenge to any Sculptor."

—GAETANO CECERE

INTRODUCTION *Lincoln as a*
Sculptor's Problem

A FEW days after the dedication of the Lincoln Memorial in Washington in 1922 there appeared in an American magazine an essay by a professional writer on art topics, in which he said: "There are sculptors of the very highest rank who have declared it to be their opinion that in spite of the greatness of the subject, in spite of the nobility of his achievements, in spite of the inspiration to be awakened by the contemplation of his extraordinary life, Abraham Lincoln is not a proper theme for sculptural treatment." The writer named John Quincy Adams Ward as an eminent sculptor who several times had refused to consider valuable commissions for a Lincoln statue because he could not think of him as a theme for the glyptic art; and, he continued, "There are several others among living sculptors who have concurred in Ward's judgment." With these opinions the writer apparently did not himself agree. He felt that the inherent difficulties in the making of a sculptured Lincoln explained the views he mentioned; he dwelt upon "the unique problem" of "representing Lincoln's lank, awkward figure in such a way as to give it the dignity and beauty demanded of a monumental work of art."

With the debate as to the relative merits and the contrasting domains of realism and idealism in art, of the uses of truth and fancy in the delineation of life, this volume has little to do, but we may point out in passing that the difficulties which the worker in plastic art must overcome in making a statue of Abraham Lincoln have not prevented scores of sculptors, not all of them with commissions in hand, from undertaking the task. A few have succeeded magnificently in the creation of their "Lincolns," many have produced statues which may be graded upwards from "good" to "excellent," and many others have not done so well.

This volume contains only accounts of Lincoln statues of heroic size. Nearly all of these are of marble or bronze. The sculptors have had to deal with a figure of unusual dimensions which in his lifetime was often derided as uncouth, and with a face that has been described both

1

as monstrously ugly and as actually beautiful. The makers of the portrait busts of Lincoln almost without exception have talked or written about the difficulties they encountered in their work.

Lincoln's was in fact one of the most plastic of human faces. Schuyler Colfax, writing in 1866, referred to his "flexible face, reflecting on its surface the deep feelings that so often struggled within him." William Howard Russell's portrayal, written in 1861, is relatively familiar — the "strange, quaint face and head," the "great thatch of wild republican hair," the "prodigious mouth," the "flapping ears." The long passage is the report of a keen observer and an able writer who deserved his wide fame, but one is justified in the conclusion that it was composed without any careful regard for accuracy. Every item in the inventory is exaggerated. The opinions, almost unknown, of two observers who were reared in homes of affluence and culture in and about Boston well illustrate the divergences of judgment which are found throughout the comments of the men and women who came into more or less intimate contact with Lincoln during the years of his Presidency. Colonel Theodore Lyman, in a letter written in 1865, told his wife that Lincoln "is, I think, the ugliest man I ever put my eyes on. There is also an expression of plebeian vulgarity in his face. . . . On the other hand, he has the look of sense and wonderful shrewdness, while the heavy eyelids give him a mark almost of genius." And Robert Gould Shaw wrote in 1861 of seeing the President at a desk "literally covered with papers," and engrossed with his work, and that he had "seldom seen a pleasanter or more kindhearted looking" man, and how "very striking" was his face.

Many women, not under obligations to the President for kindly favors or deeds of mercy, saw much to admire in the man's looks. Princess Felix Salm-Salm, writing in 1877, recalled that "people said that his face was ugly," and that "he certainly had neither the figure nor features of the Apollo of Belvedere; but he never appeared ugly to me, for his face, beaming with boundless kindness and benevolence . . . had the stamp of intellectual beauty." Mrs. M. E. W. Sherwood, sophisticated society woman, saw Lincoln as a member of Congress in 1848 and again in the war years, and recorded the opinion that he was "a great original, and distinct form, a grotesque figure perhaps, but lighted up with a pair of wonderful eyes. . . . His smile and voice were beautiful, and his eyes superb. There his beauty ended, but the magnetic result of genius remained."

2

Many have noted the facility with which Lincoln passed from grave to gay, and how easily he lapsed again into an expression of meditative melancholy. His response to humor and his reaction to pathos were equally instant. It has been justly said that no plainer man, "of barer surroundings and more unpromising outlook," ever arrived at greatness. Truman H. Bartlett, eminent in sculpture, in his remarkable essay on the portraits of Lincoln, lingered on his wonderful eyes, his swift changes of expression, the "vertical elasticity" of his body. The difficulty with which painters, photographers, and sculptors had to contend was that they could not catch him when his face did not wear the somber look which Mrs. Lincoln once alluded to as his expression when he was having a picture taken. There are more than a few today who consider the picture of Lincoln in the group painted by G. P. A. Healy in 1865 to be in important respects the best portrait ever made of him. Robert T. Lincoln is said to have preferred it to all others. The artist shows the President, in the cabin of the *River Queen* at City Point, listening intently to General Sherman's account of his campaigns in the South, with General Grant and Admiral Porter looking on. Lincoln leans forward, elbow on knee, his face lighted, the eyes shining.

No sculptor has studied the written records and the photographs and other portraits more intensively than Gutzon Borglum, and he more than once recorded his conclusions. "I do not believe," he said more than forty years ago, "that there ever was a grotesque Lincoln. . . . No; he was not an awkward man. . . . You will find written in his face literally all the complexity of his great nature."

The mobility of that face must have been something to wonder at. It would be easy for any respectable artist to make a recognizable likeness on canvas or in marble, and we have many such portraits; the trouble is to depict the man in his entirety. There is perhaps only one smiling "Lincoln" among the painted portraits, the work of Alban Jasper Conant, in 1860. He said in after years that Lincoln's features were "most puzzling," and that there never was a countenance so flexible, nor capable of such changes of expression. Thomas D. Jones, a Cincinnati sculptor, went to Springfield in December, 1860, and made a bust of Lincoln. He saw him in various moods, once at least when his face was "illuminated," and then, a fortnight before he left for Washington, that face was "transformed from mobility into an iron mask."

In an elaborate magazine article, written in 1891, John G. Nicolay dealt at length with Lincoln's personal appearance. He said: "There are many pictures of Lincoln; there is no portrait of him." He duly recorded the details — the coarse hair, the large nose, ears and mouth, the heavy eyebrows, the high cheekbones and thin cheeks. As to his figure: the arms were long, the chest thin and narrow as compared to his great height, the legs of more than proportionate length, the feet large. But the former private secretary deemed those long limbs and large and strong features to be "fitted to his unusual stature and harmonized perfectly with it." "The beholder felt that here was a strong man . . . of character and power." He had "the general western habit of an easy-going, loose-jointed manner of walking — a manner necessarily acquired by the pioneers in their forest life, where their paths over inequalities of ground, over logs and stones, made impossible the stiff, upright carriage of men on the unobstructed pavements of cities." Point by point Nicolay traced the career of Lincoln in terms of his physical makeup and of the clothing he wore. His boyhood and youth were spent among frontier people, who certainly did not dress elegantly, but let it not be inferred that they were "habitually slovenly." When Abe came back from New Orleans to Illinois "we may reasonably surmise that he wore a new suit of clothes." As a legislator at Vandalia "he saw a convocation of samples of all the good clothes and good manners in the State; but this showing could not have been too imposing." He was mingling with men "well through the transition from buckskin to blue jeans, but not yet far on the road from blue jeans to broadcloth." In the White House he gave little thought to dress, but "the world has yet to learn that General Scott, or Lord Lyons, or Bishop Simpson, or Prince Napoleon, or Archbishop Hughes, or the Comte de Paris, or Chief Justice Taney ever felt humiliated by the dress or want of dignity of President Lincoln in state ceremonial or private audience."

The earlier sculptors had to depend upon memory and photographs for their portraits, except that Lot Flannery probably had some acquaintance with the President, and that Vinnie Ream had the benefit of personal observation in the White House over a period of several months. The Volk life mask became known in 1886, and in that year more than thirty casts were made from it, some in bronze, the others in plaster. Augustus Saint-Gaudens was the first to use one of these casts; since the erection of his standing "Lincoln" in Chicago in 1887, many, perhaps nearly all, of the Lincoln sculptors have had the advan-

4

tage of the use of that famous mask. For the looks of Lincoln as a boy and a young man, artists have been compelled to rely upon a few contemporary written records and upon the notoriously fallible recollections of old men, and it was a rare man who did not enjoy sharpening the contrast between the man they had known and the martyr mourned by the world.

The first photograph of Lincoln, a daguerreotype, dates back to 1846. Between 1857 and 1865 about a hundred and twenty photographs are known to have been taken. Frederick Hill Meserve says that "he was perhaps the most photographed American of his time." In that period also, several portrait busts and painted likenesses were made. He seems always to have responded graciously to the pleas of all comers to "take" him. Abraham Lincoln understood well the uses of publicity, but he cannot be called what newspapermen contemptuously refer to as a "publicity hound." He did owe an enormous debt to such photographers as Alexander Hesler of Chicago and Samuel G. Alschuler of Urbana, Illinois, and to Mathew Brown Brady and Alexander Gardner in New York and Washington. He is said to have given credit to Brady for the aid his Cooper Institute photograph gave him as a candidate for the presidency; he made Lincoln look like an Eastern statesman. He has been portrayed by sculptors as boy and man, bearded and without a beard, as rail-splitter, orator, emancipator, standing and seated, addressing juries and rapt in meditation. Many of the images exist only in plaster, a few in wood; the great majority are in bronze, with a handful in marble, granite, and limestone. There are plaster "Lincolns" in the English High School in Boston, in the Lincoln High School in Portland, Oregon, and in many cities between. The busts of Lincoln in this country and abroad are uncountable. They may be found in Norway and Denmark, in the Lincoln Room in the Hotel Savoy and in the Royal Exchange in London, in the parish church in England's Hingham, in France, in the miniature republic of San Marino, and probably elsewhere in Europe. Such portraits, many of them the work of eminent artists, may probably be seen in every state in the Union, with the exception — unhappily — of the states below the Mason-Dixon line. Relatively small statuettes of famous "Lincolns" have been placed in hundreds of schools and public buildings; for example, there is a Saint-Gaudens standing "Lincoln" in the Harvard University Library, and one was given to the Irish Free State in 1937 by Cyril McCormack in the name of his father, the celebrated tenor. The churches have their "Lincolns." A bronze "Lincoln" kneels in prayer in the Episcopal Cathedral in Washington, and a statuette of the President, standing with the Emancipation Proclamation in his hand, is in the Cathedral of St. John the Divine in New York City. There are Lincoln windows in the Foundry Methodist Church in Washington, in the Central Christian Church in Detroit, and elsewhere. Lincoln boulders have been set apart, with tablets or other markers, across the country from Nyack, New York, to La Jolla, California. A pyramid and a bench at Council Bluffs commemorate the day in 1859 when he gazed from Point Lookout over the Missouri River valley, and still other Lincoln memorials, buildings, and rooms, with a multitude of tablets and bas-reliefs, testify to the place that Lincoln holds in the hearts of his countrymen. And as Virginia's Williamsburg has been recreated with lovely results, so has the hamlet of New Salem been reconstructed in Illinois.

What other man has been so commemorated? As one reflects upon these matters, he might fancy that nothing remains for art to do in behalf of the fame and the living influence of "the first American." We dissent. The originality of our artists is not exhausted. The historian of American sculpture, Lorado Taft, long ago recorded the conviction that in statuary one new idea per man per year was a high average, that many an artist had varied only a single theme in his whole career, and that some "respectable sculptors had never had a sculptural idea." We think the Lincoln theme is not exhausted either in literature or in art. We have had fine statues of "Lincoln the Lawyer" — when shall we have the "Lincoln," aroused to the heights of emotional intensity, standing, almanac in hand, before the jury in the "Duff" Armstrong case? We have several portrayals of "Lincoln the Orator," but we do not have as yet the Debater ablaze in his duel with Douglas, a statue to match the "Douglas" in the State House grounds in Springfield, that "Douglas" which none who see it can forget, so virile, so "alive," it looks. Mr. Fred M. Torrey has in the Lincoln Tomb in Springfield a small equestrian "Lincoln Riding the Circuit": why should we not have that, or some similar work, in life size, somewhere out on the open prairies? Lincoln was under fire at Fort Stevens in 1864; why not a group, with Lincoln looming high above the parapet peering toward Early's lines, while a future Justice of the Supreme Court of the United States orders him down? We have no recumbent Lincoln, but in 1917 such a "Lincoln," with a winged

"Fame" and a mourning "America," designed by F. Wellington Ruckstuhl, assisted by Anthony de Francisci, was exhibited in New York. It was destroyed by fire, we have been informed, and, unfortunately, Mr. Ruckstuhl was leading the opposition to George Grey Barnard's "atrocity," as he called it. Is not a rendering in marble of the attractive picture of Lincoln and "Tad" looking over an album together in Brady's studio worthy of the sculptor's art? Such a work, small in size, was done several years ago by Miss Ella Buchanan of Los Angeles.

While any extended discussion of the origin and development of American sculpture falls outside the scope of this work, there are a few matters that do not take us far afield. In one of the *Roundabout Papers,* Thackeray recalled an incident of one of his American lecture tours. "Opposite that famous old White House in Washington, whereof I ever shall have a grateful memory," he said, "they have set up an equestrian statue of General Jackson, by a self-taught American artist of no inconsiderable genius and skill." It happened that a member of Congress interrogated him about that work. "Was it not the finest statue in the world?" The novelist "was bound to reply" in the negative. " 'But you must remember,' the Congressman insisted, 'that Mr. Mills had never seen a statue when he made this.' " And the Englishman, who had written much about art and himself was no mean artist, "suggested that to see other statues might do Mr. Mills no harm." He met Mills subsequently, and found him "modest regarding his merits" and perfectly "willing to own his defects."

Clark Mills belongs in our story, for he made a life mask of the bearded Lincoln in February, 1865. It is often alluded to as a death mask. Mr. Meserve considers it "a poor representation." Mills nevertheless was a pioneer of distinction. He devised a new and cheaper method of making casts of living faces, and invented a system of his own for making busts. In spite of all the jests about his "Jackson," it ought not to be forgotten that he spent several years amid heartbreaking difficulties in its making, and actually planned and built a foundry in which to cast the statue. The statue of "Freedom" which surmounts the dome of the Capitol in Washington was cast by Mills in his foundry "at Mills Avenue toward Bladensburg." The statue was modeled in Rome by Thomas Crawford, who at the time of his death in 1857 was looking about for funds for its casting at the Royal Foundry in Munich. The plaster model was safely delivered in Washington, and Mills did the rest, so that the bronze figure was hoisted into place in December, 1863.

American sculpture has been traced back to the early work of those clever and self-reliant chiselers known as "the Yankee stone-cutters." Those who intended to adopt the art as a profession invariably hurried to Italy, and several of them settled for life in Florence or Rome. Naturally they tended to adopt the Canova tradition. The United States in those days could not provide competent art teaching nor examples of good sculpture. Italy had the Carrara marble. The right kind of sand for casting in bronze was not to be found in the States, it was believed, and anyhow the secret casting processes of the famous Munich foundry were carefully guarded. Crawford's equestrian "Washington" for Richmond, Virginia, was cast at the Royal Foundry, as was Thomas Ball's "Emancipation" group. Before the Civil War, however, the Ames Manufacturing Company, at Chicopee, Massachusetts, had in successful operation a bronze statuary foundry. There the equestrian "Washington" for the Boston Public Garden, the Concord "Minute Man" by Daniel Chester French, and the statue and the groups for the Lincoln Tomb in Springfield were cast. A claim is entered also for Robert Wood's establishment in Philadelphia, where in an early day statues were cast for many of our sculptors. Priority, however, belongs to Mills, whose "Jackson" was dedicated in 1853.

In this volume eighty-seven statues are considered. Of these, sixty-seven are originals and twenty replicas. They are the creations of fifty-six sculptors. The Mezzara and Ellicott statues no longer exist, but the reasons for their inclusion seem obvious and convincing. Various admirable "Lincolns" may be missed, and this is a matter of regret, but these omissions are clearly justified as they are not within the scope of our theme. We admit our deviation from the strict limits of our title, for while seventy-five of these statues are bronze only five are marble, while we deal with two of granite, two of limestone, and two of plaster. Our plea is that we wanted a simple, descriptive title for a book intended to be comprehensive. Of the total number, eighty-two are in the States of the Union, one in San Juan, Puerto Rico, and one in the Territory of Hawaii; there are replicas of two of our most celebrated "Lincolns" in England, and Scotland has an original.

Illinois very properly leads all the states in the number of these memorials within her bounds — fifteen in all. New York has eight, and Wisconsin seven, "Lincolns." Ohio has five and the District of

Columbia has five. Six states — California, Indiana, Iowa, Michigan, New Jersey, and Pennsylvania — follow, each with four. There are three in Nebraska and three in Kentucky, two in Massachusetts and two on the other coast in Washington, and there are seven states each with a single "Lincoln" — Idaho, Kansas, Maryland, Minnesota, Missouri, New Hampshire, Oregon, and Vermont.

The first of these statues was set up in 1866. From that year through 1899, fourteen "Lincolns" were erected. During the years 1900–1949, both inclusive, five times as many have been erected. The average is close to one a year for the entire period. Such computations might be extended. They induce questions for which satisfactory answers are not easy to find.

The sectional distribution of these tributes invites speculation. There are only four Lincoln statues in all New England; the border state of Kentucky alone has three. While Lincoln's home state of Illinois boasts of fifteen "Lincolns," the other four states which were carved out of the Northwest Territory — Ohio, Indiana, Michigan, and Wisconsin — have twenty in all. Many of our Lincoln statues were given by individuals or by families; the Grand Army of the Republic led campaigns for Lincoln memorials in many instances, and local pride has often been invoked for the marking of localities with Lincoln associations in this conspicuous manner. Probably it is true that the spirit of the populations of states, cities, and smaller communities is reflected in the financing of most of these monuments. School children and wealthy citizens have shared in their cost. Large areas have been stirred by crusades in behalf of "our Lincoln memorial." Seldom has such a campaign finally failed; interest has occasionally ebbed for a few years, but success at length has been achieved. All these facts provide an overwhelming demonstration of the magnitude of Lincoln's fame — that towering figure, the face recognized at a glance around the globe; millions who know little or no English have vague ideas of what Lincoln stands for in history and of how his career affects their own lives.

The plan of this book is simple enough, but the collection of the material for its writing has been anything but a simple task. The labor, however, has been abundantly enjoyable. For nearly every statue we record the origin of the movement for its erection, some account of the life and work of the sculptor, and the ceremonies of its dedication. In a surprising number of instances the dedication addresses have proved to be of high merit, and most of these are quite unknown. Many, not all, of these statues the writer has seen, including those which are most admired. In a few cases fundamental facts have not been accessible. Satisfactory photographs sometimes have eluded the skill of the photographer, owing to the height of the pedestals or to the shadowing foliage of the shrubbery and trees about them.

We have two concluding observations to offer. If a Lincoln memorial is unveiled before an admiring throng, and dedicated with eulogies of the man and of the artist, it surely deserves better care over the years than some of these monuments have received. A few have been disfigured by the wear of weather and climate, and a few — but only a few — have been mutilated by vandals. Far the greater number, however, have had the watchful care of local Lincolnians, and these lovers of Lincoln number many thousands today, while the influence of Lincoln tourists is also a protective factor.

We have often felt in our contemplation of these statues that they are shining examples of what a memorial ought to be. Nobody can readily miss the meaning of a Lincoln statue, whether it be a masterpiece or a run-of-the-mine product of the studio. The Lincoln story is one for art in all its forms to perpetuate. To label an auditorium with his name, or to dedicate a park or a playground to his memory, with a tablet or a marker somewhere to tell its origin, or to seize in any other manner upon the opportunity to use his name in order to provide a community with a betterment long wished for, is not a very lofty expression of gratitude for a martyred President, nor for any group of veterans who fought in the War for the Union or in any other of our wars. A real memorial ought to symbolize in an inescapable way the sentiment inspiring its erection. It should dramatize an emotion, an idea, an aspiration. A member of the Art Commission of the City of New York stated the matter on a day in 1946 with unerring exactitude. For many years he had guarded worthy art and resisted commercialization of memorials, new and old, for which the city had accepted ownership and responsibility. And he said: "A stadium, dedicated today as 'a living memorial,' is no longer a memorial tomorrow — just a stadium."

With great pleasure we acknowledge the courtesy and generosity with which our requests for aid in obtaining suitable photographs have been honored by friends and strangers, artists and sculptors, city and town officials, donors, and others who have sent information as to probable sources of supply. The sculptors themselves have sent large numbers of pictures to the author over a period of about forty-five years, some to illustrate their ideas and others as their choice for publication. Special mention must be made of Mrs. William Penn Creswell, daughter of Daniel Chester French; Dr. Louis A. Warren, of Fort Wayne, Indiana; and of Dr. Roy P. Basler and Dr. Benjamin P. Thomas, of Springfield, Illinois. Dr. Lorado Taft more than once went out of his way to aid me by direct correspondence and through his assistants.

In the writing of this volume the standard works of reference have constantly been used, among them the *Dictionary of American Biography; Who's Who; Who's Who in Art;* Charles H. Caffin, *American Masters of Sculpture;* Lorado Taft, *History of American Sculpture;* the *Encyclopedias,* both General and Annual; the newspapers of many cities, and the numerous art magazines.

For this chapter, the following have also been used: Thomas F. Madigan, *Catalogue of Lincolniana,* 1929; William Howard Russell, *My Diary North and South,* 1863; Col. Theodore Lyman, *Meade's Headquarters,* 1922; M. E. W. Sherwood, *An Epistle to Posterity,* 1897; Princess Felix Salm-Salm, *Ten Years of My Life,* 1877; *McClure's Magazine,* March, 1909; *Century Magazine,* October, 1891.

I   ILLUSTRATED PAGE 143

How the City of the Golden Gate Led the World

DURING the decade that was overshadowed by the War for the Union, San Francisco, with a population of eighty thousand, was the most cosmopolitan and the most isolated community of similar size in the United States. The "magnetic telegraph" was a new utility. There was no transcontinental railroad. To reach the Atlantic seaboard, travelers must make the long voyage around the Horn, or go down the coast by steamship and cross the Isthmus of Panama, or cross the mountains and the plains by the Overland Mail. The population of California was a vast conglomerate. The city of the Golden

Gate, with every state in the Union and half the countries of the world represented in the throngs that milled about the streets, was anything but a provincial metropolis. Solid citizens and flighty adventurers, statesmen and demagogues, realists and dreamers, the cultured and the ignorant, bankers and merchants who looked forward to a splendid future once the state should be established on a firm foundation of intelligence as well as energy, and shoddy speculators of limited vision who lived for the present alone, were so interwoven as to baffle the shrewdest observers in their study of the issues that had to be decided in 1860.

The state contained a large and influential body of men of Southern derivation, who actively sought to promote the secession movement, either by taking California into the Confederacy or by the establishment of an independent Pacific Republic. San Francisco was the center of the Union group. Thomas Starr King, the famous Unitarian minister who had left Boston to promote a new church on the other coast, toured the state as an apostle for the Union cause. Abraham Lincoln's long-time friend, Edward D. Baker, known in the West as "the Gray Eagle," thrilled great mass meetings by his eloquence. In the elections of that year the Union ticket carried the city and the state, although the pluralities were disturbingly small.

The firing on Fort Sumter ended the uncertainties. San Francisco thereafter was overwhelmingly loyal. Volunteers held the state for the Union. In the various branches of the Northern armies fifteen thousand men from California were enrolled. With the ending of the war, Dr. Henry W. Bellows, the head of the Sanitary Commission, which served as the Red Cross of that period, certified by telegram his gratitude for what San Francisco had done, hailing the city as "noble, tender, faithful, city of the heart, commercial and moral capital of the most humane and generous State in the world." Of the five millions of dollars in cash received by the treasury of the Commission, more than one-fourth came from California.

No city in the United States more deeply mourned the passing of Abraham Lincoln. The first statue in honor of the martyred President was erected there.

All that we have been able to ascertain about the man who made that statue may be recorded in a single brief paragraph. When and why Pietro Mezzara came to San Francisco we do not know. The name has an Italian cast. Several local newspapers describe him as "the well-known sculptor who for many years resided in San Francisco," and the prints agree that he maintained a studio in Pioneer Hall on Montgomery Street. From various sources we glean the titles of a few of his works. He designed the statuary for the state capitol at Sacramento. His was the statue symbolizing "Charity" for the Masonic Temple, and his "Romulus and Remus" was placed on the façade of the Mechanics' Building. In 1859 he made a bust of David C. Broderick, the senator whom David S. Terry mortally wounded in the long-remembered duel. A bust of Francis Scott Key, made in 1875, is attributed to Mezzara, and in the following year a bust of Aaron A. Sargent, congressman and senator. The rest is silence, except for the story of the Lincoln statue and the announcement of the sculptor's death, the date of his passing being variously given as September 5 and September 30, 1883. Late in October of that year the papers carried a notice of three or four lines, stating that "Pietro Mezzara, formerly of this city, [had] died in Paris, France, after a long and painful illness, at the age of sixty."

Additional information about this man would be most welcome. Sculptors probably were few in that region at that time. Judging by his "Lincoln," he cannot be ranked as an artist of more than mediocre gifts. He doubtless conceived the idea for the statue in the hushed days of grief that followed the arrival of the awful tidings from Washington. Within three months of the President's death his model was ready for exhibition. It was shown that autumn at the Mechanics' Fair, occupying the place of honor "in the centre of the Pavilion in Union Square." The statue was acquired by a group of citizens headed by William Chapman Ralston, president of the Bank of California, and placed upon a pedestal in front of the new grammar school building which had been named for Abraham Lincoln, and there it was dedicated on Saturday, April 14, 1866, the anniversary, lacking one day, of the President's death.

Few schools, private or public, have been more loved by their "old boys" than Lincoln Grammar School. David Belasco was one of those "boys" who, some forty years later, helped to organize the Lincoln Grammar School Association, still a going concern, with a membership which includes many men known far beyond the boundaries of California. It has many good works to its credit. The movement which procured the bronze "Lincoln" by Haig Patigian, now standing before San Francisco's City Hall, was substantially aided by this Association. The school building was not yet finished on the day of Lincoln's assassination. When it was opened, on June 29 of that year, the papers described it as "the only elegant building yet erected by the municipal authorities." It stood at the corner of Market and Fifth streets, a big four-story structure, costing $90,000.

In a commanding position before this building the Mezzara statue was placed, atop a pedestal of unusual height. The schoolboys themselves did the unveiling. One of them, George W. R. King, had returned in May, 1865, from a visit in the East, and when the school began to function in July he entered as a member of the "third class." As the day for the dedication of the statue drew near, King told Professor Ira G. Hoitt, the principal of the school, that on April 11, 1865, "as we were leaving Washington for New York," he had had the honor of "shaking hands with Mr. Lincoln." On that account Mr. Hoitt granted him the privilege "of being one of the boys to lean out of the window of his class room and pull the flag from the statue," a thing easily done, as a glance at our illustration will show. After a few years the building suffered heavy damage by fire, but the statue seems to have been unharmed.

Made of plaster, it stood in its original position until 1889, when the weathering of the fogs and rains of a quarter-century was plain to see. Instead of patching Mezzara's model, a replica was made of a white metal known as French bronze. This duplicate was set up on the original pedestal, with no change in the total effect. Not even a wrong date on the tablet was altered, although it informed the public that Abraham Lincoln was "re-elected March, 1865." This restoration was not made at public expense; an anonymous individual paid the bills. He also was probably an "old boy." For seventeen more years the statue challenged the attention of students and public from its vantage point at the main entrance of the school, to be finally destroyed in the great disaster of 1906. One vestige remains. Another "old boy," Frank H. DeGuerre, rescued the first finger of the right hand, and caused it to be fashioned into a gavel for the Association. It was so used at their annual reunions until the Association provided it with a permanent place for security and inspection in the Golden Gate Museum.

It is the story of this statue — the first such memorial of the Civil War President ever to be erected anywhere in the world — and not its merit as an artistic achievement that interests us. One recognizes Lincoln at a glance, which is something that cannot by any means be said of all our "Lincolns." He wears a dress coat of the sort that used to be called a "spike," with a high vest. His extended left hand holds a document. The right arm hangs at full length downward, the fingers of the hand outspread. Although photographs do not make the figure clear, we understand from an address to the Association by Lucius L. Solomons on Lincoln's birthday in 1936 that "the hand rested upon the curly head of a manumitted slave boy." The scroll in the left hand intimates that this, like most of the early Lincoln statues, commemorated him as the Emancipator, with a slave boy completing the symbolization. By far the best feature of the work must have been the face. The pose is theatrical — that of a self-conscious man, which Lincoln was not — but the uplifted face is that of a man proud of a great deed.

There are two other Lincoln statues in San Francisco: one by Haig Patigian, of which more will be said later, and another so completely forgotten that diligent inquiry was necessary to obtain even an admission of its existence, although many thousands must have seen it among the commercial exhibits sent over from Italy for display in the Palace of Manufactures at the Panama-Pacific Exposition in 1915, where it appeared in a curious marble quartet, standing in juxtaposition to Semiramis of Nineveh, while our Washington stood next to Egypt's Cleopatra. The owner and editor-in-chief of the *San Francisco Chronicle,* Mr. W. H. DeYoung, the Exposition's vice-president, obtained the "Lincoln" and installed it in the Memorial Museum which he founded in Golden Gate Park. For a long time now it has been out of sight, stored in the basement, awaiting the construction of an addition to the building where it will be shown.

This "Lincoln," lacking an inch of his actual height, presents him with a handsome smooth face. The right hand, extended forward, holds a manuscript, and the left hand is thrust into the trousers pocket — the pockets being placed forward, in the old-time manner. Behind one foot is an irregular pile of books. The statue and its base are of one piece of marble, and the base has an inscription reading "A. Frilli, Firenze."

SOURCES: *Lincoln Grammar School, a Record Compiled for the Boys,* 1938; information from the California State Library, the California Historical Society, the San Francisco Public Library, and Master Robert Lauriston Bullard, San Francisco; correspondence with Dr. Milton H. Shutes, Oakland, California.

In Justice to Lot Flannery

WHAT for many years was understood to be the first public statue of Abraham Lincoln to be erected anywhere was unveiled in Washington on an April day in 1868. Long before 2 :00 P.M., the hour of the ceremony, throngs of people, undaunted by rain, began to assemble, until more than fifteen thousand had filled the space before the City Hall, with long lines stretching through the adjacent streets. The crowd filled roofs and windows of neighboring buildings, and Negroes packed the space behind the official stand. President Andrew Johnson was conspicuous on the platform, along with representatives of the diplomatic corps, several Civil War generals, and numerous local dignitaries. The most observed spectator off the platform was the man who, within a few weeks, would be nominated for the Presidency of the United States. Entitled to a place on the stand, he had insisted on taking a position on the sidewalk. Allen C. Clark, an authority on matters pertaining to the District of Columbia, wrote, tongue in cheek, that General Grant's curious preference of position on the sidewalk may not have had any reference to the President's presence on the platform; but all Washington knew of the feud between the President in office and the President-to-be. Gideon Welles recorded that General Grant early in the following year notified the committee in charge of the arrangements for the inauguration that he would not ride in the same carriage with Andrew Johnson, nor speak to him on that day. The outgoing President, we may be sure, was equally averse to any intimate contacts with his successor.

Nor was that the only curious aspect of the unveiling. Just about everybody was there on that afternoon of April 15, 1868, the third anniversary of Lincoln's death — except the Justices of the Supreme Court of the United States and the members of the Senate and the House of Representatives. All business in the Federal departments and the municipal offices had been suspended. The public schools had closed. Flags hung at half staff. The "heavy boom of half-hour guns reminded the District of the solemnity of the occasion." But while President Johnson attended the ceremonial, he was on trial for his official life on Capitol Hill, where the jury of senators was fulfilling its constitutional function in his impeachment trial.

The statue was the work of a man whose name infallibly indicates his Irish origin. Lot Flannery was born in Limerick. His given name was not "Lott," although it has been so spelled in several dignified tomes; nor did he ever serve as a Confederate soldier — a statement that may have originated in a confusion of similar names. He did spend several years in New Orleans and St. Louis, but during the opening years of the Civil War he was in Europe, and on his return to Washington he resumed the profession which he had begun to practice in that city. Moreover, he was not a stone mason, a maker of gravestones or a chiseler of epitaphs. He may not have been an artistic genius, but he was more than an ordinary artisan. The widely-spread idea that he was a hewer of stone for cemetery uses is due to his association in business with his brother. He won the right to make the Lincoln statue in open competition; a committee chose his model as the best of those submitted. He already had to his credit an ideal representation in marble of "Grief," placed in the Congressional Cemetery, and a bust of Franklin. In later years he made many portrait busts, we are told, including one of General John A. Logan, from which, with Mrs. Logan's approval, a plaster cast was used by Franklin Simmons in the creation of the equestrian statue of the General long on view in Washington. Flannery is said also to have carved a statue of Stephen A. Douglas. An additional qualification was the claim that he had personally known Lincoln, and that the President had more than once visited his studio. In a lively debate in the House of Representatives many years after the dedication of the Lincoln statue, as will appear farther on, both the merit of the statue and the ability of its maker were discussed, but on the day of the unveiling, as might have been expected, both the sculptor and the statue were "vociferously cheered."

Only a few days after the tragedy in Ford's Theatre, "on motion of Mr. N. D. Larner, of the City Councils of the District of Columbia, a joint committee was appointed to take action with reference to the erection of a monument in the City of Washington to the memory of Abraham Lincoln." Before the end of that month of April, this committee of three members from each board formed itself into a Lincoln National Monument Association, with Richard Wallach, mayor of the city, as president; Crosby S. Noyes, of the *Washington Star,* as secretary; George W. Riggs, the banker, as treasurer; and twenty-three other citizens of the District as directors. This committee, proposing to obtain a national subscription for a monument to be placed in the capital of the nation, appointed a number of honorary directors, including a member of Congress from each state. Organizations of the same character soon became so numerous all over the land, however, that the project for a nation-wide enterprise was modified. Few contributions were obtained outside the District of Columbia, of which the only unsolicited gift came from none other than John T. Ford, the owner of the theater in which the President's life had been taken. A "benefit" in his Baltimore playhouse produced eighteen hundred dollars for the fund. Almost the entire expenditure for the monument came from small contributions from permanent residents of the District and from soldiers and sailors passing through the capital or temporarily living there. These Washington people had learned to appreciate the neighborly qualities of Lincoln. They called him their President and regarded the statue as their memorial.

The arrangements for the dedicatory ceremonies seem grotesquely old-fashioned today. A procession swung into step a half hour before the exercises, when members of the No. 2 Steam Engine Company commenced firing a salute from the fieldpiece in front of the engine house. As the memorial was to be dedicated with the Masonic ritual, the Grand Lodge and members of subordinate lodges, headed by the Marine Band, took the leading position in the line. Following in order came the Sons of Temperance, preceded by the band of the Twelfth United States Infantry, the Temple of Honor, the Good Templars with "their band of seventeen pieces," and the Grand Lodge of the United States of the Knights of Pythias. Once these fraternal orders had been maneuvered into position, Mayor Wallach opened the ceremonies with prayer by Dr. William Hamilton.

The Infantry Band having "performed 'The Heart Bowed Down' from 'The Bohemian Girl,' " the Masons proceeded with the dedication ceremony of their craft. The "implements of architecture," the plumb and the level, were applied, and the builders were certified to have done their duty well. The corn, the wine, and the oil were presented to the Grand Master "as the consecrating elements," and he pronounced a series of invocations; then, with three raps of his gavel, he declared "this foundation properly prepared, well laid, true and trusty, and this statue, erected by the citizens of Washington to the memory of Abraham Lincoln, duly and fully dedicated to the American people."

The Marine Band "performed the 'Miserere' from 'Trovatore,'" and the orator of the day, Benjamin B. French, who had written the Ode for the ceremonies of dedication at Gettysburg five years before, was introduced. His oration was long, appropriate, and reasonably adequate. Early in the address he said: "Monumental marble may crumble into dust; bronze may melt away; granite may perish from the earth; but the memory of Abraham Lincoln shall live in human bosoms and be perpetuated on the living pages of history as long as any nation or people shall exist on earth."

Closing, French referred to the statue as "the plain, unassuming, but almost speaking semblance of that plain, unassuming, but noble and Godlike specimen of human nature." The orator was correct; the statue is plain, and it looks like Lincoln. And, added Mr. French: "Here the statue stands, as it were, in the plaza of the city; and here it will stand, we hope, to be seen by generations long hence to come." From his vast audience came cries: "It will! It will!"

Other bands "performed." Colonel E. B. Olmstead "recited an original poem." President Johnson "pulled the cord," and "the covering of the statue fell." In defiance of the rain umbrellas were swung aside or lowered, and all heads tilted upward. There stood Abraham Lincoln, high above the throng, atop a slender column. From the foot of this "pedestal" to the crown of the head of the statue was forty feet. The average diameter of the tapering shaft was three feet. On the moulded capital three feet square stood the base of the statue, supporting the marble figure, a little more than life-size. Lincoln's head inclined slightly forward, his left hand resting on Roman fasces emblematic of the Union, the right hand partly opened, as though he addressed an audience. The sculptor is said years afterward to have told a Baltimore newspaper reporter why he placed the figure so far above the ground. He had been in Ford's Theatre "that night," and had heard the fatal shot and seen the President's head "fallen forward." So, when he undertook to "carve and erect this statue I resolved to place it, and did place it, so high that no assassin's hand could ever again strike him down."

If the statue did not stand high upon that column "for generations long hence to come," it did stand there, honored by diminishing numbers as the postwar generation arrived, disregarded by most and derided by many, for a full half-century. In the autumn of 1919 it was taken down. An official stated that it was "stored in the basement of the Court House," which seems not to have been true; at least if it was ever stored there it stayed only a short time.

In the Civil War years Washington had a municipal government with a mayor and council. In 1871 Congress put the District under a "territorial government," with a governor, a board of public works, and a legislative assembly. During the few years that this regime lasted, Alexander R. Shepherd, commonly called "Boss" Shepherd, a native of the city, was in succession the all-important member of the board and the governor of the District. He undertook a greatly needed although grandiose system of public improvements, and in spite of the jobbery and profitable "speculations" with which he was charged and amidst which he left the District, his statue stands in Washington today, and many express gratitude for what he did in leading the way for the transformation of the city from a sprawling, hit-or-miss sort of town into a splendid world capital.

The City Hall, before which the Lincoln statue was placed, is one of the oldest buildings in the District of Columbia, its cornerstone having been laid in 1820. The open space, now known as Judiciary Square, before which it stood is at the meeting point of Louisiana and Indiana Avenues, only a short distance off Pennsylvania Avenue. The changes in street levels ordained by Shepherd left the foundations of the Lincoln monument exposed, and this condition continued for several decades. Meanwhile Congress had terminated the territorial government and in 1878 established the present system, by which the city is governed by three commissioners appointed by the President. With this change the City Hall became the home of the Supreme Court of the District of Columbia. The old building was remodeled and rededicated in 1920, its centenary year.

The Commission on Public Buildings and Grounds, in charge of the remodeling, decided that the foundation on which the Lincoln monument stood was "very insecure." A good many sophisticated persons wanted to get rid of Flannery's statue anyhow. So it came about that a deficiency appropriation bill for the fiscal year of 1920 contained an item "for the construction of walks and a service road and the restoration and planting of grounds around the Court House in Judiciary Park, including the removal of the statue, $23,445," half to be paid from District revenues and half from the Federal

Treasury. No member of Congress said "I object." The bill passed. The statue came down, and the pedestal no longer obstructed the roadway.

Then the storm burst. State legislatures denounced the disappearance of the statue as "sacrilege." Civic organizations adopted resolutions of protest. The members of the Grand Army of the Republic unanimously condemned the "outrage." The Loyal Legion, the Aztec Club, the Sons of the American Revolution, all were heard from. Howard University asked that the statue be placed on its campus. The Society of Oldest Inhabitants, which is said to have blocked earlier attempts to consign the statue to oblivion, contributed extensively to the hullabaloo. The Commission certainly had failed to give due consideration to the probable reactions of public sentiment.

But where *was* the statue? For two years nobody seemed to know. Freeman Thorpe, an artist, then nearly eighty years of age, came to town. He missed Flannery's "Lincoln." Thorpe's portrait of Schuyler Colfax hung in the House lobby, and his oil painting of Lincoln, by order of the Senate, had lately been placed in the main hall of the Senate wing of the Capitol. Thorpe had known Lincoln, and was much disturbed when nobody could explain why the statue was not in the Court House basement. Over his signature he told in 1921 how, "after a tedious search," he found the statue "down near the river, in the rear of the old Bureau of Engraving, not stored at all, but lying outdoors, roughly crated," and "covered partly by an old piece of gunnysack." Once cleared of dust and rain spots, "the face gazed kindly upon him. The resemblance to Lincoln was startling. It was accurately done by some one who studied Lincoln from life, as I did, and was not done from photographs." Mr. Thorpe continued to express his emphatic opinion that the work "is a better likeness of Lincoln than anything in plaster, stone, marble or bronze that I have seen, and I have seen about all that have been made. Some have been made that are unquestionably great works of art, but the best of them are not accurate likenesses. This one is to those who, like myself, knew Lincoln, pleasing to look at, because it is accurately modeled, and in its simple truth is in keeping with the unassuming man we loved."

Long before this letter appeared in the newspapers Congress had taken cognizance of the wide demand for the restoration of the statue. The House Library Committee reported a resolution to that purpose in January, 1920, and held hearings in April on that and two other House bills and two House joint resolutions, the earliest of which had been introduced in the preceding December. Several of the petitioners who appeared before the committee had prepared their arguments with care, dealing, from varying viewpoints, with Abraham Lincoln's personal contacts with the sites to which they sought to have the statue trans-, ferred. The four-hour session made it plain that if the statue were to be deported from the Federal District, plenty of places would gladly provide it a permanent home.

Oscar R. Luhring, who represented the Congressional district which included the Indiana farm on which Lincoln had spent his youth, would have the statue delivered to the Nancy Hanks Lincoln Burial Ground Association, owners of a tract of sixteen acres which enclosed the grave of the President's mother. He submitted a petition from seventeen hundred of the "best people" of that region. It was fitting, said he, that the statue should be set up in the county in which Lincoln's character was formed. He was "a typical Hoosier."

Henry T. Rainey argued the case for Illinois. To be sure, Lincoln had spent "a few uneventful years" in Indiana, and the gamblers who flocked to French Lick might furnish profitable patronage for the Burial Park, but for Lot Flannery's statue the best possible site was in an Illinois State Park near Petersburg and Springfield. He referred to New Salem, and told the committee that, although it might be "almost a violation of confidence," it was his tip to William Randolph Hearst, then a fellow-Congressman, which had prevented a brewing company of Springfield from obtaining an option on the abandoned village of Lincoln's early manhood with the intention of establishing a beer garden. A Chautauqua Association had been trying to raise enough money to buy that site, and Hearst had bought it and turned it over to the Association, which later transferred the title to the State of Illinois.

It was William G. Graham of Illinois who had introduced the December bill "seeking disposition of this statue." Somewhat naively he said: "I have my own community to look after and they have asked me to get this statue, and they have some claim for it." "A gentleman from Moline," in Graham's district, had called the Congressman's attention to the proposed removal. The gentleman in question was Joseph Benjamin Oakleaf, a member of that group of Lincoln collectors known as "the Big Five." In describing the neighborhood to which his Lincolnian constituent would have this marble "Lincoln" transported,

Graham dwelt on the presence of several association sites — the Arsenal at Rock Island, the Union and the Confederate cemeteries there, and the Black Hawk War trails. Representative David G. Classon, of Wisconsin, supported a resolution for the removal of the marble waif to Green Bay in his state.

An Illinois member of Congress, Edward J. King of Galesburg, fathered a resolution to "put the statue back in the exact spot from which it was taken." He said little about Lincoln, but presented a comprehensive review of the history of the statue. It had been erected by the District, and belonged to the District; the difficulties in the way of its re-erection on the old site could readily be overcome. "However," he continued, "if I was going to put it in Illinois, I would like to have it put on the east wing of Knox College, in Galesburg, where the greatest Lincoln-Douglas debate took place."

After many months of delay the question of the disposition of the statue reached the floor of the House. Meanwhile President Harding had sent the committee a letter endorsing Mr. King's resolution. That Congressman proved to be a strong champion of the claims of the Federal District. His speeches of April 5 and April 22 are entertaining reading. He had the goods and knew how to present his case. The charge that the statue "is inartistic" had "emanated from a government clerk, a mere blameless marionette, whose simple wax cylinder mind recorded and repeated the impressions made by another." The clerk had been so long "ensconced behind the pillars of pull and preferment" that he now lived in an atmosphere which transforms "the meekest bureaucrat" into a "grim image of intolerance." It was true, of course, that nobody ever claimed "that Lincoln had the legs of Adonis, the arms of Mercury, or the fat stomach of Bacchus," so "it was unnecessary to use the triangle test." Yes, it must be admitted also that in this statue Lincoln "is dressed in his customary habiliments, the conventional unpressed trousers — a pressed article at that date indicated store clothes, and no orders from London at that time having been received — the familiar Prince Albert coat open in front; vest; a high-rolled soft collar, and large black tie." There was a rumor that "some enemies of the statue would have been less violent in their campaign, and would have admitted it would have come nearer in meeting the requirements of their ornate minds, had Mr. Lincoln been dressed in one of the . . . suits of Hart, Schaffner and Marx."

The Illinoisan denied the charge that "a grave-stone maker" had carved the statue, although it was pertinent to notice that Abraham Lincoln himself had been a "wood-chopper." In fact, however, Lot Flannery had a brother named Martin. The two had been associated in business as the Flannery Brothers. Martin had made the cemetery stones; he had nothing to do with the statue. Lot had maintained a studio in Massachusetts Avenue; "he was an artist," never having any intimate connection with "the graveyard business." Mr. King told how Miss Lillian Flannery, a daughter of Martin and a niece of Lot, had come to the Capitol to see him, and had verified his statement that Lot had been a personal friend of the President, "who frequently stopped at his studio and walked and talked with him." In answer to certain objections, Robert Luce of Massachusetts, a member of the Library Committee, explained that the intention was to dispense with the tall column, and stand the statue on an appropriate pedestal on or near the original site.

Congress adopted the resolution, the vote in the House being sixty-one to three, and the statue was provided with a more suitable pedestal and brought within easy range of the vision of passers-by.

Lot Flannery, "a very old and weary man," did not live quite long enough to witness, on April 15, 1923, the rededication of his "Lincoln." He died at the age of eighty-six, on December 17, 1922.

SOURCES: *Statue of Abraham Lincoln*, Hearings before Committee on the Library, House of Representatives, 66 Cong., 2 Sess., April 2, 1920, on H.R. 11079, 11443, 11495, H.J.Res. 269, 282; Norman J. Gould, *Re-erection of the Statue of Abraham Lincoln*, 67 Cong., 1 Sess., House Report No. 98, May 25, 1921; *Diary of Gideon Wells*, III:532 passim; Allen C. Clark, *Abraham Lincoln in the National Capital*, 1925; H. P. Caemmerer, *Washington, the National Capital*, Senate Doc. 332, 71 Cong., 3 Sess., 1932; Helen Nicolay, *Our Capital on the Potomac*, 1924; among newspapers, especially the *Washington Star*, of April 15, 1868, and Dec. 17, 1922.

Henry Kirke Brown's
Two LINCOLNS

ONE hardly knows whether to grin or to grieve over a scrap of art criticism which *The New York Times* inflicted upon an innocent public on the morning of September 21, 1870. It would be interesting to know the name of the writer of the long editorial paragraph. It reads like the screed of somebody with a grouch who had eagerly grabbed an opportunity to get it out of his system. Both for its style and for its content, the article seems even at this distant day to deserve the penalty of citation. The alleged critic declared:

"A frightful object has been placed in Union Square. It is said to be a statue of a man who deserves to be held in lasting remembrance as a true patriot, a sincere, unselfish, noblehearted chief in times of great trouble and perplexity — Abraham Lincoln. But it does not resemble Mr. Lincoln. The lines which gave his face character are not there. But the sculptor has tried to atone for this defect by putting plenty of hard lines in the clothes which are enough to distract anybody who thinks that dress need not of necessity increase the hideousness of man. The mind has not conceived such a pair of pantaloons as that which the artist has placed on this statue. To increase the beauty of their effect the designer of the work has clapped a Roman toga over the upper part of the figure, thus combining the costume of the past and the present in a manner never yet dreamt of by caricaturists. There never was such a statue seen in this world before. It is like a hideous nightmare which people have after supping on roast beef and lobster salad. How much it cost to make it and put it up we do not know, but we will gladly receive subscriptions toward the expense of taking it down and sending it off to Chicago where 'works of art' of this kind are highly appreciated. In Union Square it is miserably out of place. Nurse-maids are in the habit of taking young children to this spot, and the statue of poor Mr. Lincoln will only be the embodiment of those terrible visions of 'Bogey' which affright the juvenile mind."

While that Union Square statue of President Lincoln is not a great work of art, it was the creation of an American pioneer sculptor of established reputation, who deserved more considerate treatment at the hands of a serious critic. A companion work by the same sculptor, made in the same period, which treated the same subject in almost exactly the same manner, had been unveiled in the preceding year across the river in Brooklyn, and had been hailed as "the work of an accomplished sculptor" who had "moulded the solid yet ductile metal into the very similitude of the man." Was the newspaper paragrapher hurling a boomerang at Brooklyn by way of Chicago? In both statues the pantaloons are voluminous; in both, with slight variations in detail, the toga — which really is more of a cloak — is draped over the figure; and the face is the same in both. In Union Square the same sculptor's equestrian "Washington" is accepted today as a statue of high merit. After a few days *The Times* referred again to this "Lincoln," and in temperate tones to which no exception can fairly be taken. We are disposed to think that the public had been heard from.

Henry Kirke Brown, the artist in question, was probably the only Lincoln sculptor who dealt with the Lincoln Memorial Committees of neighboring cities at the same time, and worked on their commissions in the same period. His letters show that he intended that both of his Lincoln statues should depict the President who issued the Emancipation Proclamation. Several other sculptors have modeled more than one statue of Abraham Lincoln, but the experience of the man who produced the "Lincoln" that stands in Prospect Park, Brooklyn, and its near twin in Union Square, New York, was different and exceptional.

Brown is generally rated as "the first American sculptor," a characterization that is justified by placing the emphasis on the word "American," inasmuch as he had rebelled against the assumption prevailing in his time that American art must take orders from Europe. One historian holds that he "owed less to Europe — directly — than did any of his predecessors and colleagues." He resolutely endeavored to express national sentiments and ideals. Adeline Adams expanded the idea, holding that "he was the first of our sculptors to make any serious attempt to shake off the 'real chains' of the contemporary Italianate pseudo-classicism, but he came too early to profit by the vigorous new naturalism taught in the French schools." Born in Massachusetts in 1814, reared on a farm and given an academic education, Brown evinced an aptitude for making silhouettes, and went on to try with crude materials the painting of portraits. His parents decided that they ought not to ignore these indications of his bent, and arranged for him to study with Chester Harding, the most popular portrait painter in the country at that time. In 1836 he struck out on his own in Cincinnati, supporting himself in the main by surveying. Quite casually he undertook one day to model in clay the head of a friend. The result was so satisfactory that he forthwith abandoned the brush. He dreamed of going to Italy, and after six years he went, meanwhile earning wages and saving money by working as a surveyor on Illinois railroads and making portrait busts in Troy and Albany. He spent four years in Rome, and returned to set up a studio in New York. There, at the real outset of his career, he broke with classicism and obtained wide recognition for ability and originality with his long-remembered "Indian and Panther." More than once he traveled among the Indians in quest of subjects. He wanted American themes, and he depicted them so successfully that in 1851 he was made a full member of the National Academy of Design.

His masterpiece was given to the public on Independence Day in 1856. Lorado Taft wondered how it could have happened, and left the problem as an unsolved mystery, for Brown, after all, was only "an amiable and intellectual, but generally commonplace, sculptor." Plans had been completed by Horatio Greenough in collaboration with Brown for the making of an equestrian statue of Washington. Greenough's seated "Washington," a curious figure, half-clad, a throwback to extreme classicism, had been for years a butt for jokesters; he had felt compelled several times to explain his poetic purpose, and how, if he had made an historic portrait, such as a "Washington on Horseback," he would have put him in his ordinary dress. Greenough died, and it was left for Brown to execute what was to have been a joint production. He spent about three years on the work. On its unveiling it was greeted with universal applause by artists and laymen alike, placed as it was to dominate Union Square. There followed a long succession of works of varied character, attesting the versatility of the sculptor, among them statues of General Winfield Scott, General Philip Kearny, Governor George Clinton, Richard Stockton, and De Witt Clinton.

Brown was at work on a group for the pediment of a new State House in Columbia, South Carolina, when the Civil War came; this work was destroyed in 1865. He possessed also a considerable endowment of mechanical ingenuity, and managed to set up in his studio a miniature foundry wherein many of his smaller creations were successfully cast. In the years in which he was at work on his "Lincolns" his correspondence shows him to have been busy on a statue of Dr. George W. Bethune, the Dutch Reformed clergyman, and he was also working "very constantly" on his equestrian "Scott," spending more than six months of labor on it, which would be "nearly or quite as much time" as he "spent upon the statue of Mr. Lincoln." Also, New Jersey was negotiating with him for the "Kearny" and the "Stockton," intended for Statuary Hall in the national Capitol, and for Rhode Island he had in hand "a lifesize Nathanael Greene." Decidedly, he rated as a top-flight man.

His prices also signify his standing. He told the New Jersey negotiators that for the "Kearny" and the "Stockton" his fee would be $8,000 each, provided he received both commissions, with the understanding that the state would provide the metal appropriated by Congress for the "Kearny." For Rhode Island the honorarium for the "General Greene" would be $8,000 in gold, the equivalent of $13,000 in currency. The amount to be paid for the "Bethune" was $10,000, his "usual price for a life-size portrait." For the Brooklyn "Lincoln" he received $15,000, and for the New York "Lincoln" $20,000 "and the interest on the money invested during its execution." In those years he was a very busy man, at the top of his fame, dividing his time among several Eastern cities and his home and studio in Newburgh.

On the day of Abraham Lincoln's death, the Union League Club of New York City appointed "a committee to confer with the municipal authorities to obtain permission to erect a monument on Union Square in memory of the Martyred President." With hardly a doubt this may be accepted as the first action of the kind by any responsible group of citizens. Ten men were named on the committee; at the top of the list were George Bancroft and Theodore Roosevelt, father of the President.

Brooklyn was no laggard, however. A War Fund Committee, at its first meeting after the assassination of Lincoln, and only a week after his death, decided "to open a subscription for the erection of some suitable and permanent memorial in the city, of him for whom the nation was in mourning." No contribution of more than one dollar was to be received, in order that "all might have an equal opportunity to take part in this work of public gratitude." A Committee on Monument was constituted, having eight members, of whom James P. Wallace was listed first, followed by James S. T. Stranahan, a great citizen, whose statue by Frederick W. MacMonnies now stands in Prospect Park. Within a few years the War Fund Committee could report that "its important and delicate trust" had been completed by the erection of "the first statue, in bronze, in honor of President Lincoln, in an American city."

That city had possessed for years an area of fine developmental possibilities happily named Prospect Park. In 1860 the General Assembly at Albany took action for the improvement of the Brooklyn parks, and directed the Commissioners of Prospect Park to render annual reports to the Common Council. Relatively little was done during the war years, but the report for 1866 contains references to a plan for a Plaza which should form part of the principal entrance to the Park, and for "the erection of certain monumental designs" at this entrance, with the suggestion that "if one of these sites shall be suggested for the proposed statue of President Lincoln, it is hoped that the other will be reserved for a statue of Washington."

The successive reports of these commissioners clearly indicate that a strong civic movement was under way. The Board was composed of men of ability and vision. Stranahan's official service with that body extended from 1861 to 1882. These reports and the correspondence of Henry Kirke Brown show that the Lincoln statue project was under intensive consideration in 1865. The sculptor explained that an exterior statue should be of bronze for looks and durability, and if erected in Prospect Park should be eight or nine feet in height, with a pedestal of fifteen feet. In his judgment the subject should be treated "in the simple dignity of his character with nothing in the way of accessories." He wrote also, "My impression is that in the treatment of a statue to Mr. Lincoln, the fact of his Proclamation of Emancipation should be made prominent somehow, either in bas-relief, or on the base, inscribed on the pedestal or seen on a scroll held in his hands."

Brown further explained, in January, 1866, that "in any view of the late rebellion, the Southern interest in human slavery was its foundation and its motive power, and, in consequence, the destruction of that institution by the President's Proclamation was the final blow to it and the basis on which the war was closed. It has therefore appeared to me proper to represent the late President unfolding the sublime purpose of Emancipation — symbolized by the scroll which he holds in his hands — upon which may be engraved the body of the Proclamation and the finger of his right hand pointing to those ever-living words 'forever free.' "

Within a few days the sculptor met with the Monument Committee. The interests of the park were interwoven with discussion of the memorial and its financing. The question of the payment for Mr. Brown and the security for the first installment came up, and the possibility of his consenting to the completion of the work by another person in case of his own failure to perform. In a letter to Mrs. Brown at Newburgh the sculptor said: "I reported Mr. Ward's offer to finish it without compensation." The conference ended with the understanding that Brown would go on with his "preparations" and a contract would be made and signed in the meantime, the sculptor engaging that he would mortgage his "place as security" for the $3,000 which "they proposed to advance to him." A member of the committee followed him from the room and urged him not to mortgage his property, offering instead to serve as his security himself. In wakeful hours that night Henry Kirke Brown pondered that situation. The committee was fearful that something might happen which would imperil a portion of the subscription funds.

The artist wanted the contract. He was proud of his profession. He had a great deal of pride also in his own manhood. And he resolved to stand by his rights as an honorable man and an upstanding citizen. He sent his wife this account of his decision: "As to giving security for the first payment on the contract, in case failure to complete abrogates the whole contract, and not only deprives my heirs of any benefit from it, but compels them to pay $3000 out of my present property to cover this advance, which has been expended in the legitimate prosecution of the work — To accept my friends as security, in case of failure, compels them to pay $3000 for which they have received no possible benefit. I have resolved to do neither, for they both are most degrading propositions, and I will not submit to them. I have concluded not to return home in this frame of mind, but see it out — finish the contract. The contract shall be so drawn as to be valid to my heirs, — it shall contain no humiliating clauses or quibbles, and I will have my rights and they shall respect them."

The available sources confirm the inference that Brown won his case, and that his position was sound. In the following November invitations were sent out in the name of the War Funds Committee "to view the statue of Lincoln, designed by Henry Kirke Brown, Esquire, at the artist's studio at Newburgh" on a designated day. The Park Commissioners' report for 1867 has an outline drawing of the statue and a short statement to the effect that the War Funds Committee of Kings County had presented the memorial to the city. The unveiling must await the preparation of a suitable place for its reception. It was "a beautiful work of art." Mr. Brown was "a distinguished sculptor." The memorial was the result of dollar subscriptions and could therefore "truly be called a Peoples' Memorial." The head and shoulders of the statue had been "modeled from a bust taken from life." A "correct delineation of the other peculiarities had been secured by a vivid recollection which the personal intimacy with the deceased afforded the artist." The President had often worn a cloak, so one was thrown over his shoulders. The monument would be erected in the Plaza near the Fountain. "Our city may feel a just pride in the accomplishment of this beautiful tribute to the memory of Abraham Lincoln."

The unveiling took place on October 21, 1869. The Park Commissioners declared that the event "formed an epoch in the history of our city, as well as of our Park, and gave occasion to an interesting display of taste and of patriotism." In fact, it was a more impressive occasion than the contemporary publicity might lead one to suppose. Abiel Abbot Low, in his opening address as presiding officer, pronounced Lincoln to have been "the Providential Man of our time," and the city had proudly accepted the grateful duty of the perpetuation of his memory. The sculptor himself released the coverings that concealed the statue, "amid the cheers of the spectators and the thunders of the national salute from a battery on the adjacent hill." Mr. Wallace formally presented the statue to the Park Board, in behalf of the War Fund Committee. He paid tribute to the thousands of Brooklyn citizens who, without distinction of creed or political faith, belonging to all classes of society, had honored Lincoln's memory with their contributions — "a name with every dollar and a dollar for every name," and all the names preserved in the archives of the Historical Society. The $13,000 thus raised had been so invested as to earn $2,000 more, making up the total amount expended for the statue.

Mr. Stranahan accepted the memorial in the name of the Commission. Letters from President Grant and Governor John T. Hoffman were read. Dr. Richard Salter Storrs, the famous minister of the Church of the Pilgrims, delivered the oration of the day. It was in the familiar style of that great preacher, with numerous long and involved sentences making a labyrinth from which he always emerged with a definite and pertinent thought — a fine example of the eloquence of that time.

There is one more chapter in the story of this statue. Early in 1869

Mr. Wallace wrote the sculptor that in his own judgment and that of other members of the committee the site allotted was not the best available — that it ought to be placed inside the Park and not in the Plaza. Brown wrote in reply: "My objections to its present position are radical and decided. . . . As it now stands, it becomes simply an adjunct to the fountain, whose superior mass or size overpowers it, and renders it a secondary object instead of a principal. It sets so low in consequence of the massive steps behind it that the base seems inadequate for the statue." Moreover, it stood in a bad light: "The likeness is lost — the features become distorted and unnatural. It never can in the present position convey the full intention or expression of the work." Then, too, it must be "protected from insult and nuisance. . . . I conjure you gentlemen of the Committee never to consent to allow that noble though homely face, to be perceptibly shrouded in darkness or lit up at all by a sinister or reflected light. . . . It should be removed bodily to some other location." Only a few days before the unveiling Brown returned again to the charge.

The Park Commission stood by its original decision, however, and the statue stayed in the Plaza for twenty-five years. In 1887 a special committee reported that the Plaza was "a great failure . . . devoid of all life . . . a stony waste, suggestive of Siberia in winter and Sahara in summer," and that "the noble statue of Lincoln is dwarfed and made dismal by its surroundings." By 1893 plans were in hand for transforming the Plaza into "a delightful and attractive spot." In the following year a Grand Army Memorial Committee asked that the statue be moved to a better site, where it might be protected from injury. The Park Commissioners, in a report for 1895, stated that the statue had been removed in June, almost nine years after the death of the man who had made it and had fought for its protection. Undeniably the new site is far better. There the memorial stands, in a flower garden, approached by a wide pathway, amid splendid trees, facing a lake, where Memorial Day exercises can comfortably be conducted. Numerous photographs show the annual pilgrimages to that memorial for the placing of wreaths and the voicing of tributes.

What may be called an official description of this statue will be found in a work issued in 1909, the year of the Lincoln Centenary, by the Art Commission of New York City: "A bronze figure, heroic size, wearing / an ample cloak about the shoulders, / is standing with the left knee slightly / bent and holding in the left hand / a manuscript at which he is / pointing with the right. On each / side of the pedestal are small pro/jections supporting bronze eagles, / while the front and rear are orna/mented with wreaths, within / which are the inscriptions / U S N and U S A."

The movement in New York was well under way within a few weeks after the appointment of the original Union League Committee. In October, 1865, John C. Hamilton wrote Henry Kirke Brown of plans for the creation of a monument, "the statue to be of bronze, and it is proposed as the appropriate appendage that there be held in one or both hands the Proclamation of Emancipation — all embellishment indicating the subjection of the South to be avoided — as the object is to give to the erection a national, not a Sectional, character." He went on to suggest that Mr. Brown must compete for the commission, and that a rough sketch be drawn and submitted. "As the person of Mr. Lincoln would not be graceful it doubtless is desirable that a cloak or toga would hide much of the view." The sculptor, it seems, did not provide all the ideas. Several months later a Fund Committee invited J. Q. A. Ward, Launt Thompson, Brown, and several other sculptors to compete for a Union Square Memorial to cost not more than $30,000. Not until the last day of October, 1867, did the Committee authorize a contract with Brown.

The New York Times, in an article printed in 1870, intimated that the projectors intended to raise $150,000, but that, "although the money flowed in freely at first," the tide soon subsided, and when the books were closed only $25,000 was on hand. The Brown correspondence contains a financial statement and the names of a twelve-man committee to manage the $15,000 then paid in, invested in seventy-thirty bonds. Mr. Hamilton served as chairman of this committee, and Timothy C. Churchill as treasurer. *The Times'* opinion was that the treasurer did all the work. His letters show that he was on intimate terms with Brown. He refers to Richard Morris Hunt, the architect, as a member of the committee and "a good friend of yours who will be influential." The artist agreed that the "Lincoln" "should illustrate the great act of his life and the culminating point in his career — the emancipation of the slaves." It also appears that in his first design Brown showed the President pointing upward while looking down at a Negro with face uplifted, kneeling at his feet. The New York committee opposed any such design, "because of a fear that the figure of a negro in a public monument would arouse the resentment of the Irish citizens." Twice before Brown had proposed to portray the **Negro** in sculpture — once in a design for a pediment of the national Capitol and again for the pediment of the South Carolina State House.

The statue was placed in position in Union Square on September 16, 1870. The newspapers had much to say — about the pedestal, that its base was the largest stone ever quarried in America, weighing seventeen tons, above which were placed two other huge blocks. The statue had been completed a year before and "secreted in a bonded warehouse," awaiting the arrival of these granite blocks. *The Times* said: "The face of Lincoln is of almost photographic accuracy," but commented editorially four days later that the face did not resemble the man. In a descriptive article of October 2 this paper declared: "Of the merits of the statue as a work of art, enough has been said heretofore in these columns," and added, with becoming moderation, what is undeniably true, that it was "not one of Mr. Brown's successes." Beyond question the "Lincoln" suffers from its proximity to the well-liked equestrian "Washington" in the same square. There probably was also a measure of justification in a news writer's observation that "it should be understood that Mr. Frank Howe and Mr. Richard M. Hunt comprised the sub-committee to whom was entrusted the important task of inspecting the sculptor's models, and deciding whether or not the statue, when completed, should be accepted. On them, therefore, rested the responsibility of giving the subscribers to the statue fund a monument which certainly can scarcely be said to be a work of great merit."

For this memorial no dedication or unveiling ceremonies were held. Various newspapers had stated that October 3 was the appointed date for such a function. One searches vainly, however, for any account of such an occasion, and finds a solution to the puzzle in a paragraph at the end of *The Times* article cited above — "The statement, made in some papers, that the statue will be unveiled with appropriate ceremonies, is untrue. Nothing of the kind is intended."

It has seemed worth-while to record these details as illustrative of the conditions amid which artists did their work three-quarters of a century ago. The autobiographical materials included by H. K. Bush-Brown in his life of his uncle, Henry Kirke Brown, and especially the abundant correspondence there made available, enable a student to acquire a somewhat intimate knowledge of the hopes and fears, the cherished ideals, and the expedient concessions which checkered the working years of the sculptors of that time. We have been told that these conditions have not altogether vanished today.

One wonders if the artist himself regarded his Union Square "Lincoln" as a work of high value. He was proud of the majestic "Washington" which completely dominated the square, and without question was anxious to produce a statue of the Savior of the Union worthy of the position it was to occupy in the same square, at that time a fashionable shopping center. Several times he expressed his concern that the "Lincoln" might not be lifted high enough and have "sufficient mass" to properly offset the memorial to the Father of his Country. The Art Commission's statement is sufficiently descriptive of the work:

"A bronze figure, heroic size, / with whiskers on the lower part of his / face and with the face and eyes to the front, / stands with the left foot advanced on / a granite pedestal. His cloak, / drawn round over the right shoulder, / is gathered in ample folds against / his breast with his right hand, / while his left hand, holding a roll, / hangs at his side."

SOURCES: Manuscript biography of Henry Kirke Brown, by Henry Kirke Bush-Brown, Library of Congress; *Annual Reports of the Brooklyn Park Commissioners; Reports of the Art Commission of New York City; Official Report of the Unveiling of the Brooklyn Statue*, issued by the War Funds Commission in 1869; Charles E. Fairman, *Works of Art in the United States Capitol*, 1913; New York City Art Commission, Catalogue of Works of Art Belonging to New York City, 1909; Helen W. Henderson, *A Loiterer in New York*, 1917.

The *Dictionary of American Biography* is in error in stating that the Union Square statue was erected in 1868.

4   ILLUSTRATED PAGE 146

What a "Wisp of a Girl" Did

ONE day in the autumn of 1870 a young American woman, followed by her father and mother, climbed aboard a train running from Florence to Rome. In a businesslike manner she arranged comfortable places for her parents and found a satisfactory seat for herself. Having stowed away her guitar case in a baggage rack, she addressed "some question about time, place, or the like" to a young man whose seat was back to back with her own. She was very communicative. In a little while she was telling her new acquaintance that she was born in poverty on the Indian frontier in the United States, and had been employed in "a post-office." An "old sculptor" had discovered her talent for modeling in clay. Before long she was actually making busts of eminent Americans. And, what was most remarkable, she had come to Europe to complete a marble statue of the most celebrated American of the time, in fulfilment of a commission awarded her by the Congress of the United States, and she bore credentials from the Secretary of State to the diplomatic and consular representatives of her country. She was returning to Rome from Carrara where she had been superintending the shipment of the completed work.

The young man was Georg Brandes, the Danish critic, then in his twenty-ninth year and well on his way to fame. The young woman was Vinnie Ream. They "took to each other." "She found pleasure in talking to me," says Brandes in his reminiscences. He describes her as "rather small in stature, strong and healthy . . . with white teeth and red cheeks . . . with brown eyes, and brown hair that curls naturally about her head." She was "doubly remarkable" to him, "as being the first specimen of a young woman from the United States with whom I became acquainted." He was "not wholly attracted by her talent," although she was "a true artist and a true woman." He had "never in any woman encountered a will like hers." Of matters outside her own field she was "very ignorant," and only of her own work did she speak with passion. On the day before she left Rome, the Danish writer put on paper this statement: "I have never been in love with Vinnie Ream, but most people would think so, to hear the expressions I am now using. But I love her as a friend, as a mind akin to my own." Moreover, she had shown him "an intellect whose work is not a labor." Through her conversation there "swept a breath of the independence of the great Republic." No, she was not "a fine lady." She was vain, enthusiastic, "good." And — "there was always the very devil of a rush and Forward! March! about her, always in a hurry."

No better portrait of Vinnie Ream has been presented. It matches well that painted by George P. A. Healy, who lived in Rome during her stay there. Georg Brandes never saw this indomitable American girl again. So he wrote: "No Roman elegy. I will hide her away in my memory —

"Here lies / Vinnie Ream, / Sculptor, / of Washington, U.S.A., / Six-and-twenty years of age. / This recollection of her is retained by / One who knew her / for seventeen days / And will never forget her."

This American girl had done much during her twenty months in Europe. In Paris she had met Gustave Doré, who inscribed a drawing to her. There also she had modeled what Brandes pronounced "a really excellent bust" of Père Hyacinthe. She had visited London, Berlin, and other cities before settling down in Rome. There she achieved a degree of popularity, receiving visitors in scores and obtaining numerous orders. Franz Liszt sat to her for a bust, and she amazed the informed by obtaining permission to execute a bust of Cardinal Antonelli. All she did, she explained, was to "dress in her most beautiful white gown and ask for an audience of the dreaded cardinal." He appears to have been impressed by her "intrepid manner." As a matter of course she made the most of all available opportunities as a student; she studied under Léon Bonnet in Paris and with Luigi Majoli in Rome.

The commission which she was completing in Italy had not been easily obtained. Many men of influence in Washington had ridiculed the idea that the first award by the United States government to a woman for a life-size statue for the Capitol should be entrusted to an inexperienced girl only nineteen years of age. At the climax of the impeachment trial of President Andrew Johnson she had also to weather the threats of his enemies, who charged her with using her influence with a United States Senator in Johnson's behalf, and intimated their intention to turn her out of her studio in the crypt of the Capitol regardless of the peril to the plaster model then almost completed.

Just at the turn of the year she arrived back in Washington, and on January 7, 1871, the official preview of her statue took place. By the terms of the contract, the Secretary of the Interior must accept her work before its formal unveiling. Besides Columbus Delano, the Secretary, there were present Senator Lyman Trumbull of Illinois, several members of the House of Representatives, and a few of the sculptor's personal friends. She stood, pale of face, while the covering was slowly raised until the towering figure of Abraham Lincoln loomed high above her, and then through minutes of stillness until rounds of applause assured her that her toil had not been in vain.

Georg Brandes was in error about her age, for Vinnie Ream, the daughter of Robert Lee and Lavinia (McDonald) Ream, was born on September 25, 1847 (not 1844), in the frontier town of Madison, already chosen as the capital of the soon-to-be state of Wisconsin. Her father's employment as a surveyor for the General Land Office made family removals imperative from time to time. For a few years Vinnie attended Christian College at Columbia, Missouri. Robert Ream's health became undermined by the hardships to which his occupation had exposed him, and early in the Civil War he brought his family to Washington where he obtained a clerkship in one of the departments, while Vinnie and her older sister Mary found employment in the Post Office Department, and their mother contributed to the support of the group by taking a few boarders into their home on Capitol Hill. One of these was a Senator from Kansas, Edmund G. Ross, the man whose vote was expected to decide the fate of President Johnson.

Midway of the war occurred the incident which determined the course of the younger daughter's life. Columbia, Missouri, was on the way to becoming an educational center. Christian College was the first institution chartered by the state for the collegiate education of Protestant women. The University of Missouri had also been opened there, in 1841. The man who was proud to be called "the Father of the University," James S. Rollins, lived in Columbia, and represented the district in the United States Congress from 1861 to 1865. He became interested in Vinnie Ream and regarded her as a protégée. At his suggestion, Clark Mills, the "old sculptor" of Brandes' narrative, undertook to make a bust of her for the Missouri college. The quick-eyed and nimble-fingered girl watched him at his work, and exclaimed: "Why! I could do that." Mills handed her a bucket of clay and told her to mould a portrait of himself. Both the girl and the veteran were pleased with the result. Mills decided that she had talent, and took her into his studio. Within a year she was making busts and medallions of public men. This seems to be the authentic one of the several versions of how Vinnie got her start.

The eager girl conceived the project of making a portrait of Lincoln, and her patron, Senator Rollins, interceded for her with his friend in the White House, who agreed to give her half an hour a day for sittings. These intervals he set aside for relaxation, doing little business and seldom receiving callers. The sculptress in after years liked to talk about that experience. The sittings took place at intervals in the last five months of the President's life. Vinnie never met Lincoln the storyteller. Her Lincoln was a sad man — "a monumental melancholy always weighed upon his heart." Tucked away in a corner of the room, she watched him. There came a night in April when her parents came home very late and told her that the man for whom she had developed an intensely reverent affection had been murdered. For that ardent and impressionable girl the tragedy was a shock almost unendurable. She believed that she had been studying the looks and habits of a very great man. Before many weeks had gone by, she was using every means she could devise in behalf of the project which was to take her overseas a few years later.

There was a competition for the making of a marble statue to be placed in the rotunda of the Capitol. No one put on a more strenuous campaign than Vinnie Ream. During the lively debate over the award of the commission in Congress, Jacob M. Howard, a Senator from Michigan, stated that he had met her frequently, and that she "surely had shown no lack of that peculiar talent known as 'lobbying' in pressing forward her enterprise." Some newspapers charged her with sitting "conspicuously" in the galleries, "bewitchingly" dressed, and smiling upon the legislators. Perhaps these things are true; Georg Brandes recorded the opinion that she was "cold, deliberate, and composed as a man of strong character; . . . but ingratiatingly coquettish towards any one whose affection she wished to win."

This, however, could not account for the imposing endorsement which she obtained — a paper dated April, 1868, signed by President Johnson, General Grant, three Cabinet members, thirty-one Senators, and one hundred and four Representatives. The list of House members was headed, significantly, by Thaddeus Stevens. There were thirty-one other signers, among them five sculptors (including Clark Mills), several military men, and William Cullen Bryant. In their statement at the top of the paper the signers evinced "a national pride in Miss Ream" and a "desire to aid her in the development of her unquestionable genius." In a roster of her works they named the portraits of eleven eminent men, including Stevens, Rollins, Richard Yates of Illinois, John Sherman of Ohio, Horace Greeley — and Abraham Lincoln.

On July 26, 1866, a Joint Resolution was reported in the House by the Committee on Public Buildings and Grounds, authorizing the Secretary of the Interior to contract with Miss Vinnie Ream for a life-size model and statue of Abraham Lincoln, to be executed at a price not exceeding $10,000, "one-half payable on completion of the model in plaster, and the remaining half on completion of the statue in marble to his acceptance." With an insertion requiring the Secretary's approval of the model, the House passed the resolution that day.

In the Senate debate on the resolution the next day, some pretty caustic things were said about this "wisp of a girl." Charles Sumner of Massachusetts unlimbered some of his heavy guns to lead the attack. They were to commission "an unknown artist" and to "give away $10,000." They "might as well place her on the staff of General Grant." In his judgment they could not expect "even of Lincoln more than one statue in Washington," and "whoever undertakes that work must be of ripe genius."

Senator Nesmith of Oregon took Sumner on. "This young scion of the West" comes from Lincoln's country; she "manifests intuitive genius." The Senator from Massachusetts "has pandered so long to European aristocracy that he cannot speak of anything that originates in America with common respect. . . . If this young lady and the works she has produced had been brought to his notice by some near-sighted, frog-eating Frenchman, with a pair of green glasses on his nose, the Senator would have said that she was deserving of commendation." Others also becudgeled Sumner. Yates, of Lincoln's home state, had known the President well, and to him Miss Ream's bust was an exact likeness. In his reply Sumner kept his temper well, arguing that it is one thing to make a bust and another to make a statue. "It is no small thing to set a man on his legs," he declared. Cowan of Pennsylvania ended the discussion amid laughter by saying: "It is no ordinary girl who can shake and agitate this chamber to its very centre." The Senate passed the resolution by a vote of twenty-three to nine. President Johnson approved it on July 28, and on August 30 the contract was signed by Secretary of the Interior James Harlan and by Vinnie Ream.

The ambitious young artist had won her first campaign. Another, and a fiercer one, awaited her in 1868. In the meantime, a few days after the signing of the contract, Sumner received a letter from Mrs. Lincoln, inspired by a letter from *"Miss Vinnie Ream"* just come to hand. "Washington lobbying has evidently *not* improved the young lady very greatly," wrote Mrs. Lincoln. "The tone of her letter was self-satisfied and rather presuming. Nothing but a mortifying failure can be anticipated, which will be a severe trial to the Nation, and the world, and the country will never cease to regret that your wise admonitions were disregarded. . . ."

In 1868 the trial of Andrew Johnson approached its climax. On May 16 the Senate voted on one of the charges formulated by the House Committee against the President. Of the fifty-four Senators, thirty-five voted "guilty" and nineteen "not guilty" — falling short by one vote of the two-thirds necessary for conviction. The Senate recessed until May 26. During that interval extreme exertions were made to round up that single vote, but when the Senate voted on two other charges on the twenty-sixth, the count both times stood the same, 35 to 19. The attempt to impeach Lincoln's successor had failed. But the House managers, not ready to concede defeat, put through the lower chamber a resolution to the effect that there was "probable cause" to believe that "corrupt means" had been used "to influence" the vote. The managers were empowered to "summon witnesses, seize persons and papers, and look into the foul crime." They used methods reminding one of Hitler's Gestapo. They broke open desks, read private correspondence, examined bank accounts, and ransacked telegraph offices in Washington and Baltimore.

Vinnie Ream found herself dragged into the imbroglio, for Senator Ross lived at her mother's house, and, along with many other visitors including members of both houses, the Senator had visited Vinnie in the room in the Capitol assigned to her for a studio, where for many months she had been at work on the life-size model for her statue. It had been whispered about that a few members of the upper chamber, which constituted the impeachment jury, had found it convenient to confer both in the studio and in the Ream home. George W. Julian, a representative from Indiana, admitted on the floor of the House that he had descended to the studio to see Miss Ream when he heard that she was trying to induce Ross to vote for Johnson. He denied having threatened her, however; he had merely suggested that "such rumors would injure her in the estimation of the public and of Congress." The girl declared that she had never taken sides at all in the sensational proceedings, and Julian had accepted her denial. His was only one of several "friendly warnings."

Before long Miss Ream confronted a more serious peril. One Charles Wooley, who gambled at racetracks and speculated in Wall Street, was reported to have wagered large amounts on the acquittal of the President. Summoned before the House Committee in charge of the management of the impeachment proceedings, Wooley answered many questions, but refused to answer others. Charged with recusancy, he disappeared for a time, and then, on that memorable May 26, the Sergeant-at-Arms produced him at the bar of the House. He asked for a copy of the charges against him, and for time to prepare a reply.

On motion of George S. Boutwell of Massachusetts the Sergeant-at-Arms was directed to hold the obstreperous witness in close custody until the end of the session, or until discharged by the House. But where should he be kept? No rooms in the Capitol were designed for such uses. After a long parliamentary mêlée the House voted that "Room A" in the crypt should be fitted up as a guard room.

The fur began to fly — for that was the very room Vinnie Ream was using as a makeshift studio. Representative James Brooks, a New York Democrat, declared bitingly that "the honorable managers are gratifying a double sentiment — one beyond the creating of a Congressional dungeon under the Capitol, over the dome of which, as if in mockery, a bronze statue of Liberty presides; and that sentiment beyond is an insult to a clever young lady to whose genius as an artist the Lincoln party in this House, when it existed, voted some thousands of dollars to mould a plaster cast for a statue of Abraham Lincoln." To move that cast in its present condition would destroy it. The managers "are ready to forget and forego all their admiration of Lincoln to punish this young lady" for her alleged attitude toward Johnson's impeachment, and all because her mother "took an old Kansas acquaintance to board with her." For this Miss Ream was to be "hunted out of the Capitol," and the "money contracted to her is to be withheld." Ben Butler, in his domineering style, allowed that "the woman ought not to be left in rooms in the Capitol where she is exposed to such suspicion. Let her and everybody else who visits her there be cleared out, and if the statue of Mr. Lincoln, which she is supposed to be making, is spoilt in so doing, as one of his friends I shall be very glad of it, for, from what I hear of it, I think it is a thing that will do neither him nor the country credit." Columns of such remarks appear in the *Congressional Globe*.

In the end Wooley changed his mind, appeared before Butler's committee, and answered their questions. A resolution of May 30 granted Vinnie Ream permission to continue to occupy the dreary quarters called, by courtesy, her studio, but not until July 20 did it get to the floor of the House, when "Thad" Stevens, extreme radical though he was, rallied the legislators in her behalf. Many Congressmen resented his course, but none had the temerity to cross swords with him. So in that dark and gloomy basement room the young sculptress completed her model, and from there it was sent overseas to Italy.

The formal unveiling took place on the evening of January 25,

1871, in the great rotunda of the Capitol, in the presence of President Grant, a large assemblage of government dignitaries, representatives of foreign nations, and unofficial spectators. Lincoln's old Illinois friend, David Davis, whom he had appointed to the Supreme Court in 1862, raised the veil, a flag sent from Lyon, France, as a testimonial of respect for the American President, with the request that it be placed somewhere in the Capitol in the name of the weavers of France. There were addresses by Senator Lyman Trumbull and Representative Shelby M. Cullom of Illinois, General N. P. Banks of Massachusetts, Representative Brooks of New York, Senator James W. Patterson of New Hampshire, and Senator Matthew H. Carpenter of Wisconsin. The sculptress stayed in the background, remaining on the platform only a few minutes while the final speaker presented her to the assemblage. For that young woman, then in her twenty-fourth year, this was the greatest triumph in a life which did not end until 1914.

Kind things were said of Vinnie Ream and her work that night, although the speakers, almost as though by prearrangement, evaded any definite opinions on the artistic merits of the statue. Trumbull considered it a correct representation of the pensive expression habitually worn by Lincoln when "burdened with great responsibilities," but declared that others must judge of its artistic execution. Carpenter declared it to be "Abraham Lincoln all over," although he was no judge of it "as a mere [*sic*] work of art." Davis declared the statue "an admirable representation of Mr. Lincoln in a mood of serious contemplation." Patterson read a letter from the American painter George P. A. Healy, who had seen Miss Ream's work in Italy, praising it "as in the very manner of our noble patriot martyr."

Critical opinions varied. One writer in 1871 praised the head and features of this "Lincoln" as "boldly and powerfully executed" and affirmed "the unfathomable melancholy of the eyes" to be exactly right, but this same critic in 1873 saw the work as "mechanical and unilluminated by one mental or spiritual characteristic." Henry Kirke Brown, in 1867, in a letter to his wife, said some caustic things about Miss Ream's model. Writing in November of that year, he told of a call at her "studio" in the Capitol, where she had "a figure of Mr. Lincoln set up in clay mud in some respects better than I expected to see." But "there were a good many people in her room, so I could not do anything to her statue, nor would if the opportunity had offered, for the changes required to make it a work of art are radical, not partial." On the other hand, the *Washington Evening Star,* edited by Crosby S. Noyes, commenting on the official inspection of the statue early in 1871, alluded pointedly to Henry Kirke Brown as it asked: "Could it be that the fragile, youthful figure standing there, pale and anxious, and rendered more childlike in her appearance by her petite form and Dora-like curls, had made a success where so many older sculptors — Brown notably and recently — had failed?"

Vinnie Ream's later career was notable. In January, 1875, she obtained the contract for the bronze statue of Admiral Farragut which was unveiled in 1881 in Farragut Square, Washington. Meanwhile she had married Lieutenant Richard Leveridge Hoxie, of the United States Engineers. He built a home for her on that square, and there for some years she maintained what might be called a salon. After a long interval she resumed her work, modeling many portrait busts, several statues, and a series of ideal figures. Her idealization of Sappho was placed in the National Gallery. Her husband, who had become General Hoxie, caused a reproduction of this work in bronze to be erected above her grave in Arlington National Cemetery, with a stone seat opposite "for meditation and rest."

A few days after the unveiling of her "Lincoln," the statue was taken to Statuary Hall in the Capitol, where each state was to be represented by the statues of two distinguished citizens. Presently, perhaps on the theory that Abraham Lincoln belonged to the nation, the "Lincoln" was brought back to the rotunda, where it stands today — the figure partially draped in what some call a Roman toga and others a shawl, with the head bent forward and the eyes downcast, as though the subject occupying the mind of the man was the Emancipation scroll in his hand. The consensus today would seem to be that it is not an inspired work, although marked by genuine feeling, and that, taken in connection with the story of the sculptress, it must be considered a remarkable creation. The work belongs to a period long gone by. It is dated by the accessories which Vinnie Ream thought she must employ. But, after all is said, it may justly be denied that the more extreme jibes which have been directed upon it are deserved.

SOURCES: Richard Leveridge Hoxie, *Vinnie Ream,* 1908; the *Congressional Globe;* Mary Clemmer Ames, *Ten Years in Washington,* 1873; Charles E. Fairman, *Arts and Artists of the Capitol,* 1927; Georg Brandes, *Reminiscences of My Childhood and Youth;* Henry Kirke Bush-Brown, "Biography of Henry Kirke Brown" (MS), Library of Congress; "Letters of George Caleb Bingham to James S. Rollins," *Missouri Historical Society Quarterly,* October, 1938; letter of Mary Todd Lincoln to Sumner, Harvard University Library.

Many of the magazine and newspaper articles about Vinnie Ream proved to be unreliable.

5

ILLUSTRATED PAGE 147

A Monument that "Marked an Era"

THE Park Commissioners of Philadelphia, in a report dated January 31, 1872, recorded their conviction that the dedication of the Lincoln Monument in Fairmount Park "marked an era in the progress of the development" of that famous municipal playground. The dedication took place on September 22, 1871, the ninth anniversary of the preliminary Proclamation of Emancipation. With a good deal of rhetorical exuberance the Commissioners described the events of the day. On that "bright, autumnal afternoon, the sloping acclivities were rich with verdure, their summits crowned with fully equipped batteries of artillery, their slopes covered with dense masses of people. Regiment after regiment passed with measured tread to blare of trumpet and beat of drum, the sabres of the cavalry and the bayonets of the infantry alike flashing in the genial sunlight. The natural terraces, leading by sinuous paths to the crest of Lemon Hill, provided an advantageous point for the gay groups who gazed from the glades of evergreen on the spirited spectacle below. The Schuylkill, dotted with glittering barges and spanned by shapely bridges; the busy city close at hand, its long lines of massive structures relieved by turret and spire and dome — all combined to constitute a picture which it would be difficult to match, and, of its kind, impossible to surpass."

Those officials were proud of their "Lincoln," and probably they were aware that the dedication of the memorial provided them with a rare opportunity to publicize their work. There is a degree of similarity between the work of the Commissioners in the creation and extension of this park and the erection of a memorial to Abraham Lincoln therein, and the movement under way in that same period for the development of Prospect Park in Brooklyn. The Philadelphia Park Commission was established in 1867, and entrusted with the care and management of Fairmount Park on both sides of the Schuylkill River. By 1870 the domain under their control had attained "the magnificent area of three thousand acres." Certain gifts of land had been made, and for land and buildings there had been expended more than three million dollars. The Commissioners were not unmindful of the probable significance of a visit lately made by a deputation from Washington; Congress was looking forward to the celebration of the centennial of American independence.

Just five weeks and five days after the death of Lincoln, the movement for a memorial was initiated. An Association was organized, and later in the year a Committee of One Hundred was endowed with power to control collections, disbursements, and the location and design of the monument. A resolution for the erection of a bronze statue of Lincoln was adopted in December, 1866, and at a meeting in February, 1868, the Executive Committee examined the designs which had been submitted, and approved the general scheme offered by Randolph Rogers, an American then residing in Rome. In due course the Association was organized as a corporation, with Charles Janeway Stillé as president, J. Raymond Claghorn as secretary, and James L. Claghorn as treasurer. Dr. Stillé, lawyer and scholar, had been a leader in the work of the Sanitary Commission, and in 1868 he became the provost of the University of Pennsylvania. It was his pamphlet, with the attractive title *How a Free People Conduct a Long War,* that President Lincoln read aloud to his friend Senator Orville H. Browning in December, 1862. Contracts were made — one for $9,800 for granite, and another with the sculptor for $19,300. The Association obtained from the city permission to erect the monument at the intersection of Broad Street and Girard Avenue, but the Fairmont Park site was substituted. In December, 1870, the Association in formal session listened to the reading of a letter from Mr. Rogers telling of "the satisfactory completion of the bronze." The following May the statue arrived in New York.

For almost a third of a century Randolph Rogers lived in Italy, a popular and respected member of the American colony and intimately known in the art circles of Rome and Florence, returning to the United States for professional visits which sometimes lasted a year or more. He was born in 1825, at Waterloo, in central New York, the son of a millwright. The family moved westward stage by stage, finally settling down at Ann Arbor, Michigan, where for several years the boy attended the common schools. There he manifested his bent by handiwork with a jackknife, whittling out wooden heads readily recognizable as portraits. During his later apprenticeship in a bakery, it was said that "his cakes were all dough, for he forgot to watch his oven while moulding his raw material as a sculptor would work with clay." In those early years he also experimented with the painting of portraits and acquired a rudimentary knowledge of engraving on copper. He became known also as a clever mimic, with a keen sense of humor, a gift which won friends in later years in Rome, where he was frequently called on to assist in private theatricals. As a young man he somehow found employment in the wholesale dry-goods establishment of John Stewart in New York City, and there his knack for modeling soon brought him to the attention of his employers. One of his superiors was much impressed by the portraits of his young children made by the future sculptor, and by an ambitious attempt to mould a bust of Lord Byron. Mr. Stewart himself furnished the funds for Rogers to go abroad for study. In the three years which Rogers spent in the studio of the celebrated Lorenzo Bartolini, he earned money to repay the loans of his American benefactors by the sale of two or three of his symbolic figures — one of them an ideal bust which he called "Night."

He now boldly set up for himself. In his own studio in Rome he produced his most popular figure, his conception of "Nydia," the blind heroine of Bulwer-Lytton's *The Last Days of Pompeii*. He now made a visit of two years to his native land, obtaining commissions for various works, including a contract for the bronze doors at the main entrance to the Capitol in Washington. These doors were made by him in Rome in 1858, and cast at the Royal Bavarian Foundry in Munich at a cost of $17,000.

The rest of his story may be simply told by listing a few of his more notable works. Thomas Crawford, who had designed the well-known Washington monument for Capitol Square in Richmond, Virginia, and had completed for it the equestrian "Washington" and four of the sub-statues, including the "Jefferson" and the "Marshall," did not live to complete the work, and Rogers moulded the two additional sub-statues and six allegorical figures. What is called his "great opportunity" arrived with commissions for colossal soldiers' and sailors' monuments for Detroit and Providence. As an example of the then current conception of what such a memorial should be, we observe that the Detroit monument, sixty feet in height, was to have "at each of the four corners at each of three sections, rising one above the other, bronze figures representing United States infantry, marines, cavalry and artillery, and others suggesting Victory, Union, Emancipation and History, with a design to symbolize the State of Michigan surmounting the whole structure." Rogers made many portrait busts, the "Genius of Connecticut" for the capitol at Hartford, an equestrian group of Indians which he called "The Last Arrow," and an idealization called "The Lost Pleiad," which became nearly as popular as the "Nydia" had been. An often-repeated story, which has found its way into some history books, is to the effect that his statue of William H. Seward, in Madison Square, New York, was designed in Rome as the statue of another man, and then, with a new head, made to do duty for the Civil War Secretary of State.

Many high honors were bestowed on Rogers in Italy. He was decorated by King Humbert; he succeeded to Crawford's chair in the Roman Academy of St. Luke, and in 1875 he was made an Academy Councilor. He is described as a large, powerful man, of distinguished looks and manners, with strong features and a magnificent beard, a genial and generous comrade, who might be found entertaining such a visitor as Nathaniel Hawthorne one day and receiving royalty the next. He was overtaken by paralysis in 1882 and died in the Eternal City ten years later. He is said to have announced his intention to give all his original casts to the University of Michigan at Ann Arbor, but we are advised that "the inventory of his casts and their present whereabouts are not definite," and that a replica of the "Nydia" is the only one of his marbles on the campus.

The Park Commissioners placed the Rogers "Lincoln" on what they described as a broad plateau in Fairmount Park, where it could readily be seen from both sides of the Schuylkill, a situation "conspicuous in itself and appropriate and picturesque in its surroundings." When the day for the formal ceremonies arrived, the treasurer reported that the total of gifts received amounted to $23,700, and that the funds had been so managed that interest and premiums on investments and profit from certain sales had increased this sum to $36,200. With all expenses paid, the treasury contained a balance of $4,300, which would be "absorbed" by extra bronze work and the expenses of dedication day.

That September day was beautiful enough to justify a considerable expenditure of rhetoric. More than fifty thousand persons witnessed the unveiling. The monument was covered with canvas. Flowers banked

48

the exposed base. The invited guests marched from the Lemon mansion to the speakers' stand. Among them were numerous municipal dignitaries, Senator Simon Cameron, Lincoln's first Secretary of War, and several Civil War generals, including George Gordon Meade, who at that time was in command of the Military Division of the Atlantic with headquarters in Philadelphia, and was serving as one of the Park Commissioners. His daily horseback jaunts, it was said, had made him familiar "with every haunt in the Fairmount." Dr. Stillé, in a "Preparatory Address," alluded to the "two-fold purpose of the Monument Association — to make a lasting tribute to Abraham Lincoln and to help to keep alive his great example." His short and admirable speech ended: "The Commissioners of Fairmount Park having consented to assume the care and guardianship of this monument, I now formally commit it to their charge. I dedicate it, in the name of a grateful people, to the perpetual memory of Abraham Lincoln, President and Martyr, and I direct it to be unveiled and publicly inaugurated."

The canvas was lifted. The multitudes shouted. The bands struck up national airs. From a hill overlooking the park the Keystone Battery fired a national salute. The national colors were run to the top of the flagstaff, and in unfolding dropped myriads of little flags upon the statue and the people. The Knights Templar, the military, the guard of honor composed of soldiers' orphans, presented arms before the monument. "The moment was thrilling" and "vast numbers of people manifested their emotion."

A long description of the monument in the official report indicates the pride with which the Commissioners regarded their work, as well as the great changes which have taken place since in the public taste. There is "an oblong base with projecting buttresses at each corner," upon which rests "a moulded plinth, with consoles at each angle resting upon the buttress of the base." Each face of the base bears "an ornamental panel with a carved inscription." One reads simply: "To Abraham Lincoln from a grateful people." Another face carries a sentence from the Emancipation Proclamation, which, if the official record of the Commission quotes it correctly, does not perfectly correspond with the words Lincoln wrote. Upon the third face the closing passage of the Gettysburg Address is presented, also with clumsy alterations. On the fourth face appears a portion of the final sentence of the Second Inaugural Address. "Surmounting the plinth on which these inscriptions are cut," the record continues, "is a second pedestal plinth. At each corner . . . are eagles of bronze with half-spread wings . . . between the eagles are festoons of oak and laurel. This pedestal in turn is ornamented with four panels . . . crossed swords . . . the coat of arms of the United States . . . American flags crossed and draped. . . . At the top a projecting cornice," and then the statue.

We are told that this "Lincoln" in bronze was modeled by Rogers in Rome, and "cast at the celebrated foundries in Munich"; also, that it represents the President seated in a cushioned chair, facing south; that in his right hand is a quill pen and in his left a scroll; that the face is an excellent likeness, and the posture easy and natural; that the figure is colossal in size — nine feet six inches high in the sitting posture, and standing its height would be nearly eleven feet.

We admit our own lack of enthusiasm for this statue. The posture is not "easy and natural." The outstretched arm and the quill in hand are awkward and artificial, conveying no sense of either motion or emotion. The President might have poised a pen for a few moments while he thought about the significance of the Proclamation he was about to sign, but there is nothing to indicate anything of the sort in Frederick W. Seward's description of the actual signing; the President had done his pondering before he issued the preliminary Proclamation the previous September. Some observers have suggested that this "Lincoln" ought to be seated at a table. The facial likeness is adequate, but not inspiring. It conveys no hint of the emotional atmosphere of the hour. With all deductions made, the monument, by virtue of its size and elaborate accessories, is impressive — the sort of work that would be welcomed with enthusiasm in 1871.

The oration of the day was delivered, "with almost electrical effect," by Colonel William McMichael. "In your presence, fellow-citizens," he began, "in this chosen spot, in the chosen city where the nation was born in whose cause he died, and in sight of heaven whither his spirit has ascended, we unveil this statue of the greatest man of our time." The orator depicted Lincoln as "in defeat hopeful" and "in victory calm." He dwelt upon his "words of forgiveness and mercy." Then, he said, with the war won, amid the jubilee for peace, "grief conquered the conquerors. . . . Again we gathered in old Independence Hall. The shadow of the grave had fallen there. The nation's cradle was now its martyr's bier." In closing he reminded his auditors that Lincoln in 1861 in his Independence Hall address had said he would rather be assassinated on that spot than surrender the concept of liberty embodied in the Declaration of Independence. "May the whole nation ever recall with gratitude the services of Abraham Lincoln, and still renew his noble resolve 'that government of the people, by the people, for the people, shall not perish from the earth' !"

SOURCES: *Sketch of Fairmont, Lemon Hill, and the Adjoining Grounds as a Public Park,* Philadelphia, 1855; *Reports* of Philadelphia Park Commissioners, 1867 and subsequent years, with Appendices; J. Thomas Scharf and Thompson Westcott, *History of Philadelphia,* 1884; George Gordon Meade, *Life and Letters of General George G. Meade,* 1867; correspondence with Dr. Lewis G. Vander Velde and Mrs. Jane Thompson Lemish, of the University of Michigan.

6

ILLUSTRATED PAGE 148

The Shrine in Oak Ridge Cemetery

THE place for the burial of President Lincoln was decided by his widow in accordance with a preference which he himself expressed a few days before his death, while he was enjoying the nearest equivalent to a vacation that had come to him during four years of war. On an April afternoon in 1865, during the fortnight which Lincoln spent at General Grant's headquarters at City Point, he and Mrs. Lincoln went riding on the banks of the James River. The spring had come early that year, and the Virginia countryside was beautiful. The Lincolns left the carriage to walk through an old graveyard, in a retired spot shaded with trees; many of the mounds were already covered with flowers. The President was silent and thoughtful. As they resumed their ride, he said: "Mary, you are younger than I. You will survive me. When I am gone, lay my remains in some quiet spot like this."

We accept this incident as authentic, although its authority rests on the statement of one of Lincoln's friends, who incorporated it in a biography of the President, copyrighted in 1884, as having been told to him ten years previously by Mrs. Lincoln.

Just what did happen, and the exact order of events in the wild days of rush and confusion that followed the assassination, are extremely difficult, if not impossible, to determine. It would be both uncharitable and unreasonable to hold Mrs. Lincoln responsible for all the remarks attributed to her while the funeral arrangements were under way. Orville H. Browning, in his *Diary,* records that Robert T. Lincoln told him on the day of his father's death that his mother did not wish the remains to be taken back to Springfield, and an entry for the following Monday states: "We all think the body should be taken to Springfield for interment, but Mrs. Lincoln is vehemently opposed to it, and wishes it to go to Chicago." According to the biographer upon whom we depend for the account of the visit to the Virginia cemetery, Mrs. Lincoln said that she preferred Oak Ridge Cemetery to any other site in Springfield, as a "retired" place in consonance with her husband's wish.

The Illinois capital was swift to insist that the body must rest in the town which had been most closely identified with his life. A local committee, with the approval of the majority of their townsmen, selected a large square within the city limits, known as the Mather Block, for "the deposit of the remains." There a temporary tomb was made ready while the funeral train moved slowly westward over the roundabout route from Washington. The Mather Block became the site of the imposing Capitol of Illinois of today.

Four days before the funeral train arrived in Springfield, however, a telegram from Secretary of War Stanton gave the committee official notification that Mrs. Lincoln wished the body placed in the receiving vault at Oak Ridge. That evening John T. Stuart, Lincoln's former law partner and a relative of Mrs. Lincoln, wired back that her wishes "shall be complied with." It was at Oak Ridge, therefore, that the funeral services were held on May 4.

The popular impression persisted nevertheless that the permanent memorial would be erected on the Mather property, and that in good time the remains would be removed thereto. One who now undertakes to weave his way through the somewhat puzzling records is bound to feel that the committee was strangely tactless, even if not coldly indifferent to the wishes of the one person to whom most sympathetic and thoughtful deference was due. It seems, in fact, that Mrs. Lincoln's source of information as to the plans of those in charge of the burial arrangements, and the erection of a "proposed memorial," was the newspapers! It is no wonder that when she learned that the committee was holding on to the Mather Block, within "full view of the Chicago and Alton Railroad" and very "convenient of access to visitors," she sent an "ultimatum" — with a time limit of ten days: her wishes must be respected, and, if the committee refused to assent to them, she would accede to the preferences of her husband's Eastern friends and allow his body to be placed under the dome of the Capitol in Washington. Two members of the committee went to Chicago to see Mrs. Lincoln, but again they allowed her to learn of their mission through the press! She was not the only woman who would have resented what looked at least like a lack of courtesy, if not an affront to the widow of a former President of the United States; and she had lived in Springfield long enough for her old neighbors to know her temperament, even without taking into account — as they well might have — the agitation which during those weeks of mourning had at times reached the extreme limits of emotional distraction. The committee members failed to see her, but her son handed them a letter reaffirming her determination. By the bare margin of a single vote the Springfield committee finally came to terms. Paul M. Angle cites a letter written by Jesse W. Fell on June 1 of that year, stating that he had "reliable information" that Lincoln himself had expressed his wish to be buried in the cemetery in which, thanks to the insistence of his widow, his body was deposited. The coffin was transferred to a temporary vault built for its reception on December 21, thus releasing the receiving vault for its normal public use. On September 19, 1871, the remains, encased in a metallic casket, were removed to the crypt of the monument then in course of erection.

The Springfield committee of nine members, which had been organized to supervise the funeral arrangements, appointed in turn a group of thirteen men — later expanded to fifteen — which was incorporated as The Lincoln National Monument Association, whose duty was defined as the construction of "a monument to the memory of Abraham Lincoln, in the city of Springfield, State of Illinois." The directors of the Association were men of eminence in the city and the state. Governor Richard J. Oglesby was president of the board, and Ozias M. Hatch, a former Secretary of State, served as its secretary. Other members, most of whose names are familiar to Lincolnians, were Orlin H. Miner, the Secretary of State; John T. Stuart, State Auditor; Jesse K. Dubois, State Treasurer; James C. Conkling, Superintendent of Public Instruction; Samuel H. Treat, Judge of the United States Court; Thomas J. Dennis, mayor of Springfield; Jacob Bunn and John Williams, bankers; David L. Phillips, United States Marshal; Sharon Tyndale; Dr. S. H. Melvin; James H. Beveridge, who served as treasurer of the Association; and the well-remembered educator whom Lincoln, with his diminutive stature in mind, described as "my little friend, the big schoolmaster of Illinois," Newton Bateman.

The Association opened books in the city's banking houses for subscriptions to the Monument Fund the day before the funeral train arrived in Springfield. Only sixteen donors, with gifts amounting to fifty-seven dollars, came forward on that day, and the next two days saw no subscriptions at all. In the anxious months that followed no wave of enthusiasm was discerned; but the incorporators never wavered, nor were they dilatory. They named an agent for each county in Illinois, sent out form letters, issued special appeals to public schools, fraternal organizations, and societies of many types, and in particular to the men who had fought on land and sea in the war. The amount sought was $250,000, but at the end of 1866 the treasury contained only a third of that sum. More than 17,000 Sunday Schools had given $18,000. Veterans had contributed $28,000, almost a third of which came from colored troops. In 1867 the State of Illinois came to the rescue with an appropriation of $50,000. Other states responded, New York with a conditional gift of $10,000, Missouri with $1,000, Nevada with $500.

With $134,000 in hand, the Association decided to advertise for a design for the memorial. A "friendly competition of American artists" was announced, the designs to be ready on April 14, 1868 — later extended to September 4. The Association also issued an "Address to the Public," hoping to increase the fund to $200,000, and to avoid the necessity of adopting a plan which would reduce the required expenditure. The amount was large for that day. Such a competition was almost unknown in the United States. Architects, sculptors, engineers, artists of all sorts and grades of ability saw an opportunity of extraordinary value offered to them.

For ten days in that September, the designs — thirty-seven of them, sent in by thirty-one competitors — were on view in the Illinois State Capitol. Twelve states and the District of Columbia were represented by entrants. Six of them submitted two designs, among them Leonard W. Volk, C. G. Volk, Larkin G. Mead, Jr., and Thomas D. Jones, who had modeled two busts of Lincoln from life. Two women were on the list, the indomitable Vinnie Ream and Harriet Hosmer, the Massachusetts girl who had been in Europe most of the time since 1852 and had won recognition as a sculptor of distinction. Although her design was submitted from Boston, it must have been made in Europe in 1867, for Gladstone and other notables had seen it in London that summer.

With a single dissenting vote, the Association accepted one of the designs submitted by Larkin G. Mead, Jr. Mead was a Yankee from Brattleboro, Vermont. He had been living in Italy, but returned to America with a plaster study of the successful entry. This was a real triumph for a man then only in his thirty-fourth year. Mead, while still in his teens, had received excellent instruction in the studio of Henry Kirke Brown, and almost at the end of his twenty-first year had challenged the attention of the Green Mountain people by moulding one night a huge figure of snow and ice at a crossroads near his home. Mead called this figure "The Recording Angel," a welcome and a warning for the New Year of 1857, due on the morrow.

What he wanted, and needed, was publicity. He got it. Orders began to come in. At twenty-two he moulded a colossal "Vermont" for the dome of the Capitol at Montpelier. Four years later his marble "Ethan Allen" was chosen for a place of honor in the interior of the building. In the first year of the Civil War he spent several weeks at the front, making sketches for *Harper's Weekly* — an experience which proved of value when he was modeling the groups of service men for the Lincoln monument. Mead went to Italy in 1862, and lived and worked in Florence through most of the half-century which remained of his life.

In several respects fortune had befriended this ambitious young American. In his Brattleboro home he had been surrounded by artistic activities. His brother William R. Mead was one of the founders of McKim, Mead and White, the celebrated firm of architects. A sister, Elinor, herself an artist, met in Columbus, Ohio, the author William Dean Howells, then serving a literary apprenticeship as a newspaperman. Since Howells had compiled one of the campaign biographies of Lincoln in 1860, his friends considered it proper that the new President should do for him what Franklin Pierce had done for Hawthorne, by providing him with an income and an opportunity through an assignment to an overseas consulate. Venice fell to him, and when Larkin Mead crossed the Atlantic in 1862 he took Elinor with him and duly delivered her to the man whom she married on the day before Christmas. The young sculptor himself married a Venetian in 1866.

Mead is described as an amiable and companionable man. He watched the trend away from Italy to France for the study of art, but steadfastly maintained his first allegiance. He belonged to what is known as the "Old School" of sculptors, but he found work to do almost to the end of his life. He readily made friends. They found in him a rare comrade. Many of his letters bubbled with humor, and he was on intimate terms with some masters in the fine art of correspondence. Writing to Charles Follen McKim about a sculptural decoration for the Agricultural Building at the World's Columbian Exposition of 1893, he discoursed about "as drunken looking a Silenus as you would care to see; a sprightly young Bacchus, a lively Satyr playing cymbals, a gay young Bacchante playing flutes, a rather stunning Flora, and a pretty good Jason," and added: "I have been working today on Mercury and Proserpine. . . . Mercury looks a little sick at the stomach, but he will get up in style in the large." One wishes that the letters about the Springfield competition were accessible; who knows what he might have said about the Lincoln monument in the numerous letters he must have written while that commission was under execution, if not to the Springfield committee, then to the friends to whom he wrote without restraint and with his inborn sense of humor?

With contract in hand, Mead returned to Italy. He was "to mould, cast, and deliver" a statue of Lincoln, not less than ten feet high, together with four groups representing infantry, cavalry, artillery, and the navy, and a coat of arms of the United States, for a total amount of $70,000, these to be sent on at intervals to suit the convenience of the Association. The Association itself assumed the responsibility for the architectural work, accepting a bid of $136,550 by W. D. Richardson of Springfield for the erection of the monument in exact conformity with the specifications of the sculptor. Ground was broken with appropriate ceremonies on September 9, 1869. The capstone was placed in position atop the central obelisk on May 22, 1871. On July 15 of that same year, Thomas Lincoln — "Tad," the captivating boy of the White House years — died in Chicago, and his body was brought to Springfield and deposited in the crypt beneath the structure. On September 19 the remains of the President were brought there from the temporary vault, with the bodies of Willie and Edward Lincoln. Of the Lincoln family only Mrs. Lincoln and her eldest son Robert remained alive.

Not until 1874 was the Lincoln statue in place. It happened that the annual reunion of the Army of the Tennessee was to be held that year in Springfield, and October 15 was chosen as the dedication date to coincide with the presence of the thousands of Union veterans. Meanwhile the Association had been busy raising funds to meet the terms of the contract for the sculptural groups. In the summer of 1871, Governor Oglesby and David L. Phillips obtained, almost by chance, from a few Chicago businessmen, a pledge to buy one of the four. This stroke of fortune encouraged them to go East, and in New York, with former Governor Edwin D. Morgan leading the way, they obtained an understanding for the financing of the naval group. They had no luck whatever in Boston, and abandoned their contemplated trip to Philadelphia. The great fire of 1871 was a staggering disaster for the Chicago contributors, and the Association at once released them from the obligation they had assumed, but they insisted that their group be ordered at once. Oglesby, who had become a senator, renewed his solicitations in the East. New York made good, but no money was forthcoming either from Philadelphia or from Boston. Once more Lincoln's own state came to the rescue with a $27,000 appropriation in 1877. The naval group, which had been on exhibition at the Centennial Exposition in Philadelphia in 1876, was the first to arrive in Springfield, followed closely by the infantry group, given by Chicago. Both these groups were erected in 1877. The artillery and cavalry groups were not placed in position until 1882 and 1883, at last completing the Monument Association's work — eighteen years after its beginning. Seldom have the zeal and unselfish service of this body been matched in the promotion of such an enterprise.

That day in mid-October of 1874, when the statue was unveiled and the monument dedicated, therefore, antedated by nine years the full realization in stone, brick, and mortar of the artist's design. Many thousands of visitors flooded the prairie capital; arches spanned the streets; flags flew everywhere. The procession to the tomb was two miles long. The Association had some trouble in finding an orator for the occasion. William H. Seward, Lincoln's Secretary of State, who had been stabbed almost to death on the night of the President's martyrdom, had been their first choice, and Governor Oglesby had called on him in person at his Auburn home in 1872, but Seward, after a day's consideration and consultation with his family and his physician, felt constrained to decline, and his death that same year validated his decision. President Grant pleaded inability to do justice to the subject. Governor John A. Dix of New York found his "official engagements" in the way. Gideon Welles, the Civil War Secretary of the Navy, delayed his decision and then declined. Governor Oglesby went to Indianapolis with an invitation for Governor O. P. Morton, and found him enfeebled by ill health. Thereupon the Association turned to the Illinois governor himself. Oglesby well fulfilled the difficult duty thus thrust upon him. As a matter of course he reviewed the life of Lincoln, quoting from several of his speeches; he devoted some time to contrasting Lincoln and Douglas; he pictured Lincoln as entering upon the Presidency "like one feeling his way amid precipices in the darkness of night"; and, at the end, he said:

"And now, by the authority and under the direction of the National Lincoln Monument Association, in the presence of this vast assemblage, who bear testimony to the fact, and under the gracious favor of Almighty God, I dedicate this monument to the memory of the obscure boy, the honest man, the illustrious statesman, the great Liberator, and the martyr President, Abraham Lincoln, and to the keeping of Time. 'Behold the image of the man!'"

The waiting multitude watched in silence while the veil of red and white silk slowly moved down before the statue. Two nuns from Jacksonville, representing an Order which had labored in camps and hospitals in wartime, drew the cords releasing the cover. The choir sang. James Judson Lord read a dedication poem in tribute to

> . . . one of the noble few
> Who saw the right and dared the right to do.

President Grant made what for him was a long address. Among other speakers were Jesse K. Dubois for the Association; Vice-President Henry Wilson of Massachusetts; Usher F. Linder of the Illinois bar, an old friend of Lincoln's; General William T. Sherman; former Vice-President Schuyler Colfax; and William E. Forster of the British House of Commons. The sculptor was introduced and roundly cheered.

Since that dedication day the monument has been twice rebuilt. From the beginning there were numerous objections to the inadequate height of the central obelisk; it did not conform to Mead's design, and photographs clearly reveal its lack of proportion to the rest of the structure. It looked like a truncated shaft; some of the original contributors even intimated that they had been short-changed. In time it became known also that the foundations, aside from the supports for the central shaft, were inadequate, and that the structure was falling into disrepair. Also there was irritation over the charge of an admis-

sion fee and over the sale of relics by the custodian of the monument —
and in 1876 there was a grotesque and almost unbelievable attempt to
steal the body of the President! Discontent became widespread, and a
demand arose that the state should take over the structure as a public
trust. Suitable legislation was enacted, and on July 9, 1895, the monument passed out of the control of the Association. In the presence of a
large number of state officials, in the chamber of the House of Representatives, ex-Governor Oglesby, who is said to have been the last sur-
vivor of the original committee of 1865, made an impressive presentation address, to which Governor John P. Altgeld responded.

A few years later, Governor John R. Tanner sent a special message
to the General Assembly, pointing out that, while the obelisk was sunk
to bedrock, the other footings rested only on clay; in consequence there
had been an uneven settling, so that the preservation of the structure
depended on the correction of these unstable foundations. Tanner held
the design to be "admirable" and the workmanship "excellent." An in-
vestigating committee confirmed the Governor's statement, and split
over the question of the remedy. Historians allude to the extensive
"manipulations" which took place during that session of the Legislature, as a minority found the monument "crude in design" and "faulty
in construction," and demanded "a grand new structure" to be erected
in the center of the city. The rebuilding plan finally won; all but the
obelisk was reconstructed, at a cost of about $100,000, and the height
of the shaft was increased. This work was finished on June 1, 1901.

After another quarter of a century the necessity of further repairs
became evident, and afforded an opportunity for remodeling the interior of the structure. The obelisk showed signs of deterioration, and
was rebuilt along with the superstructure to within six feet of the
ground. Except for an air of newness, the exterior appearance was not
altered.

The monument as it stands today was completed, at a cost of nearly
$200,000, in early June, 1931. What one now looks upon is a huge
structure of brick and Quincy granite, with only the stone visible. The
base, sixteen feet in height, would make a square seventy-two and a
half feet each way, except that rounded chambers project from the
middle of the north and south sides, enlarging that dimension to one
hundred nineteen and a half feet. Stone steps lead to the top of the base,
which is balustraded and forms a terrace, above which rises the obelisk.
At the angles of the shaft are pedestals upon which rest the sculptured

groups. A higher pedestal on the south side carries the statue of the President. At the entrance stands a bronze replica of the huge marble head of Lincoln by Gutzon Borglum, the original of which is in the Capitol at Washington.

Within the rotunda of the tomb the visitor confronts a reduced replica of the seated Lincoln conceived by Daniel Chester French for the Lincoln Memorial in the nation's capital. In the corridors leading around the interior of the base stand eight bronze statuettes which picture Lincoln in successive periods of his life. Two of these — both showing Lincoln as a horseman, the first as a "Ranger" and the second as the circuit rider — were made by Fred M. Torrey especially for this memorial. The others are replicas: of Leonard Crunelle's statue of Lincoln as a soldier of the Black Hawk War, which stands in Dixon, Illinois; of Crunelle's "Lincoln the Debater," in Freeport; of the Weinman seated "Lincoln," at Hodgenville, Kentucky; of Lincoln the lawyer addressing a jury, by Lorado Taft, at Urbana; of the contemplative "Lincoln" by French, at Lincoln, Nebraska; and of the standing statue of the President by Saint-Gaudens, in Chicago. At the rear one enters the sarcophagus chamber. The walls are lined with black marble. Within one wall are buried Mary Todd Lincoln and three of her sons; Robert, the oldest, rests in Arlington. The body of the President lies in a cement vault ten feet below the floor and six feet within the opposite wall. A cenotaph in the chamber, surrounded by the Stars and Stripes and the flags of all the states associated with the Lincoln family, bears the simplest possible inscription — "Abraham Lincoln — 1809–1865." The bronze grilles at the entrance and exit of this chamber may be closed on occasion.

No sensitive and informed observer can miss the overwhelming significance of his surroundings. The marbles and the gold leaf, the stars and the flags; the bronze plaques carrying the farewell to Springfield, the Gettysburg Address, a portion of the Second Inaugural, and a sketch of Lincoln's life, produce the atmosphere of a shrine. All voices are hushed, steps are slowed, and many eyes are dimmed under the emotional tension which floods this quiet and solemn chamber. The most casual and careless tourists cease their chatter and leave this place in reverence.

Just below the statue of Lincoln is placed what is known as the Servius Tullius stone, derived from a wall said to have been erected in Rome by a more or less legendary king twenty-five centuries ago.

Visitors who ascend to the top of the base, or the "terrace" as it is often called, may obtain an idea of the historic justification for the conspicuous and permanent position which has been given to this fragment of an ancient structure. The stone is small, roughly hewn, and irregular in shape, with an incised Latin inscription. The translation of this inscription is chiseled below, in the granite slab in which this unique relic is sunk, together with an additional inscription explaining how the Roman relic came to be where it is. A group of Italian patriots, who had watched with appreciative interest the progress of the American Civil War, sent this stone to Washington in 1865 — whether before or after the President's death we do not know. The inscription, in translation, reads: "To Abraham Lincoln, President for the second time of the American Republic, citizens of Rome present this stone from the wall of Servius Tullius, by which the memory of each of those brave advocates of liberty may be associated. Anno 1865." This inscription accepts as fact the tradition that this ancient king endowed the plebeians of Rome with the rights of citizenship, and gave liberty to the serfs, making them citizens also. The stone is therefore conceived as a link between the lives of two Liberators, although separated by a vast interval of time. Through the efforts of Representative Shelby M. Cullom of Illinois, the stone was sent to Springfield "to be placed by the Lincoln Monument Association in the monument" then under construction.

Governor Henry Horner caused it to be given its present position, and formally made it a part of the Lincoln tomb on October 11, 1936, with ceremonies including an address in which the Governor said: "There is no beauty in that stone to make it attractive. Still, the association of ideas that cluster around the stone will always cause it to be an object of interest. During the time that has elapsed since it was placed by human hands in the wall surrounding the city of Rome, continents have been discovered; empires have risen and fallen; and more than seventy generations of human beings have sprung from the earth, acted their busy parts, and sunk back into its bosom. Servius Tullius at the beginning and Abraham Lincoln at the close of that long period of time were influenced by the same spirit of humanity. Both loved and trusted the common people, and both were loved and trusted in return; and because of that mutual love of the Roman patriots who sent this stone to us, the names of 'those brave advocates of liberty' are and will be associated from this time henceforth."

We may profitably spend the early hours of a summer morning strolling about the eminence in Oak Ridge Cemetery on which this monument stands. The crowds of sightseers are not yet arriving. Quiet and beautiful are these surroundings, conducive to reflection upon the strange career of a man incontestably great, yet admittedly unfathomed. Many of his old friends are resting under the oaks in this neighborhood — including his law partner William H. Herndon. Did any of them really *know* Lincoln? As the sun floods the monument with warm light, we obtain the most satisfactory impression of the work as a whole by looking from the ground at a little distance from the entrance, as the sculptor intended us to do.

The President appears as he looked near the end of his life, with furrowed and meditative face, one hand slightly lifted and the other clasping the scroll of Emancipation. By present-day standards it is not a great statue, but for many years the statue and the monument as a whole were rated first among such memorials in this country. Joshua Fry Speed, the most intimate friend Lincoln ever had, attended the dedication of this "Lincoln" in 1874, and years later pronounced Mead's statue the best likeness of his old friend that he had ever seen. The orthodox explanation of the sculptor's purpose is that the President stands on the Constitution as his warrant for calling on the armed forces of the nation for the preservation of the Union.

On the right of the figure of Lincoln is the naval group, depicting a scene on a gunboat, with a mortar poised for action. On the left is represented a group of infantry surprised on the march. On the north side of the obelisk are the artillery group, in a scene which Mead himself is said to have witnessed at Yorktown, and the cavalry group, with a rearing horse and a dying trumpeter supported by a dismounted comrade. Mead was undoubtedly a sincere artist, a man of ability and imagination, and in its principal features the monument stands today substantially as he conceived it.

On June 17, 1931, a President of the United States arrived at the Wabash Railroad station in Springfield, from which in 1861 Abraham Lincoln as President-elect started on the circuitous journey to Washington for his inauguration. Herbert Hoover, in the Illinois capital for the dedication of the reconstructed memorial, had a busy day: he visited the Lincoln homestead, made an impromptu address before a joint session of the state legislature, inspected the interior of the monument — writing his name at the top of a new register as the first visitor admitted to the rotunda — placed a wreath of palms before the cenotaph, and delivered the dedication address from a stand erected to command the many thousands of auditors who crowded the open space before the tomb and filtered through the surrounding groves of trees. The President's address was simple, suitable, earnest, and thoughtful. The tomb was "a shrine for all Americans. . . . Lincoln after all these years still grows in the hearts of his countrymen and in the hearts of the peoples of the world. The very greatness which history and popular imagination have stamped upon him obscures somewhat the real man back of the symbol which he has become. It is not amiss to reflect that he was a Man before he became a Symbol." There was one interpolation in the prepared address, in which the speaker affirmed Abraham Lincoln to be "our greatest American."

When the new register was signed that day, visitors were told that the old one contained two million names. Every day since, visitors have been coming — coming from every State in the Union and from every country in the world. People visit Mount Vernon more to see the home of Washington than his grave. There is no tomb in the magnificent Lincoln Memorial in the national capital. It is probably true that more pilgrims come to Springfield to see the grave of Abraham Lincoln than visit any other similar shrine in the Western world.

SOURCES: John Carroll Power, *Abraham Lincoln, His Life, Public Services, . . . with a History and Description of the National Lincoln Monument,* 1889; Paul M. Angle, "The Building of the Lincoln Monument," *Lincoln Centennial Association Papers,* 1926; Fred L. Holmes, *Abraham Lincoln Traveled This Way,* 1930; Cornelia Carr, ed., *Harriet Hosmer Letters and Memories,* 1913; *Ceremonies Incident to the Placing of the Servius Tullius Stone in the Tomb of Abraham Lincoln,* a document issued by the State of Illinois, 1937; Bess King, *The Tomb of Abraham Lincoln,* 1941; Paul M. Angle, "New Plans for the Lincoln Monument," *Bulletin of the Abraham Lincoln Association,* No. 17; James Judson Lord, *Lincoln Monument Dedication Poem,* 1907; folders and pamphlets issued by the State of Illinois.

The account of the visit to the old graveyard in Virginia may be found in Isaac N. Arnold, *The Life of Abraham Lincoln* (1885), p. 435.

Slavery's Own Tribute to Lincoln

ON HEARING of Lincoln's death, without the delay of a day, a colored woman brought a five-dollar greenback to Dr. William P. Rucker, a Union "refugee" from Virginia, then living in Marietta, Ohio, with the request that the money be used "to make a monument to Massa Lincoln." The woman's name was Charlotte Scott. She had been a slave in Dr. Rucker's household, and her gift was understood to be her first earnings as a free woman. Dr. Rucker placed the money in the hands of General T. H. C. Smith, who had entered the Civil War as lieutenant-colonel of the First Ohio Cavalry. General Smith in turn sent it to Mr. James E. Yeatman, of St. Louis, with an explanatory note: "A poor woman of Marietta, Ohio, one of those made free by President Lincoln's proclamation, proposes that a monument to their dead friend be erected by the colored people of the United States. She has handed to a person of Marietta five dollars as her contribution for the purpose. Such a movement would have a history more grand and touching than any of which we have account. Would it not be well to take up this suggestion, and make it known to the freedmen?" This was the first of a series of events which ended after a period of years in the dedication of the famous Emancipation Memorial in Washington, a duplicate of which also stands in the Massachusetts state capital.

The several persons who shared in the promotion of the movement for the erection of this memorial are equally entitled to honor, although they constitute a group of most diverse types. At the time that Charlotte Scott offered her gift, Negro men and women all over the United States were mourning the death of the Emancipator; many of them must have wished to express in some way their affection and gratitude for "Massa Lincoln," and it fell to this former slave, of whom we know so little, to show what might be done.

Dr. Rucker had come to Marietta more than a year before the ending of the war. He was a Virginia loyalist, described in the North as "a gentleman of property and influence" who had "done a great deal for our cause," and denounced in the South as "a notorious spy and bridge-burner" who had been guilty of larceny and treason. For about seventeen months he was in the hands of the Confederates as a prisoner of war. His life was in peril. The Federal government set aside certain Southern prisoners as hostages for his safety. His home had been at Covington, in what is now West Virginia, but it was from Marietta that his wife wrote in his behalf to President Lincoln in February, 1863. Richmond and Washington were still exchanging argumentative letters about his case when he solved his own problem by escaping from jail. In November, 1863, he arrived at Gauley Bridge, and soon afterward crossed the Ohio River and rejoined his family.

James Erwin Yeatman, banker and philanthropist, was a leading citizen of St. Louis. During the war he devoted almost his entire time to his duties as president of the United States Sanitary Commission, which had been organized to do in the West a work similar to that done in the East by the Commission founded by Dr. Henry W. Bellows — establishing hospitals, recruiting nurses, distributing sanitary supplies, looking after the welfare of prisoners, attending to the multitudinous details of caring for sick and wounded soldiers and sailors, and raising money for the cause — a Civil War forerunner of the Red Cross.*

This Western Sanitary Commission had been established at the behest of another Unitarian clergyman. Dr. William Greenleaf Eliot was born in New Bedford, Massachusetts, graduated from the Cambridge Divinity School, and was ordained in William Ellery Channing's Boston church in 1834. At the age of twenty-three Eliot went to the then distant city of St. Louis, where for years he served the whole community in various religious and benevolent enterprises. He became the founder of a great university, a preacher of liberal views in a stronghold of orthodoxy, and an advocate of gradual emancipation in a slave state. It was by accident that Dr. Eliot came into contact with the Negro slave Archer Alexander, but it was no accident that he became his protector in the troubled times of war. Archer was born on a plantation about thirty miles from Richmond, Virginia. He had been a playmate of the "young master" who migrated with him to Missouri. This master was "kind and considerate," but later sold Archer to a new owner, living near St. Louis, who was a Unionist but proslavery. Midway in the war Archer learned that a party of secessionists had

* Winston Churchill is understood to have drawn his portrait of Calvin Brinsmade for his Civil War novel *The Crisis* with Mr. Yeatman in mind.

sawed the timbers of a bridge over which a Union regiment was to march. That night he walked five miles to tell a Unionist antislavery man of the trap, and the troops were warned in time. Somehow word got around that Archer Alexander had been the "traitor." He managed to reach St. Louis, and there found a friend in the respected clergyman Dr. Eliot, who rescued him from the jail into which a gang of slave-snatchers had put him, employed him, and kept him in security until the state became in fact free soil. Archer Alexander is said to have been the last fugitive taken in Missouri under the old slave code. He lived long enough to know that he and Abraham Lincoln, portrayed in bronze, were to constitute the first group in memory of emancipation ever to be erected in America.

The sculptor who modeled that group was born almost on the slope of Bunker Hill, in Charlestown, Massachusetts. Thomas Ball was a versatile and lovable man. In his ingratiating autobiography he related how he served as a choir singer in Boston, and in 1848 sang the title role in *Elijah* in the first performance of that oratorio in this country. He became a portrait painter and practiced modeling in clay. For twelve years he lived in a "spacious old garret in Tremont Row," where he "labored, studied, slept, played, and sometimes took his frugal meals," and where, "far above the noisy crowd . . . he could bellow to his heart's content." Fortune befriended him. In 1854 he sailed for Italy, and after several years returned to Boston, where, in 1864, he completed the equestrian statue of Washington which now stands in the Public Garden at the foot of Commonwealth Avenue. This was the turning point in his long career. By leisurely stages he went back to Italy with his family, spending some time in London, and leaving there just as the tidings of the fall of Richmond arrived. They went on to Munich, and "on leaving our hotel to continue our journey," he records, "the landlord came to our carriage to tell us of the terrible news, just received from America, that Abraham Lincoln, and his Secretary of State, Seward, had both been assassinated." That horror remained with Thomas Ball for many days. In Florence he found a temporary studio in the Casa Guidi, where the Brownings had lived and Mrs. Browning had died. A project had been "impatiently bubbling in his brain" ever since the German landlord had told him of the calamity which had fallen upon his country. For Charlotte Scott, "Massa Lincoln" must have a monument; Thomas Ball was dreaming of what was to become the "Emancipation Group." Each in his own way had conceived the idea of what ought to be. The sculptor set to work to make his dream a visible reality.

He relates that while waiting to find a studio he began a half-size study of the group, and goes on to explain the expedient by which he overcame a serious difficulty when he began the modeling of the nude slave. He could not find a good life model; "so, as it was warm weather," he wrote, "I decided to constitute myself both model and modeler. By lowering the clay so that I could work upon it while in a kneeling position (that of the slave), and placing a looking-glass on each side of me, I brought everything quite conveniently before me. As I did not require an Apollo for a model, but one who could appreciate exactly the position I desired, and could not only see but feel the action of each muscle, I could not have had a better one — certainly not for the money. At any rate, I succeeded in making one of the best of my nude figures, though under difficulties"; and he added, again with a fleck of humor, "but that was not the first nor the last time that I conquered difficulties in a similar way."

The sculptor made no further mention of this work until a few years later, when Dr. Eliot visited the studio and noticed the group. "In the summer of 1869," Eliot wrote, "I was in Florence, Italy, and at the rooms of Thomas Ball, sculptor, I saw a group in marble which he had designed and executed immediately after President Lincoln's death. It had been done under the strong impulse of the hour, with no special end in view, except to express the magnificent act which had given new birth to his country, and for which the beloved and heroic leader had suffered martyrdom."

The Sanitary Commission had issued a letter inviting all freedmen to send in contributions for a monument to "Massa Lincoln," and $12,150 had been received from "colored soldiers under command of General J. W. Davidson," whose headquarters were at Natchez, Mississippi. From other sources this was increased to $16,242. Then the enterprise lost its momentum; there came "a revulsion of feeling," due, so Dr. Eliot thought, to the clash between Congress and President Johnson. The inadequate fund was held at interest. When Dr. Eliot told Mr. Ball of the project, the sculptor at once responded to the opportunity for a patriotic service, placing his group in the hands of the Commission, charging nothing for supervision of the work, and asking only that the cost of its reproduction in bronze of colossal size at the Royal Foundry in Munich be made good to him. He pronounced the amount actually on hand "amply sufficient."

Photographs in hand, Dr. Eliot went back to St. Louis. The Commission gladly approved the proposal, suggesting only one change: in the marble group the countenance of the slave wore a pensive, submissive look, the eyes gazed quietly outward with no glint of emotion, the head was covered with a "liberty cap," and the right arm was bent at the elbow with the hand reaching across so that the fingers rested on the left arm. The slave seemed to receive the gift of freedom "passively." In the bronze group the head is raised, the eyes gleam upward, and the right arm is extended straight outward from the body with the hand clenched. Action is suggested; the slave helps to break his own chains. The artist cheerfully gave his assent to so obviously valid an alteration. Another set of photographs crossed the Atlantic from St. Louis to Florence. These were pictures of Archer Alexander, and it is the head of that fugitive slave upon which Abraham Lincoln looks in the bronze Emancipation Group. The likeness was pronounced by Dr. Eliot to be "as correct as that of Mr. Lincoln himself." Presumably only slight alterations were made in the delineation of the muscles of the body.

By an act of June 23, 1874, Congress authorized the erection of this monument in Lincoln Park, a quiet and handsome open space about six acres in area about a mile east of the Capitol in Washington, and appropriated $3,000 for a pedestal. The park, named for the President in 1866, was not developed until 1870, but the variety and number of the shrubs and trees give it a much older look. Not now so popular for residential purposes as it once was, it is a beautiful, quiet spot, at the intersection of several streets.

There, on April 14, 1876, the eleventh anniversary of Lincoln's assassination, a vast throng assembled to await the long procession, with the place of honor assigned to the colored troops of the Civil War. It was a great day for the Negro population of the District of Columbia. A legal holiday was declared. A dozen Negro benevolent and charitable organizations were in line, flying their banners and displaying their regalia — the Knights Templar, the Knights of St. Augustine, the Sons of Purity, the Sons of Levi, the Good Samaritans, the Labor League. On the speakers' stand sat the President, the members of the Cabinet, the justices of the Supreme Court, foreign diplomats, Senators and Representatives, and a group of local citizens. The Marine Band played; the Emancipation Proclamation, and a poem by

Miss Cornelia Ray, a Negro girl of New York City, were read. A correspondent for a Boston newspaper described how "a silence of breathless expectation fell on that dense mass when the supreme moment came." Professor John M. Langston of Howard University, distinguished son of a mother once a slave, accepted the memorial in the name of the nation and invited President Grant to uncover the group. "All eyes turned to the mass of flags, and the man of deeds, not words, hopped up, and, with hat in one hand, pulled the cord — and sat down again, without having moved a muscle of his thin lips."

"While the air was ringing with shouts and music and cannon," continued the watchful correspondent, "we looked at the statue. . . . It is conceded by all to be the best figure of Abraham Lincoln yet made. He is standing beside a monolith upon which is the face of Washington in bas relief, and holding in one hand the Emancipation Proclamation, his right hand stretched over the slave, on whose ankles are shackles, but the chain that connects them has been cut, and he is in the act of rising and looking full into Mr. Lincoln's face." The Negro was "the ideal slave," continued the writer, "although the figure is said to be a photograph," and he is "by far the best looking of the two." This reporter, a woman, "hardly thought any of us would take Mr. Lincoln as our Apollo; yet the grandeur and dignity of his mien make one forget the face, and read, in the words of Frederick Douglass, the orator of the day, in every line, feature and figure, something of the exalted character and the great work of the first Martyr President of the United States." On the face of the pedestal the correspondent read that the monument was erected by the Western Sanitary Commission, with funds contributed solely by emancipated citizens, the first contributor having been Charlotte Scott.

In the mature judgment of the historian of American sculpture, Lorado Taft, "Ball's conception of Lincoln is a lofty one . . . conveyed in a language intelligible to all, and in terms as well of sculptural significance. The Lincoln monument is one of the inspired works of American sculpture; a great theme, expressed with emotion by an artist of intelligence and sympathy who felt what he was doing. It is a pity to lose sight of its nobility and of its simple sculptural beauty because its surface lacks vivacity of treatment. We are not wrong in prizing this quality, but there are things in art, as in life, which are more important than charm of surface."

With the statue unveiled, all eyes turned upon the orator of the day, himself a former slave, sitting upon the platform among the nation's dignitaries. Brown of skin, his leonine face framed in white hair and beard, "Fred" Douglass was the most noted American Negro of that time. The son of an unknown white father, he had borne the tyranny of a cruel master, until he had been sold to a kind mistress in Baltimore, who had assisted him to learn to read and write. Ambition kindled; he escaped to New Bedford, Massachusetts, where he became a common laborer. He ventured to attend an antislavery convention on Nantucket Island, where his speech, stumbling though it was, proved to be the sensation of the meeting. Within a few years he had become celebrated as an orator of extraordinary powers. To him, as the representative of his race, had been assigned a service which he was proud to perform. In any assemblage he would have been a marked man. Twice at least he had had interviews with Lincoln, received both times *as a man*. In the second instance, in the presence of a large assemblage in the White House, the President, noticing him some distance away, had exclaimed so that all about him could hear, "Here comes my friend Douglass."

From any lips the orator's speech would have been rated eloquent and fitting, but from the lips of a man whose early years had been spent in slavery it was justly pronounced remarkable. Surrounded by a sea of black faces, Douglass referred to his hearers, with pardonable pride, several times as "fellow citizens." Nothing "could better illustrate the vast and wonderful change which has taken place in our condition as a people than the fact of our assembling here for the purpose we have today. . . . No such demonstration would have been tolerated here twenty years ago." He congratulated both whites and blacks "upon the contrast between now and then: the new dispensation of freedom with its thousand blessings to both races and the old dispensation of slavery with its ten thousand evils to both races — white and black." His people had come "to express as best they could, by appropriate forms and ceremonies, their grateful sense of the vast, high, and preeminent services rendered to ourselves, to our race, to the country, and to the whole world, by Abraham Lincoln."

Apt in analysis of the character of Lincoln, Douglass penetratingly examined his policy. "His personal traits and public acts," he said, "are better known to the American people than are those of any other man of his age. He was a mystery to no man who saw him and heard him. Though high in position, the humblest could approach him and feel at home in his presence. Though deep he was transparent; though strong he was gentle; though decided and pronounced in his convictions, he was tolerant towards those who differed from him, and patient under reproaches. . . . The image of the man went out with his words, and those who read them knew him. . . . Few great public men have ever been the victims of fiercer denunciation than was Abraham Lincoln during his administration. He was often wounded in the house of his friends. . . . He was assailed by abolitionists; he was assailed by slaveholders; he was assailed by the men who were for peace at any price; he was assailed by those who were for a more vigorous prosecution of the war. . . . But now the judgment is . . . that infinite wisdom has seldom sent any man into the world better fitted for his mission. . . . And so today we have done a good work for our race. In doing honor to our friend and liberator, we have been doing highest honor to ourselves. . . . And when in the future we shall be charged with ingratitude we may calmly point to the monument we have this day erected to the memory of Abraham Lincoln."

On a day which Thomas Ball does not date definitely, a commission came to him in Florence for a replica of this Lincoln group. Moses Kimball, the owner of a huge collection of curiosities and art works of many kinds from many lands, which he exhibited in a handsome building known as the Boston Museum, had interested himself in Ball's ambition and struggles during the sculptor's youth, had from time to time entrusted to him small commissions as a painter, and, in Ball's words, "when fortune had smiled on us both, and I had acquired the ability to make, and he the means to pay for it, . . . he gave me the munificent commission for the colossal bronze group, 'Emancipation,' which he presented to the city of Boston."

Mr. Kimball formally offered the group to the mayor of the city on May 30, 1879, stipulating that it should be placed "upon the triangular lot at the junction of Columbus Avenue, Park Square and Pleasant Street, and that the city will cause the area to be suitably enclosed and annually cultivated with flowering plants and shrubs." The municipal officials accepted the terms, and the monument was duly erected in what is now known as Park Square, in front of what was then the Providence Railroad station. Then as now this space was a crowded crossroads of traffic, although the character of that traffic has vastly changed. The replica was dedicated on December 6, 1879.

Bad weather compelled the transfer of the dedication exercises to

Faneuil Hall. Phillips Brooks offered prayer. A recent graduate of the Boston Latin School read a poem by John G. Whittier. Mayor Frederick O. Prince delivered the formal address, covering many phases of the slavery and secession conflict and ending with a judicious eulogy of Lincoln. For reasons difficult to trace, this bronze duplicate is considered by most observers not so pleasing as the original work in Washington, although it was also cast in the famous Munich foundry.

The "grand old sculptor," as Lorado Taft called Thomas Ball, was much loved by his pupils, among whom were Martin Milmore and Daniel Chester French. The latter said of Ball: "I respect his work and I love the man." No serious American art student who went to Italy in Ball's day ever visited Florence without finding there a friend. There the sculptor maintained his studio until 1897, never lacking important commissions. Then he returned to what he fondly alluded to often as "the homeland"; during all his residence abroad he kept closely in touch with affairs in "the States." Not until 1911, in his ninety-third year, did he pass away.

SOURCES: Thomas Ball, *My Three Score Years and Ten — An Autobiography*, 1891; Charlotte C. Eliot, *William Greenleaf Eliot*, 1904; *Bronze Group Commemorating Emancipation*, Boston City Document No. 126, 1879; Frederick Douglass, *Life and Times of Frederick Douglass, Written by Himself*, 1881; *Official Rebellion Records*, Series 1, Volume 2; Series 2, Volumes 4, 5, 6 (for Dr. William P. Rucker); Lorado Taft, *History of American Sculpture*.

The report of the 1876 unveiling may be found in *The Congregationalist*, April 19, 1876. The text of Douglass' dedication address was taken from a booklet issued by the Frederick Douglass Historical and Cultural League, 1940.

Augustus Saint-Gaudens

IN THE mellow light of a midnight moon in late May or early June of 1881, a man stood for a long time looking at a statue in Madison Square, New York City. He might have been about seventy years of age. The lifted face was strong, the hair was gray, the eyes were shining. He held his hat in his hands. His attitude and expression indicated emotions deeply moved. He knew that he was standing before the work of a master. The swelling chorus of praise which had followed the unveiling of the statue a few days before had told him what to expect, but the reverent pose of this plain man could only mean that he understood what he saw. His appearance was that of a laboring man, but his eyes were filled with the vision of the significance of the bronze figure of Admiral Farragut, standing, glass in hand, upon the swaying deck of a ship at sea, scanning the horizon.

A little group of pedestrians, a lady and two gentlemen, came down the Avenue and with definite interest noted this quietly contemplative man. Suddenly one of them exclaimed: "Why, that's father." He walked over to him with the question, "What are you doing here at this hour?" And the old man answered: "Oh, you go about your business. Haven't I a right to be here?" The father and the son looked at each other for a long moment; then their faces broke into smiles, and the younger man joined his friends and went on, leaving the father alone with the statue in the moonlight.

The incident is amusing, suggestive, and beautiful. The old man was Bernard Saint-Gaudens, shoemaker. The son was Augustus Saint-Gaudens, whom the world long ago accepted as a very great sculptor. The French father was born almost under the shadow of the Pyrenees. The son inherited various qualities of his father's, blending with them certain characteristics of his mother, who derived from Bally Mahon, County Langford, Ireland. The imagination of the father came to full flower in the genius of the son. Both were men of intense, although rigidly restrained, emotions. The son must have been profoundly moved by that meeting before the monument which was earning for him the reward of high fame after years of dreaming and striving.

The "Farragut" was the first of a series of masterpieces. The shoe-maker must have looked upon it not only with the proud tenderness of a kindly father, but in some measure with the discernment of an artist.

Where did the son get the ability to create that statue? The question has been discussed many times. He is understood to have said that "no one ever succeeded in art unless born with an uncontrollable instinct toward it." Was there something in his ancestry, in the mingling of French and Irish blood, that would justify the theory of inheritance, or must we fall back on the dictum that there is no accounting for genius? As a child Saint-Gaudens revealed the "urge" by making sketches of the shoemakers in his father's shop. Bernard was a skilled craftsman, with original ideas of what a shoe ought to be, and he could boast of the patronage of many of the first families of the city. He could not have been much surprised when the thirteen-year-old Augustus, in answer to the suggestion that he go to work, and the query as to what he would like to do, replied that he didn't care much, provided his job would help him to became an artist. The father thoughtfully apprenticed him to a cameo-cutter. It was a good trade; cameos were fashionable in those days. He spent six years at the lathe, and became a master of the craft on which in the following years of struggle he several times had to depend for bed and bread. Meanwhile he spent his evenings in study, first at the Cooper Institute, then in the National Academy of Design. He was nineteen when the observant and sympathetic father arranged for him to go to Paris to see the Exposition of 1867, paying for his passage in the steerage and provid-ing a hundred dollars in cash saved from the son's earnings. Before he sailed young Saint-Gaudens modeled a bust of his father and drew a portrait of his mother. It was a heavy blow to him when after many years these were destroyed in the burning of his studio at Cornish, New Hampshire. Today one looks with respect upon the pictures of these early products of his trained fingers and penetrating eyes.

The rest is the story of his upward climb, the privations he endured, the friends he made, his first commissions, the development of his characteristics as a man and of his gifts as an artist. He believed in himself, but he made haste slowly. He refused to surrender to the tra-ditions of the past which had become the conventions of the present. The five years abroad were divided between Paris and Rome. It was his luck to find in the Italian city a friend whose aid lifted him over what might have been an insurmountable hurdle. Montgomery Gibbs had watched him at work on his first statue, the now well-known "Hiawatha" in Hilton Park, Saratoga. This benefactor provided the funds for finishing the work and shipping it to the United States for exhibition; it was acquired by Edwin D. Morgan, former governor of New York. Through the Gibbs family the young sculptor obtained commissions to make copies of busts of Cicero and Demosthenes for William M. Evarts, together with an agreement that the distinguished lawyer would sit to him for a bust on his return home. It was also arranged that he would model portraits of Mr. Gibbs' two daughters.

The real turning of the tide took place in 1876–77, and it seemed like a tidal wave. Governor Morgan told him one day about a project for the erection of a statue of Admiral David Glasgow Farragut in New York City. The commission was about to be awarded. Saint-Gaudens entered the competition on very short notice, but the committee gave him the order by a six-to-five vote. Another former New York governor, John Adams Dix, heard of this award. The Dix family patronized Bernard's shop, and the governor commissioned the young man to model a statue of Robert R. Randall for the Sailors' Snug Harbor on Staten Island. John La Farge named him to make a series of high reliefs for the chancel of St. Thomas' Church. Young Saint-Gaudens had found powerful friends who believed in him and his future. He always rated La Farge as perhaps the most inspiring influence in his career.

One day Stanford White, while climbing the stairs to Saint-Gaudens' first New York studio, heard the sculptor bawling out the *andante* of Beethoven's Seventh Symphony and the "Serenade" from Mozart's *Don Giovanni*. Immediately the architect and the artist became comrades and friends. The relationship was of vast value for the sculptor, for the architect, already well started on his celebrated career, had a knack for designing pedestals which matched the sculptor's gift for modeling portraits. Saint-Gaudens loved music and liked to sing at his work. His confrères used to "rag" him during his student days in Paris; they made him sing the *Marseillaise* in English again and again. He knew good music, and went to hear singers and instrumentalists, in opera and concert, whenever opportunity offered. As early as 1882 he began to arrange for Sunday afternoon concerts in his studio; in time an invitation to attend one of these gatherings was prized almost like a decoration. White's partner, Charles Follen McKim, also became an intimate.

Augustus Saint-Gaudens was a mighty personality. His schooling had been sketchy and scanty. Only when he was well established in his career did he begin to read assiduously. A "subtle clairvoyance" has been ascribed to him, and his insight served him well in divining the secrets of character in the men he studied and portrayed. When he began work on his standing "Lincoln" he had only an imperfect idea of the man. He had seen him twice, once at a distance in life, and again, in a hurried near view, in death. In an autobiographical fragment Saint-Gaudens recalled a few memories of the outbreak of the Civil War — the mobs before the newspaper offices, the departure of Ellsworth's Zouaves for Washington, and what remained in his mind above all, "seeing in a procession the figure of a tall and very dark man, seeming entirely out of proportion in his height with the carriage in which he was driven, bowing to the crowds on each side. . . . The man was Abraham Lincoln on his way to Washington."

Young Saint-Gaudens was close to his thirteenth birthday when he saw Lincoln en route to his inauguration; four years later the President's body lay in state in the City Hall, and Saint-Gaudens stepped slowly along in the interminable line that led up to the bier at the head of the staircase, then "went back to the end of the line to look at him again." The funeral, which he viewed from the roof of the old Wallack's Theatre on Broome Street, "deepened the profound solemnity of my impression," he recorded, as he noticed everyone uncover while the funeral car went by. With the commission for the statue on his mind, he told Richard Watson Gilder, the editor and poet, that he thought of Lincoln as a good, kind, benevolent man, summoned to a high executive office. Gilder asked him about the poet, the prophet, the dreamer, who also was Lincoln. Saint-Gaudens asked how he might learn more about Lincoln, and Gilder "loaded him up" with books.

His work absorbed all his faculties. H. H. Richardson once saw him at the Boston Museum of Fine Arts, intently studying a cast of an Athens theatre seat. An hour later he found the sculptor still so withdrawn from time and place as to be entirely unaware of the presence of a friend. He was at work. His mind was busy with the details of the chair which he proposed to put behind his figure of Lincoln. Mrs. Saint-Gaudens once saved for him a fine commission when its loss was threatened by his habitual forgetfulness, while at work, of everything but the present task. The committee to designate the sculptor for a seated "Lincoln," also in Chicago, had made an appointment with

Saint-Gaudens for a Sunday morning at the Century Club, and the sculptor had marked the hour for the conference plainly on the blackboard in his studio. But his wife had her misgivings; she went to the studio and found her husband alone and hard at work. Had he met the committee? "No!" She hurried to the clubhouse and found some of the committeemen angry. How could they entrust such a work to so careless a man? She argued that a man so rapt in his work was the very man they wanted — and carried the day. And how that man did work! His enthusiasm for work was fairly matched by his high conception of what his work ought to be. The last decade of his all-too-short life of fifty-nine years was marked by a struggle for health and strength which increased in intensity as he neared the end. He would lie on a couch and direct his assistants, or be carried about in an improvised sedan chair while sketching his conceptions on blocks of paper.

A poet's soul resided in the body of Augustus Saint-Gaudens. In Rome he loved the plashing of the waters in the numberless fountains. In New York, the janitor of the old building in which he set up his first studio hunted for weeks to find the leak which boosted the water bills, and found it at last in the sculptor's studio. He let the water run because he liked "the tinkle." He was gay and generous. Not the least of his possessions was a valuable sense of humor. He was sensitive and thoughtful, eager to help promising juniors, fierce in denouncing the cheap and shoddy in art. One of the first to establish a summer home in Cornish, he became the founder of that New Hampshire colony. In 1905 his neighbors and other friends celebrated the twentieth anniversary of his coming with a masque amid the trees of his estate. For weeks artists and writers worked on plans and program. It was a beautiful tribute, remembered with affectionate satisfaction. Saint-Gaudens died on August 3, 1907.

Not only was he a master sculptor; he led the movement for the deliverance of American sculptors from their servitude to Italy, and prevented the substitution of Paris for Rome as a dominating influence. True, they profited greatly from their study of French technique, he said, but why should they borrow their themes from past times and faraway lands? A hint of what ought to be, he no doubt derived from John Quincy Adams Ward, but the idea of the modernization and Americanization of our sculpture burned within him, and found expression in his own work and in ready sympathy and eager aid for the establishment of the Society of American Artists. Shortly before Saint-Gaudens' death, Gilder told the sculptor's son that he had often said that the Society "was founded on the wrath of Saint-Gaudens." How long must the exponents of new ideas, the young artists who were coming on the scene, endure the complacency, the smugness, with which the Academy of Fine Arts refused to find room for the exhibition of their work? Neither a writer nor a speaker, Saint-Gaudens still became a powerful force in the movement for emancipation. He abandoned neither Paris nor Rome, but what he had learned abroad he used in his own way.

Four years of civil war had profoundly affected the thinking and the emotional reactions of all Americans who had any comprehension of the meaning of that awful experience. It fell to Saint-Gaudens to produce in enduring art the supreme expression of that catastrophe. He portrayed Farragut, alert and steady, watching the horizon, with only the fluttering of his heavy coat to suggest the force of the winds. He carved Sherman riding to victory. He made the black regiment and their white commander march before the State House in Boston, a work which justified the twelve years he spent on its creation. His was a "Lincoln" rising from the chair of state to speak to the people whom he loved and served.

There were other masterpieces, very different in character, in the long roll of his works. His "Puritan" stands for a faith which moved the world. The Adams Memorial, a purely imaginative work, with the waiting, brooding figure, meditating in silence and solitude, reminds us all of the enigma of life and the immutable destiny of mankind.

The man who provided the city of Chicago with the funds for the creation of the bronze "Lincoln" which has now stood for sixty years in the park which bears his name, achieved eminence and honor in the face of difficulties which fairly match those the President had overcome. Born in Springfield, Massachusetts, in 1806, Eli Bates as a boy suffered an amputation that crippled him for life. A clergyman received him into his home and fitted him to become a teacher in the common schools. In middle life he migrated west, and in 1853 entered the employ of a Chicago lumber company. At that time his savings amounted to $2,000; twenty-eight years later he drew a will disposing of an estate of more than a half million, a large fortune for those days. The quality of the man is demonstrated by the pains he took to repay, with compound interest, the loans and gifts of those who helped him in his youth, and by his numerous anonymous benefactions, amounting to perhaps another half million dollars.

The largest single bequests in Bates' will were $25,000 for a fountain in Lincoln Park, and $40,000 for "the erection of a statue of the late President Lincoln" in that park. The trustees whom Bates appointed to administer these bequests proved themselves men of sound judgment, abandoning any competitive scheme for the choice of a sculptor, and, as one of them explained on dedication day, deciding "to rely upon reputation for genius, fidelity, and skill, established by the execution of similar commissions, rather than upon crude designs hurriedly prepared." Thereupon they gave Saint-Gaudens, whose "Farragut" had been dedicated about the time of Bates' death, the commissions for both the statue and the fountain, "without restriction as to design, and with an ample allowance of time." The settlement of the estate had taken about three years, and on receiving these awards the sculptor spent three more years on the statue.

The newspapers of the time recorded the intensity and the reverence with which Saint-Gaudens discussed his great opportunity with his friends. Cass Gilbert, the American architect, in a letter to the London *Times* on the day of the dedication of the replica of the Saint-Gaudens statue "under the walls of Westminster Abbey," told of the time when the original of that "masterpiece of sculpture" was taking shape in the mind of the artist. Standing in the rain with the waiting crowd on that day in London, Gilbert recalled a journey with Stanford White and Saint-Gaudens from Helena, Montana, to St. Paul, Minnesota, in the early autumn of 1883. The three men were together constantly for three days aboard the train. The sculptor was always a charming companion, but on that trip he had been singularly taciturn. At St. Paul he refused to stop over for a few days at Gilbert's home, because, as Gilbert relates: "He told me in strict confidence that he was hurrying on to Chicago to close a contract with the committee there for a statue of Lincoln which should, he hoped, be the greatest work that had come to him. He said that he was absolutely absorbed in the thought of it, that he could think of nothing else, and that his journey from New York across the continent and back had given him a volume of impressions. He had never before realized the vastness and extent of the country; he never before had seen the Western men among whom Lincoln had passed his youth and early manhood, and he was going forward to the work with a sense of great responsibility. . . . Years afterwards, when we were in Paris together, he recalled the journey and how his hopes had been centered on the work, first, as a great artistic opportunity. . . . He was never satisfied with his own work. His passion for perfection drove him relentlessly to infinite pains and almost endless study not only of the superficial features of his subject, but yet more deeply into the study of the character, the life, the emotions and the very soul of the man whose features he so marvelously portrayed."

At about this time Saint-Gaudens discovered Cornish. A friend had told him there were "plenty of Lincoln-shaped men up there." In a barn a century old, on the estate which is now his memorial, he made the original sketches for both his standing and his seated "Lincoln." Luck favored him in finding a model. Just across the river in Vermont lived an angular giant, exactly of Lincoln's height, a respected citizen derived from a long line of New England ancestors. An ambitious young photographer, also a Vermonter, made scores, probably hundreds, of pictures of this model in experimental attitudes, and signed an agreement to make no prints except for Saint-Gaudens' use. They worked together harmoniously. In later years at his home in Illinois the photographer told this story to a historian, who published it in the *Journal of the Illinois State Historical Society*. The account is convincing as to the patience with which Saint-Gaudens worked upon every detail. It has been said that the model provided the statue with its classic shoulders and stalwart form, although the sculptor probably widened the shoulders somewhat. But for the magnificent head Saint-Gaudens relied on the life mask made by Leonard W. Volk. Gilder told Homer Saint-Gaudens, the sculptor's son, that the mask was of great help to his father, and recalled with more than a little pride that he had obtained the sculptor's aid in buying the original mask for the National Museum. Gilder was no less proud of his influence with Saint-Gaudens in poising the head of the statue, a matter which he mentioned in two letters in 1909. He wrote the son that after one of his visits to the studio he noticed that the sculptor "had thrown the head down a little, giving the contemplative look which is so fine, and so characteristic of Lincoln"; and to another friend he said, "I remember when I got Saint-Gaudens to alter the statue and give it the contemplative look it now has."

The man who financed the work is said to have indicated the site on which he thought it should be erected. In the last years of Mr. Bates' life the park, its name changed from Lake Park to Lincoln Park in 1865, had been a favorite resort. Bates was confident that the park would be of vast benefit to the people of that city of miraculous growth. The statue must occupy a commanding position in the open, "far from the madding crowd's ignoble strife" in the hurly-burly of the business center, with trees at its back and paths converging toward it.

The sculptor considered it important that the work be mounted upon a suitable pedestal. Stanford White, who had designed the pedestal for the "Farragut" and was to design other perfect architectural settings for Saint-Gaudens' masterworks, including both the Chicago "Lincolns," would see to that. Working, now alone, and again in consultation with the sculptor, White delighted the whole public, laymen and experts alike, by the exedra within which the statue stands. The high-backed semi-circular bench is sixty feet across from end to end and thirty feet deep. The few steps before the statue are flanked with low bases, each bearing a bronze globe with inscriptions in raised letters; on one a portion of the Gettysburg Address, on the other a few sentences from the letter to Horace Greeley. At the left as one faces the statue, there are cut in the stone on the outside of the exedra the opening phrases of the final paragraph of the Second Inaugural: "With malice toward none, with charity for all, with firmness in the right, as God gives us to see the right, let us strive on. . . ." In the corresponding position at the right is chiseled the final sentence of the Cooper Institute address: "Let us have faith that right makes might, and in that faith let us to the end dare to do our duty as we understand it." Before the bench, midway of its sweeping curve, stands the massive block which supports the chair of state and the figure of the President. Over him, high in the air, flies the flag of the Union.

The day of the unveiling, Saturday, October 22, 1887, was far from pleasant. Every one of the thousands who witnessed the ceremonies carried an umbrella.* The Park Commissioners, in the name of the public, accepted from the Bates trustees the splendid gift. The official address was delivered by Leonard Swett, who for about eleven years had ridden the Eighth Judicial Circuit with Lincoln, and after 1865 had become a leader of the Chicago bar. Besides dealing with the matters which such an occasion compels, his speech was interwoven

* The statement in *The Reminiscences of Augustus Saint-Gaudens,* edited by Homer Saint-Gaudens (I:353), that on account of the rain the unveiling took place "without the ceremonies that might have lent consequence to the occasion" seems to be erroneous, on the basis of contemporary newspapers and official records.

with references to his personal intimacy with his old friend. Lincoln's "tactics as a politician," said Swett, were unique. His "sublime and crowning characteristic" was self-reliance. He was the most inquisitive man Swett had ever known, pumping information from stage-drivers and crossroads blacksmiths. Lincoln had "bridged back" from middle age to youth, and learned to spell well. The Declaration of Independence was "his perfect standard of political truth." He "believed in God as the Supreme Ruler of the world," and in himself "as an instrument and leader in the forces of freedom."

The moment for the unveiling came. A boy in his fifteenth year, the son of Robert Todd Lincoln, named Abraham for his grandfather, stepped forward and pulled the cord which loosed the huge flag covering the bronze giant. Cannon boomed. But, according to the official account, there was no applause; a "deep hush" fell upon the multitude. And at that moment the sun struggled through the clouds to shine for a little while upon the scene. After a time the cheers came. Tears were shed by many who had known the man in life.

They looked at the symbol of the office he had held and of the cause he had represented. The chair was not merely an ornamental accessory, but an essential element in the composition, inseparable from the statue itself. The people had heard the chairman of the trustees say in his presentation speech that it had been the sculptor's purpose "to present Lincoln, the President, burdened with the responsibilities of the hour, giving audience to a delegation of the people, who presented for his consideration matters of great public concern." It is a thoughtful Lincoln who stands before them. He is pondering. Presently he will lift his head and tell them, out of his greater knowledge of the conditions besetting the Administration, all that he can safely publicize, and why he may not be able to grant all they ask.

Ever since the day of dedication, men and women from every corner of the Union and from all the lands of the globe have gone to Lincoln Park to look upon that statue. It was instantly recognized as a great work of art. It is so regarded today. It has never been surpassed as a portrait in bronze or marble of the best loved of all Americans. We have many noble sculptured "Lincolns" today, but it is a question — one of those questions that can never be conclusively decided — if any of them equals this in the beauty of its conception and the artistry of its execution.

That foreign-born American patriot, Franklin K. Lane, once recorded that he never passed through Chicago "without visiting the statue of Lincoln by Saint-Gaudens and standing before it for a moment uncovered." Let us linger for a time, hat in hand, within the atmosphere of this monument, and look, remember, and meditate. We see a plain man, a giant in stature, with huge feet, powerful hands, and long limbs, standing erect in an attitude which carries no hint of the actor or poseur. The figure is not dependent upon extraneous factors for its suggestion of physical and spiritual power. This man plants his feet solidly on the ground. Many artists have commented upon the astonishing triumph achieved by Saint-Gaudens in handling the problem of the clothing worn by the men of Lincoln's time. He did not drape a toga or a shawl over Lincoln's shoulders. It has been said that he "actually made coat and trousers decorative." We know that his Yankee model had to acquire a stance that would put the wrinkles in the right places. The costume does not in the slightest degree detract from the quiet dignity with which the President awaits the moment when he shall speak. The chair suggests the office he holds, the power he wields, the responsibility he must never ignore. Nothing indicates an extraordinary occasion. We see Abraham Lincoln as he might have appeared scores of times during the four years of war. The face holds our attention. People called him ugly, yet more than a few artists have pronounced his face to have been not only impressive but beautiful. For the moment he is pensive, sad. He must be cautious, he reflects before he speaks, but he is calm and unafraid — a man one can trust.

Memory comes to our aid. This man was called "Old Abe" — in derision by his foes, in affection by his friends. He was known as "Honest Abe," a tribute to his integrity. In war time he was "Father Abraham," recognized by the people as their friend, protector, and guide. Our hearts swell as we recall the wonderful story of his life. Unschooled, he became one of the best educated men of his time, the writer of imperishable letters and addresses; a logician who could "snake a sophism out of its hole better than all the trained logicians of the schools"; a statesman whose magnanimity is unsurpassed in the history of mankind. In the fear of God he occupied the seat of power, never forgetting what he had been, nor ever boasting of what he had become. The long hard years of wielding an ax had knotted his muscles and gnarled his hands; midway of the war he objected to the statue of a woodchopper in the east pediment of the Capitol because he did not make a clean cut. His inherent greatness unfolded progressively during the ordeal he had to endure, vexed sometimes but never bitter, suffering with and for the South, mourning for and with the North, never flinching in fidelity to a cause that must be "nobly saved" as "the last best hope of earth." We note the lines in that face and mark the brooding sadness in those eyes. We study the "human, humorous mouth," and we remember with satisfaction the relief he found in going to the theater and in telling the stories he brought from the West.

A unique man — none like him ever, anywhere. A great soul guided the fingers that moulded this statue. What we see in this bronze giant depends on what we are, but few there are who can resist the spell of this triumphant achievement. Augustus Saint-Gaudens gave us the man whom we love as our comrade and friend, the statesman whom we revere as our leader. We turn away from this memorial accepting anew Abraham Lincoln's vision of what ought to be.

In the nerve center of the British Empire, in what is known as the Canning Enclosure, almost under the shadow of the Houses of Parliament and facing the entrance to the north transept of Westminster Abbey, there was unveiled on July 28, 1920, with appropriate international ceremonies, a replica of this "Lincoln." Certain details of the unpleasant episode that ended with the substitution of this statue for the one by George Grey Barnard, which had once been accepted by the public authorities as a gift from an individual American, will be noted in another connection. What began as a squabble developed into a bitter controversy, but a satisfactory adjustment was finally arranged, with the Barnard "Lincoln" handsomely placed in Manchester and the British government accepting the Saint-Gaudens replica from the trustees of the Carnegie Endowment for International Peace in behalf of the American people. Dr. Nicholas Murray Butler has an account of the substitution in his autobiography, which differs in important respects from the newspaper accounts. Writing as one familiar at first hand with the facts, Dr. Butler explains that Robert Todd Lincoln deposited an ample sum of money with a New York banker to meet the cost of a Saint-Gaudens replica, and appealed to Butler, then president of Columbia University, to manage a movement for the substitution. The Carnegie Endowment entered the field, making it unnecessary to draw upon Robert Lincoln's fund for the statue or for any other expense. Dr. Butler quotes with justifiable pride Lincoln's letter of thanks to him after the tangled skein was unraveled.

The weather on dedication day, July 28, 1920, in London was worse than it had been on the corresponding day in Chicago. Nevertheless, a great crowd assembled at the Enclosure. Cass Gilbert saw in the throng princes and statesmen, prelates and soldiers, Westminster Abbey choir boys and American Boy Scouts, artists, authors, men and women of all ranks — "as representative a group as could have been gathered at any time or place in the world." Before the pedestal as a guard of honor stood fifteen veterans of the American Civil War.

The proceedings, however, with the exception of the actual unveiling, were held near at hand in Central Hall. Viscount James Bryce, who presided, concluded his introduction of Elihu Root as the principal speaker with a passage which was hailed with cheers. "Here, in the midst of our great Englishmen," he said, "let this great American stand, majestic in his simplicity, a witness to what one indomitable will — bent on high aims, always hopeful because inspired by faith in freedom and in the people whence he sprang — could achieve for all mankind." Mr. Root formally presented the statue to the British people, and went on to outline the life of the American martyr, mentioning and illustrating various of his high qualities. It is reported that there were tears when Mr. Root recited Lincoln's reply to the message of sympathy and support which the suffering cotton workers of Lancashire had sent him just at the end of 1862 — how the President had pronounced theirs "an instance of sublime Christian heroism, which has not been surpassed in any age or in any country." Mr. Root quoted the conclusion of the Second Inaugural and the letter to Mrs. Bixby. There were prolonged cheers when he ended by saying that "the statue of Lincoln, the American, stands as of right before the old Abbey where sleep the great of Britain's history."

Prime Minister David Lloyd George accepted the statue on behalf of the people of the British Empire in a brilliant short speech. In a few minutes, he said, they were to see the presentment in bronze of the best-known face in the Anglo-Saxon world, one of the few best-known faces of the whole world. "In his life he was a great American. He is no longer so. He is one of those giant figures, of whom there are very few in history, who lose their nationality in death. They are no longer Greek or Hebrew, English or American; they belong to mankind." Again the cheers were "loud and prolonged."

The crowd waiting in the pelting rain — among them Ignace Pad-

erewski as the representative of the Polish Associations in America —
shouted a welcome as the company arrived from the Hall. Mr. Root
formally invited the Duke of Connaught, third son of Queen Victoria,
to unveil the statue. In defiance of the storm the Duke delivered
his brief speech, lauding President Lincoln and thanking England's
American friends for "their noble gift." He then released the coverings which concealed the work. The Union Jack and the Stars and
Stripes parted and fell on either side; all hats came off; the choir led
the assemblage in singing Julia Ward Howe's "Battle Hymn of the
Republic," and the walls of the Abbey echoed back the chorus. Wreaths
were laid at the base of the memorial, among them a circle of laurel
by a Nigerian bishop for the native races of Africa. The final poignant
touch was reached when an offering of roses was deposited by a Cotton
Managers' Association of Lancashire.

Parliament Square was re-planned in 1950, and a smaller garden
has been made, in which the "Lincoln" stands atop its high pedestal,
with the Canning statue in the same enclosure as before. The most
noticeable change is that the "Lincoln" now faces the Houses of Parliament.

In the year of Saint-Gaudens' death, a score of years after the dedication of the statue in Lincoln Park, he completed another "Lincoln,"
also for Chicago, which there is reason to believe he liked better than
the first. We know that he welcomed the opportunity to model this
later portrait. While at work on the original commission his mind had
been divided between two conceptions of what his design should be —
whether a standing or a seated figure. Not that he deprecated the enormous popularity of the statue in Lincoln Park, for his son has intimated that "even late in life" the one change he might have made
would have been to reduce its height somewhat.

On the back of the pedestal on which is mounted the statue now commonly called "Saint-Gaudens' seated 'Lincoln' " is a simple bronze tablet informing the visitor that "this statue was given to the people of
Chicago through the generosity of John Crerar." That great citizen
had provided in his will that $100,000 should be used for the erection
of a "colossal statue" of Abraham Lincoln. The gift was not only remarkable in size, but there were detailed directions that when mounted
the statue must "face south" and be placed in "some south-side Chicago park."

John Crerar was the son of Scottish parents, a man notable for the orthodoxy of his Presbyterianism, the quiet manner in which he lived, and the lofty ideas he cherished of what a great city should be. He had begun life as a bookkeeper in Boston and New York. Coming to Chicago in 1862, he accumulated a large fortune in the manufacture of railroad supplies and materials for contractors. He died in 1889, leaving many legacies for friends and philanthropic agencies, the largest of which, and those of widest public interest, were a large sum for the creation of what is known as the Crerar Library and the provision for the Lincoln statue.

Between Mr. Crerar's death and the dedication of the statue yawned a gap of over a third of a century. Certain cousins of the bachelor Crerar contested the will, but the courts sustained it in 1893. Then Saint-Gaudens spent about twelve years on the execution of the commission, laboring with tireless patience in the Cornish studios amid annoying difficulties. The largest of the sculptor's studios was destroyed by fire in 1904, when the new "Lincoln" was nearly completed, and many of his most valued possessions were lost. Saint-Gaudens attacked the task and others in hand with characteristic determination. A suitable model was found. We are told that he clothed his man in broadcloth and had him tramp about the countryside to fit the costume to his figure. We do not know just how the development of Saint-Gaudens' ideas and the solution of the problems involved in their execution were divided between the years before and after the fire, but in spite of his illness the indomitable sculptor finished the work a few months before his death.

Still another and a longer period of waiting followed. Chicago had difficulty deciding upon a site for the statue in compliance with the terms of the Crerar will. At last a place was made for it, so to speak; a new park, named for General Grant, was created on the lake front, across the Illinois Central Railroad tracks from Michigan Avenue, and on this "made land" the statue was erected. In several ways the site is admirable. The seated figure does face the south. Eastward is Lake Michigan, westward the busy thoroughfare lined with towering buildings on the landward side, whence one crosses the depressed railroad tracks on wide and handsome bridges. The seated statue was put on display at the Art Institute in a memorial exhibition of the sculptor's work, then shipped to San Francisco for the Panama-Pacific Exposition in 1915, only to be "stored" in a Parks Department warehouse on its return, covered with dust and almost forgotten; but now at last it found a worthy place in which to abide.

Memorial Day, May 31, 1926, was chosen for the unveiling. During the thirty-seven years since the death of Mr. Crerar, the original group of trustees provided for in his will had passed away and been replaced once and again. Of the third group, William Louderback and Leonard A. Busby were present on that day. There were introductory remarks by Mr. Busby and a formal address by Charles S. Cutting, former probate judge. Norman Williams, Jr., a lad in knickerbockers, grandson of one of the original trustees, pulled the cords which held the shroud in position, unveiling the bronze figure.

The setting for this second "Lincoln" of Saint-Gaudens was also in large part designed by Stanford White. White granite steps lead up to the platform on which stands the pink granite pedestal, within a semi-circular bench more than 150 feet in diameter, at each end of which rises a lofty column of white marble. The pedestal is high and the figure huge, so much so that one must stand at a distance and lift his eyes to study the face. The bearded President sits in a chair of the Roman type in an attitude of complete passivity. The right hand, with fingers spread, rests upon the knee; the left hand, with fingers folded, falls upon the arm of the chair. The left elbow lies within a fold of a fringed flag of the Union, wrought in bronze and draped over the back of the chair. The face is lowered. The expression is that of an earnest man lost to the world about him as he studies the problems of his time. The hint of dejection which some observers find in the eyes and the poise of the head is lost when one examines the features in profile. The man is resting and pondering; he always had been "considerin' like," his stepmother had said. There is no suggestion of weakness in the pose of the body or the set of the lips. The muscles have been released from tension, but the mind is grappling with questions which he alone must answer.

The key to the sculptor's purpose is found in the suggestion of loneliness. During four years of the greatest civil war known to history Lincoln abode alone. He was at the center of the whirlpool, badgered and buffeted, with raw human nature exposed to him at its worst — and sometimes at its best — living on a level too high for most men to reach, and he was compelled, in spite of his love for human contacts, to live alone. The surroundings of the monument stress the idea of isolation. On one hand is one of the world's busiest streets, throbbing with activity, and on the other hand roll the waters of one of the Great

Lakes. The big park itself is relatively empty. The vicinity of the statue is kept clear of objects that might divert attention from that brooding figure who sits there, in silence, aloof, at grips with the problem of saving the Union.

SOURCES: Homer Saint-Gaudens, ed., *The Reminiscences of Augustus Saint-Gaudens*, 1913; Rosamond Gilder, ed., *Letters of Richard Watson Gilder*, 1916; Frank E. Stevens, "The Story of a Statue," *Journal of the Illinois State Historical Society*, April, 1931; *Ceremonies at the Unveiling of the Statue of Abraham Lincoln at Lincoln Park, Chicago*, 1887; Anne Winter Lane and Louise Herrick Wall, eds., *Letters of Franklin K. Lane*, 1922; Tyler Dennett, ed., *Lincoln and the Civil War in the Diaries and Letters of John Hay*, 1939; Nicholas Murray Butler, *Across the Busy Years*, 1940; Charles G. Baldwin, *Stanford White*, 1931; Pamphlet No. 156, published by the American Association for International Conciliation; William Webster Ellsworth, *Golden Age of Authors*, 1919; C. Lewis Hand, *Augustus Saint-Gaudens*, 1908.

Cass Gilbert's letter may be found in the London *Times* of July 29, 1920.

9   ILLUSTRATED PAGE 152

"This bronze Doth Keep the very form and mould of our great martyr's face . . ." *

THE rare service rendered to his own and later generations by Leonard Volk was the making of the famous life mask and the casts of the hands of Abraham Lincoln in 1860. At that time Volk was more attached to the fortunes of Stephen A. Douglas, the Senator from Illinois, than to the interests of the man who had failed to oust Douglas from the senatorship in 1858. Upon his son, then four years of age, Volk had bestowed the full name of his patron. In after years the son found it too cumbersome and called himself Douglas Volk. The elder Volk spent most of the winter of 1859 in Washington "publishing a statuette" of the Senator.

Douglas was a cousin of Leonard Volk's wife, and had provided the funds which enabled Volk to spend nearly two years in art studies in Rome. The young sculptor expressed his gratitude to his benefactor in many ways, and meanwhile was alert for opportunities for the ad-

* From Richard Watson Gilder's sonnet.

vancement of the professional career on which he had embarked. He made inquiries as to the probable nominee of the new Republican Party for the presidency, "hoping that he might model a bust of him in advance." Presumably it was a lucky chance rather than any formal arrangement that brought him into contact with Lincoln a little while before the Republican National Convention met in Chicago. While his own account of the incident, published in 1881, is accepted in the main as trustworthy, it is fallible in some details.

Less than two months before his nomination, Lincoln spent nearly a fortnight in Chicago in attendance upon the United States Circuit Court as counsel for the defense in the third trial of what is known as the "sandbar case," involving the ownership of accretions of land on the waterfront of a city obviously destined to become one of the greatest in America. At that time Volk had a walk-up studio on the fifth floor of the building opposite the Sherman House in Clark Street. There Lincoln kept a promise, said to have been made at some previous time, that he would "sit for a bust" if his engagements permitted. Volk offered to save time for Lincoln by taking measurements of his head and shoulders and making a cast of his face.

Volk's account of the sitting reads: "He sat naturally in a chair when I made the cast, and saw every move I made in a mirror opposite, as I put the plaster on without interference with his eyesight or with his free breathing through the nostrils. It was about an hour before the mold was ready to be removed, and being all in one piece, with both ears perfectly taken, it clung pretty hard, as the cheekbones were higher than the jaws at the lobe of the ear. He bent his head low and took hold of the mold, and gradually worked it off without breaking or injury; it hurt a little, as a few hairs of the tender temples pulled out with the plaster, and made his eyes water."

On Sunday, May 20, the day after Lincoln received formal notice of his nomination, Volk came to the Lincoln home in Springfield to make casts of his hands. "The right hand appeared swollen as compared with the left," Volk tells us, "on account of excessive handshaking the evening before." Volk wished Lincoln to hold something in his right hand, and the candidate went to the woodshed, sawed a few inches off a broom handle, and whittled the edges, so that the cast showed the hand gripping this round stick. For this mask and these casts nearly all subsequent Lincoln artists are grateful to the ambitious young sculptor.

Several association items which Volk carried back to Chicago were destroyed in the conflagration of 1871, and the sculptor "saved the casts of the face and hands" by taking them with him on a trip to Rome. He is said to have made two busts and two statues of Lincoln. One of the statues is in the State House in Springfield, showing the figure standing before a chair, an arrangement used in a very different manner by Saint-Gaudens in 1887. As this is a plaster model, however, it falls outside the scope of this volume.

Leonard Wells Volk was born in Wellstown, New York, on November 7, 1828. With little schooling and much experience in farm work, he undertook to learn the trade of marble cutting in his father's shop at Pittsfield, Massachusetts. He made up his mind to become a sculptor, and taught himself the art of modeling by the trial-and-error method. He went west, setting up "studios" successively in Buffalo, St. Louis, and Galena, Illinois, in which latter place he came into contact with Douglas. Perhaps Volk's copy of another sculptor's bust of Henry Clay interested his cousin-in-law. In 1855 Volk "deposited" his wife and boy in the family home in Pittsfield, and departed for Italy. On his return in 1857 he opened a studio in Chicago, and for several years appears to have been the only sculptor in that astonishing community, where, in spite of the preference of most people for corner lots rather than marble ornaments, he made his influence felt. He was a founder of the Academy of Design and for eight years its president, and he organized the first art exhibition ever held in Chicago. His bust of Lincoln was completed on June 7, 1860, and the *Tribune* "boosted its sale — in life size at $10, in half-size at $4." This probably is the bust which Volk exhibited in Paris in 1867; it was destroyed with the burning of the building of the Chicago Historical Society in 1871, but the original model was rescued from the flames. Volk visited Europe twice after the Civil War, and in 1872 he ordered at Geneva the first shipment of Carrara marble ever sent directly to Chicago. Among his productions are a soldiers' monument at Rock Island, Illinois; the statue of James Shields in Statuary Hall in the national Capitol; various ideal figures, and many, and more successful, authentic busts of public men, including such friends of Lincoln as Elihu Washburne and David Davis. His bronze "Lincoln" is in Rochester, New York, and his "Douglas" surmounts a marble shaft which soars toward the sky in Chicago. He died in 1895. His son became a portrait painter of note.

The Rochester "Lincoln" is the topmost figure in a Soldiers' and

Sailors' Memorial. The original suggestion for such a monument was put forward in 1870, at the observance of the third annual national Memorial Day, but nothing definite was done until the proceeds from an entertainment in 1872 were set aside as a nucleus for a monument fund. A lag of nine years ensued, ending in 1881 when the *Rochester Morning Herald* initiated an organized campaign, which brought in $13,500, and the George H. Thomas Post of the Grand Army of the Republic gave $1,000. The fund did not become sufficient until 1889, and the contract between the committee and the sculptor is dated October 31 of that year. The total cost of the memorial was $26,000.

The dedication took place on Memorial Day, 1892, in the presence, it would seem, of almost the entire population of the city, and many thousands from outside its bounds. It was distinctly a Grand Army day; every veteran who could hobble marched in the two-mile parade, along with the Sons of Veterans and numerous civic and fraternal organizations. President Benjamin Harrison, Governor Roswell P. Flower, and many other prominent political figures, were present — quite possibly mindful of the fact that 1892 was a campaign year. The platform before the monument in Washington Square was packed with dignitaries, and not the least observed of them was "Fred" Douglass. General John A. Reynolds, as master of ceremonies, reviewed the work of the Monument Committee. Five little girls pulled the cords that released the blanketing flags, the "Lincoln" itself, forty-two feet above the pavement, being uncovered by Alice Little.

The Civil War President is depicted in an unusual posture, with the right foot well advanced, and the hands holding a large scroll which he has unrolled across his body. This has been classed as a Gettysburg Address statue; we consider it more probably an Emancipation design. The gesture is that of a man who proudly displays a great document. The figure is ten feet in height, and is placed at the top of a shaft of granite set in a pedestal which rests on a base twenty-one feet square. On smaller pedestals at the corners of the base are four figures representing the national services — infantry, artillery, cavalry, and marines. The panels at the foot of the shaft carry bas-reliefs of battle scenes. The style dates the monument, but of that style it is probably as artistic an example as the country contains.

The orator of the day, David A. Hill, President of the University of Rochester, was cheered many times in the course of his long historical address. In a series of glowing sentences he defined the debt the country owed to the "men who had defended the Union." In a long poem, written for the occasion by Samuel H. Lowe, President Lincoln and a score of Union generals were lauded. President Harrison, introduced both as President and as a comrade in the G.A.R., delivered the shortest address of the day. In his remarks we find a few allusions — not to say illusions — indicating how times have changed; he declared that "we are happy in our great national isolation," and added that "no nation in the world is able to wage war on our soil."

The Governor's speech also was very short, but it sounded a note missing from the other addresses: "The same green sod covers the grave of the Union soldier and the Confederate soldier, and the firm texture which Nature has woven over the dead bodies of those who were once in mortal conflict is symbolic of that close feeling of affection and sympathy which now binds together the people of the North and the South." At that time Appomattox was only twenty-seven years away. The embers of the war were still alive, and could easily have been fanned into flames.

That was indeed a Grand Army day. The record of Rochester and of Monroe County in the war had been such that the new and the old generations could contemplate it with pride. Abraham Lincoln would not have been altogether pleased with many things said that day, although he would not have cared at all that so little was said about himself. More pleasing to him would have been the lines chiseled on the base of the pedestal below one of the battle scenes: "To those who, faithful unto death, gave their lives for their country 1861–1865."

SOURCES: Leonard Volk, in *Century Magazine,* December, 1881; Philip Kinsley, *The Chicago Tribune,* I :126; information from the Rochester Public Library and the Illinois State Historical Library.

In "The Grey Metropolis"
of Scotland

"ONCE a year, in the merry month of May, Edinburgh forgets that she is very old" and packs into a single week enough gaieties and ceremonies for a much longer time, recorded an American observer who spent the last week of May, 1897, in the proud city "throned in crags" which delights to be known as "the grey metropolis of the North." In that week were held the annual meetings of the General Assembly of the Church of Scotland, and the Lord High Commissioner came to open the series of services with such pomp as might mark a purely secular anniversary. In the midst of that busy week, with the city crowded with ministers and eminent laymen, while the Commissioner was laying cornerstones, visiting hospitals, and giving garden parties, occurred a very different sort of ceremony — the observance of what is known in "the States" as "Decoration Day," witnessed by few persons, most of them Americans. The American observer quoted above, Marian Prentice Piatt, describes the "imported ceremony" feelingly in an article published in 1900, whence our quotations are taken.

At the foot of Calton Hill is a "pretty, shady old graveyard," where, "under the shadow of the tomb of David Hume and near the obelisk to the Scottish Lords of Session who passed the reform laws, stands a fine monument to the Scottish soldiers who fell fighting for the Union in our War of the Rebellion." Upon a high granite pedestal stands a statue of Abraham Lincoln, the first to be erected in his honor outside the United States, and understood to be the only one of its kind in Europe. At the foot of the pedestal a slave stretches up his arms, the fetters struck off. On the base are carved the colors of the regiment known in the annals of the Army of the Potomac as the 79th New York Highlanders, "with their peculiar Scotch cap with two quills thrust through one side." This monument "is decorated each year by a party of Scotch and American ladies."

On the pedestal of this monument the present writer found some years ago the following records:

Sergeant Major John McEwen, Co. H, 65th Regiment Illinois Volunteer
Infantry;
William L. Duff, Lt. Col. 2d Illinois Regiment of Artillery;
Robert Steedman, Co. E, 5th Regiment Maine Infantry Volunteers;
James Wilkie, Co. C, 1st Michigan Cavalry;
Robert Ferguson, Co. F, 37th Regiment New York Infantry Volunteers.

The movement for the erection of this monument was initiated by
the man who served as American consul at Edinburgh from 1889 to
1893. Poet and orator, born in New York State and educated at Yale,
his name was Wallace Bruce. How could a man with such a name have
failed in such an undertaking — in Scotland? The story which led to
Bruce's conception of a modest project which finally grew to the dimensions of this memorial came from the widow of Sergeant Major
John McEwen. McEwen, before he met the girl who became his wife,
had enlisted as a private in "the Scotch regiment" from Illinois, serving under colonels bearing the good Scottish names of Daniel Cameron and Walter Scott Stewart. This regiment left Chicago nine hundred strong for Annapolis on June 24, 1862. McEwen was under fire
many times. He made the Atlanta campaign with Sherman. At the
end of the war he returned to Scotland and married a mill girl in Gala-
shiels, only to fall ill from the lingering effects of his wartime ex-
posures and to die in Edinburgh. His widow came to the American
consul for aid in obtaining a pension from the government in Washington, telling how she was working for five shillings a week and
struggling to keep her children with her. At one of the interviews with
this desperate woman Mrs. Bruce was present, and was much moved
by many of the details she heard. McEwen had loved to dwell upon
the incidents of his army life, and when he died he had had his old
army musket beside him under the coverlet. Mrs. Bruce proposed to
go with Mrs. McEwen to place flowers on the soldier's grave, but the
widow "couldna mark the spot." She had visited it "on the Sabbath
after his death with the bairns" and found another funeral party
claiming the same grave — so the tale was told in Scotland. Bruce obtained the necessary evidence, and the pension was granted.

Mr. and Mrs. Bruce agreed that some suitable burial place in Edinburgh ought to be made available for such soldiers. After consultations
and a formal exchange of letters, the Lord Provost, the magistrates,
and the Town Council granted the American consul a plot of ground
in an ancient and historic cemetery. The consul had promised Dr.

John H. Vincent, the Methodist bishop and leader of the enormously popular Chautauqua movement, to make an address on Grand Army Day, August 12, 1892, at the Chautauqua Assembly on the grounds beside Chautauqua Lake in western New York. In that address, made before thousands of Civil War veterans with no less a personage than ex-President Rutherford B. Hayes, a sturdy Grand Army man, serving as chairman, Bruce made the first public announcement of the plan he had matured, the project for a soldiers' memorial and a Lincoln statue in Calton Hill Cemetery in the heart of the Scottish capital.

The idea was hailed with enthusiasm and a committee was organized forthwith. A contract was made with a sculptor who was also a war veteran. The highest cost estimate came to $8,000, and before Bruce started back to Scotland about three thousand dollars had been raised. The balance of the final total of $6,300 came through correspondence, only about two hundred dollars of it from persons in Scotland. The list of contributors was headed by Levi P. Morton, lately Vice-President of the United States, and contained many other equally well-known names. One contribution came from Arizona, another from a Caledonian Club. But newspaper accounts are in error in stating that the United States government subscribed or was solicited for aid.

The unveiling ceremonies took place on August 21, 1893. It rained that day. Tourists would say that "it always does," but this was a downpour with windy blasts sweeping the official platform. The conditions did not dampen the enthusiasm of the large company that came, well wrapped, with umbrellas in hand, for that unprecedented occasion. The Lord Provost and other municipal officials wore their robes of scarlet and white. Among the military men present was Lieutenant-General Arthur James Lyon-Fremantle, formerly of the Coldstream Guards, who spent three months in the Confederacy in 1863 as an observer; he was with Lee at Gettysburg, and there gave General Longstreet a drink out of a silver flask, which "he begged he would keep in remembrance of the occasion."

The Scottish newspapers recognized the dedicatory ceremonies as of high news value. A guard of honor, two hundred fifty men in all, led by a band and pipers of the Argyll and Sutherland Highlanders, marched from the Castle to the cemetery. Dr. Robert Christie of Pittsburgh — every inch a Scot, born on the field where Bannockburn was fought — was very appropriately chosen to offer the dedicatory prayer. The chairman of the day was Sir William Arrol, the celebrated engineer who had built the Forth Bridge. Abraham Lincoln would have liked that man, for about thirty years earlier he had tramped the streets of Ayr with his blacksmithing tools in hand, asking for work. The Scottish standard waved on the platform, and the monument was draped in the Stars and Stripes and the Union Jack. Consul Bruce's daughter drew the cord which removed the flags and disclosed the monument. Cheers sounded. The Highlanders' band played "Hail, Columbia!" and "Rule, Britannia." The sculptor was called to the front. The consul made the speech of presentation to the city, and the Lord Provost accepted custody of the monument in behalf of the Town Council.

That was a great day for "the Honorable Wallace Bruce," who had arrived in Edinburgh to assume the consulship exactly four years before. Now he was about to return home, endeared to the people of the city. Earlier that afternoon, in the chambers of the Town Council, he had been presented with a handsome solid silver loving cup of the old Scottish pattern, weighing seventy-five ounces, as "a mark of esteem and in recognition of his services to Scottish literature." And in the evening of that crowded day he was entertained at a public dinner, where a company of eminent citizens and city officials bade him good-bye and God-speed.

Many things, always appropriate and often eloquent, were said at the various functions of the day. There were allusions to the men of letters of Scotland and America, to the wonders which were knitting the nations into a single fabric, to the Magna Charta and the Declaration of Independence, to the men buried in Calton Hill Cemetery and to the martyred President of the United States.

Calton Hill Cemetery is enclosed by a high wall; one might easily pass the small entrance without a glance within. This small remnant of what once was a much larger graveyard is crowded with tombs. The tall obelisk to the memory of the five men who were "exiled in the cause of liberty" stands in the center. The Constables who published Scott's novels lie there, as does the founder of *Blackwood's Magazine*. The circular "temple-like" monument to David Hume is notable for its size and shape. The high pedestal, on which stands the statue of the American martyr, and its base are of polished red Aberdeen granite. At the front sits a bearded and barefooted former slave in bronze, with his face and right hand lifted toward the Emancipator above. The slave's other hand holds a book, and beside him are battle flags and a wreath, also in bronze. The life-size bronze Lincoln stands upon a bronze slab about nine feet from the ground, so that the monument is more than fifteen feet in height and one must stand well back to examine it. The bearded, frock-coated figure stands with the right foot advanced, a small scroll in the right hand, and the left hand behind his back. The inscription about the base gives the dates and facts of the memorial. On the front across from the Negro are chiseled the words: "To preserve the jewel of liberty in the framework of freedom. Abraham Lincoln."

George Edwin Bissell, the sculptor of this statue, had served with a Connecticut regiment in the Civil War, then for two years as a naval paymaster. Entering the marble business with his father and brother in Poughkeepsie, he manifested a talent for modeling, and in 1875 crossed the ocean to spend two years in study at Paris, Florence, and Rome. Thereafter a long series of portrait busts and statues came from his studios in Poughkeepsie and Mt. Vernon. For years he divided his time between America and Paris. His work was popular, and he was flooded with commissions. Everyone loved him as a kindly man. His protégés, of whom there were more than a few, affectionately called him "Père Bissell." Although as a rule the critics pronounce him a realist, he was not altogether lacking in idealization. The American who visits the old cemetery within the wall on the hillside is likely to feel both the drama and the beauty of the sculptor's conception of the Emancipator President, heightened as these are by the monuments surrounding the memorial and by its situation in one of the most attractive Old World cities. Wallace Bruce had written a poem for the unveiling ceremony, the reading of which he discreetly postponed on that stormy day of dedication. Its stanzas, like the two here quoted, reflect the spirit of both the poet and the sculptor:

> With tendrils reaching west to rear
> The highest type of manhood's power,
> Born of the soil, without a peer,
> Our Lincoln stands, the noblest flower
> Of freedom in its widening course
> From Chatham, Fox, and Wilberforce:
>
> To whom an anxious nation turned
> When gathering clouds the sky o'ercast,
> A pilot brave with soul that yearned
> To guide the ship before the blast;
> To hold the faith our fathers knew,
> To keep the stars within the blue.

In a small town in northeastern Iowa stands a replica of this "Lincoln," with the slave omitted. This was the gift of William Larrabee, an Iowa pioneer, born in Connecticut, who prospered as a business-man and agriculturist in the West and became governor of the state. Larrabee acquired bronze busts of various war leaders for his house, and provided several memorials for his home town of Clermont. He saw Bissell's "Lincoln" in Edinburgh, and arranged with the sculptor for the duplicate, which was dedicated to the soldiers and sailors of the Civil War on June 19, 1903. The pedestal carries four tablets showing war scenes executed by Bissell.

SOURCES: *The Lincoln Monument in Memory of Scottish-American Soldiers,* Edinburgh, 1893; John J. Piatt, ed., *The Hesperian Tree,* 1900.

I I   ILLUSTRATED PAGE 154

An Equestrian LINCOLN

WHEN Henry Kirke Brown's "Lincoln the Emancipator" was removed from the entrance Plaza of Prospect Park, Brooklyn, in 1895, to another and better site inside the Park, the Plaza was not left with-out a presentment of the President. A bronze "Lincoln" in high relief is set into one of the piers of the Soldiers' and Sailors' Memorial Arch in the Plaza, and because it is so nearly equivalent to a full statue, and is the only equestrian "Lincoln" known to us, it shall have a little space in this volume. True, it is not highly regarded as a work of art. It is so "different" as to be quaint, amusing rather than inspiring. The New York City Art Commission described it as "An equestrian high relief in bronze, / showing President Lincoln mounted on a horse / standing quietly, with its right side to the / spectator and the rein hanging loosely on / its neck. His face is toward the spectator / and his right arm is extended downward with / the hand holding a high-crowned hat, while / his left hand, idly holding the reins, / rests on the pommel of the saddle."

By way of contrast, an art critic, after an inspection of this "Lincoln" and the companion work on the opposite side of the archway in which General Grant is shown in relief, observed: "Works of art they are not. . . . O'Donovan seems to have moved in sublime ignorance of the fundamental facts of sculpture and beyond the warmth of the

99

sacred fire of genius. His men are droll caricatures of the heroes they are supposed to represent. Lincoln sits stiffly, his right arm extended downward, with the hand holding the curious old top-hat as if to catch the stones with which the bad boys of the neighborhood used to keep it constantly filled." That hat is certainly so slanted as to invite contests in marksmanship. The unsmiling Lincoln is understood to be responding to the salutes of marching troops. Few of the other Lincoln bronzes have so much of a posed look. Lincoln was not a bad horseman, but, as has many times been said, he seems here to be embedded in his steed.

The Memorial Arch is an imposing structure, eighty-one feet in height, with a span of thirty-five feet, and piers fifty feet deep at their base. Sculptured groups representing the army and navy are carried by supporting columns on the fronts of the piers, and the panels of Lincoln and Grant face each other across the roadway. The Arch is surmounted by the much-admired quadriga by Frederick MacMonnies.

For the figures of Lincoln and Grant, William Rudolf O'Donovan was responsible, while Thomas Eakins modeled the horses, and of the twain the latter did the better job. Both men knew horses well; O'Donovan served four years in the Confederate artillery, while Eakins was an excellent amateur scientist who had mastered the anatomy of the animal. They decided not to manufacture composite steeds by patching together fragments of many horses, using only their best points and ignoring their blemishes — but what a time they had finding satisfactory mounts for such august riders! It did not matter so much about the President's horse; for him they used "Billy," a mount of great strength and endurance which Eakins found in the West. But their "Grant" was to be the general, not the president, and they wanted a horse of the type he had ridden in the war. They watched the cadets in action at West Point and made many pictures there; they studied the horse-show prize winners at Long Branch and Newport; at length Alexander J. Cassatt, president of the Pennsylvania Railroad and an ardent horseman, loaned them his favorite mount, and the panel in the Arch displays Grant on "Clinker."

Most of the sculptors' work was done on a farm near Avondale in Pennsylvania, where Eakins rode about a field mounted on a pony, studying the looks and action of "Billy" and "Clinker" as they were ridden by a colored boy. The artists posed for each other. Eakins sat sidewise, hat in hand, on "Billy" for O'Donovan, who in turn "sat" for Eakins on "Clinker." The final modeling was done in O'Donovan's New York City studio.

Just why these painstaking and earnest men failed to produce panels worthy of applause is baffling. They did not lack experience. Although O'Donovan was self-taught, he maintained a studio for fifty years and seems never to have lacked friends and patrons. He proudly recorded himself as one of the little group that founded the Tile Club in 1877. His name is listed in the membership of numerous important public commissions. He was a painter as well as a sculptor, and those who knew him praised the poetic quality of his work. The roster of his sculptural productions is long, including busts, statues, and monuments. Among those who sat for him were Walt Whitman, Edmund Clarence Stedman, General Daniel Sickles, and Theodore Tilton. He produced the "Washington" for Caracas, Venezuela.

Eakins, too, was a versatile and popular man whose professional career in Philadelphia covered many years. Among the masters with whom he studied in Paris was J. L. Gérome. He did more painting than moulding, together with much teaching and lecturing. He had a scientific mind. His favorite occupations were studying surgical operations, mastering the anatomy of the horse, watching boat races, and riding bronchos; and all of these interests, including those which might be classed as recreative, are reflected in some degree in his works. His paintings of surgical clinics are celebrated.

Eakins' representations of "Billy" and "Clinker" are accurate, no doubt, but the horses do not come alive. O'Donovan's "Grant" and "Lincoln" are equally self-conscious and statuesque. It would be difficult for any sculptor, no matter how great his genius, to create a successful equestrian "Lincoln," although Fred M. Torrey has two excellent statuettes of this type in the Lincoln tomb at Springfield, Illinois. And we venture the hope that somebody, some time, will try his hand at depicting the prairie lawyer driving out of Springfield in his old-fashioned buggy.

SOURCES: *Catalogue of Works of Art Belonging to New York City,* 1909; Helen Henderson, *A Loiterer in New York,* 1917; Cleveland Moffett, article in *McClure's Magazine,* October, 1895; biographies in *Who's Who* and the *Dictionary of American Biography; Annual Reports of Brooklyn Park Commissioners;* and a few newspaper items.

The Seven Pelzers

THIS chapter contains an account of a Lincoln statue which has six duplicates — and the word "duplicate" is used advisedly as more accurate than "replica." The original member of the family is in New Jersey, while the other members are scattered almost across the continent — one in Pennsylvania and one in Ohio, two in Michigan, one in Nebraska and one in Idaho. The story of these "Lincolns" is the more remarkable, because, although made of bronze, they were not cast in the usual manner but constructed by a very different process. They are the work of a German who came to this country about sixty years ago.

Two bachelor brothers, Hubert and Alfonso Pelzer, established a business of making church furniture and statuary in Salem, a small city in northeastern Ohio which had been a station on the "Underground Railroad" and an antislavery center in the years before the Civil War. The Pelzers are said to have been experienced and talented sculptors of plaster statues for inside display. Hubert, the older, died, and Alfonso sold the small shop to William H. Mullins, son of the founder of the now widely known Mullins Manufacturing Corporation, and turned to the making of plaster statues for reproduction in metal by the Mullins firm.

The Mullins process is difficult to describe in non-technical terms. Pelzer made the model for a statue in wax over a wooden frame. Plaster of Paris dies in sections were taken from this model and sent to the foundry in the Mullins plant, where they were moulded into zinc dies. Each die was then "anchored in the bed of the press," and from it a lead die was obtained and bolted to the hammer. The next process was similar to that by which a typescript is produced by clamping a sheet of paper against a cylinder and subjecting it to the blows of the type bars. The metal sheets inserted between the dies were hammered into shape, and annealed and quenched in water, or air-cooled, depending on the metal used. The sections then were joined by riveting and soldering, and the seams plated. The result was a statue of much lighter weight — and of much lower cost — than a similar work of cast bronze.

It was by this process that the Saint-Gaudens "Diana," for years poised at the peak of the tower of the old Madison Square Garden, was finished "in hammered copper." All the Pelzer "Lincolns" were thus made in bronze. At the time of William H. Mullins' death in 1932, a local newspaper stated that the Pelzer brothers had lived in Salem for many years, and had modeled hundreds of figures of animals and birds, as well as statues, in hammered or pressed copper, bronze, and zinc, and that they had conducted for a time "a little school of sculpture" in the city. Atop the Wayne County Building in Detroit stand four large copper figures, representing Commerce, Industry, Justice, and Liberty, which the Mullins firm attributes to Pelzer. The firm also constructed, while that German artist and artisan was in Salem, what was said to be the largest statue ever undertaken in the United States. This is the statue of Hermann, or Arminius, the German national hero, thirty-two feet in height, made for the city of New Ulm, Minnesota. The Mullins firm discontinued the statuary business many years ago.

What the Corporation refers to as "our original Lincoln statue" stands in the square facing the railroad station in Lincoln, New Jersey, a community next door to Menlo Park and well within the range of the suburbs of New York City. This statue is said to have been erected in connection with a real-estate development undertaken by the town a half-century ago. The cornerstone for the pedestal was laid on Lincoln's birthday in 1898, and the statue was unveiled on the following Memorial Day. The funds for the purchase of the statue were raised by school children. It is of sheet bronze, showing Lincoln with the left foot advanced, the right arm extended in a low gesture with the hand open, while the left hand holds a half-unrolled scroll containing the Emancipation Proclamation. Lincoln, with head held high, is depicted as an orator, in an expository phase of a persuasive address. On the face of a large block of smooth stone beneath the feet of the President one reads in raised letters a portion of the final sentence of the Second Inaugural: "With malice toward none, with charity for all, with firmness in the right as God gives us to see the right." This stone is one of the blocks which truncate the pyramidal pedestal. It is a pleasant statue, by no means great; nor is it calculated to create an emotional response in an observer. In moulding his model the sculptor is understood to have used photographs and to have reproduced the face "from a death mask furnished by the government." This is a mistake, of course, as no death mask was made.

Seventeen years passed before there was a demand for the duplication of this statue, and then, in 1915, four "Pelzers" were erected: two in Detroit, one in Wooster, Ohio, and another in Boise, Idaho. The statue in the Idaho capital was unveiled on the anniversary of Lincoln's birth. It stands on a pedestal of white sandstone, seventeen feet in height, in front of Lincoln Hall at the Idaho Soldiers' Home. A bronze tablet on the pedestal carries the full text of the Gettysburg Address, and another an extract from the Second Inaugural.

At least five Lincoln statues are related to the transcontinental highway named for Lincoln, and three of these are "Pelzers." The others are the seated "Lincoln" by James Earle Fraser, in Jersey City at the point where the highway turns westward, and the statue by Granville Hastings in Jefferson, Iowa.

As a matter of course many business men interested in the development of the automobile industry actively promoted the movement for the creation of a nation-wide network of highways suitable for motor traffic. The Lincoln Highway Association was organized under the presidency of Henry B. Joy, at that time president of the Packard Motor Car Company. In 1913 Carl Fisher suggested that "the impracticable and impossible task" of building a three-thousand-mile highway from ocean to ocean should be undertaken. The name for the projected highway having been adopted — not altogether for business reasons — memorials of Abraham Lincoln of various types began to appear along the selected route. Some time in 1915 William H. Mullins presented one of the Lincoln statues made by his firm to Mr. Joy, and another of the duplicates to Henry M. Leland, president of the Lincoln Motor Company, which has since become a component of the far-flung Ford empire. Mr. Leland was a devoted admirer of President Lincoln, and had named his company for him.

The Packard "Lincoln" was placed in the visitors' lobby in the company's administration building, and remained there until alterations in 1919 made its removal necessary. Then, locked away in storage, it was more or less forgotten until, at the suggestion of Major W. C. Greany, an employee of the company and later its plant protection engineer, who was at the time a Northwestern District Boy Scout official, it was given to the Boy Scouts of the Detroit area and set up by them at their Camp Brady, near Waterford, where it was dedicated as an official Lincoln Shrine on July 25, 1936. Mounted upon a pedestal of field stone against a wooded background, this statue probably appeared to better advantage in this location than any other of the "Pelzers." In April, 1946, this camp was sold, and the statue was taken to the new Charles Howell Boy Scout Reservation at Brighton, about twenty-five miles from the Detroit business center. The other Detroit statue has remained in the possession of the Lincoln Company throughout. The only outdoor statue of Abraham Lincoln in the city, it holds a commanding position on a pedestal of medium height on the lawn before the office building, where, year by year, Lincoln Day ceremonies are conducted.

The Wooster "Lincoln" was a gift to the College of Wooster by James Mullins, the father of William H. Mullins, who at the time was a resident of the city. The statue is well placed upon the lovely campus.

In the Borough of Wilkinsburg, a suburb of Pittsburgh, at the junction of the William Penn Highway and the Lincoln Highway, the motorist encounters the only Lincoln statue in western Pennsylvania. The pedestal informs him that it was "erected by Wilkinsburg school children, June, 1916." The children saved enough small coins to pay for it, and proud they were of their campaign. There were unveiling ceremonies on June 9, in the midst of a three-day celebration by which the community expressed its jubilation over the Pennsylvania Railroad Company's elimination of several undesirable grade crossings.

Henry B. Joy was wont to use his vacations for driving from coast to coast over the route of the highway he had fathered. It was an adventure, and he had enlisted for the duration. In the great farming states of the West, riding was easy in dry weather, but in days of rain when time was "of the essence" cars often went down to their running boards in gumbo. Mr. Greany, then a captain in the United States Army Motor Transport Corps, serving as adjutant and statistical officer, compiled the official report of the first transcontinental expedition conducted by the Army over the Lincoln Highway. General Eisenhower, then a lieutenant colonel, went along. The convoy train started from the zero milestone near the White House on July 7, 1919, and arrived at the Presidio in San Francisco on September 6 — sixty-two days, at an average speed of 6.07 miles per hour. There were eighty-one vehicles in the train and nearly three hundred men; twenty-one were lost en route through various casualties. The convoy moved as though under war conditions in enemy country, self-sustaining in all respects. For hours at a time the men built wheel paths of timber, brush, or canvas. Dangerous mountain trails, where a slip meant destruction, had to be traversed. Eighty-eight wooden bridges that broke down under the weight of the caravan were rebuilt. The expedition surmounted the Continental Divide, 8,427 feet up, in Wyoming. If this paragraph be regarded as a diversion from our real theme, we suggest that this enterprise would have had the warm endorsement of the President who signed the bill for the building of the Union Pacific Railroad, and that Lincoln would have highly appreciated the bestowal of his name upon the great motor highway.

The West hailed the new highway with enthusiasm. Distance and name signs were put up. Towns competed with each other for inclusion in the route. "Old Abe's" portraits were hung on hundreds of walls; sometimes Lincoln busts were displayed, and in a few instances Lincoln statues erected. These incidents covered a period of years; the highway was not constructed as an emergency job. The seventh and last of the "Pelzers" was dedicated on May 30, 1921, in a park at Fremont, Nebraska, about forty miles from Omaha. The ceremony was admirably arranged. A former slave, Thomas M. Watts, unveiled the statue, the gift of Lucius Dunbar Richards, who came from Vermont, served in the Civil War, and spent the latter half of his life as a business man in Nebraska.

Why were these Pelzer statues so many times duplicated? A conclusive answer is yet to be found. It seems that three besides the original were purchased in the usual way, while three were gifts by the manufacturing company. Possibly the answer is to be found in an old inventory in the Salem offices of the company, indicating that the price of the statue was about five hundred dollars.

SOURCES: Correspondence with the Mullins Manufacturing Corporation; information from Thomas I. Starr, Detroit, W. C. Greany, Packard Motor Car Company, Detroit, F. H. Richards, Sr., Fremont, Nebraska, and Dr. Louis A. Warren, Lincoln National Life Foundation, Fort Wayne, Indiana; courtesies by Earl Schenck Miers, Rutgers University, and from the Burton Historical Collection, Detroit Public Library.

A Monument that
"The Man with a Dinner Pail
Will Understand"

A MEMORIAL bust of Charles Henry Niehaus was unveiled in the Hall of American Artists in the rotunda of the Gould Memorial Library at New York University on December 3, 1938. Adolph A. Weinman delivered a discriminating eulogy. Years before, "somewhere back in 1896," he said, he had been associated with the older man. Niehaus at the time needed an assistant in his work for the façade of the building for the University Club of which McKim, Mead and White were the architects. Weinman "liked the sculptural quality and vigor of Niehaus' work," and besides, he needed a job fully as much, if not more, than Niehaus needed an assistant.

The studio with which he then became familiar was perhaps the best adapted for a sculptor's workshop of all in the city. It was large; the skylights were high; and it was readily accessible from the street, so that large blocks of stone could be moved in and finished works of whatever size moved out without difficulty. This had been the studio of Saint-Gaudens, who was leaving America for a time in order to finish and exhibit his equestrian "Sherman" in Paris. In that studio Weinman modeled the portrait which was accepted as a memorial to Niehaus in the Hall where American painters and sculptors are honored.

Weinman described Niehaus as "being rather of a nervous temperament," so that "it was somewhat of a task to get what might be called a regular sitting. He was most willing to give his time and attention freely, but he just could not keep still for long." Weinman found that by telling stories and listening to accounts of Niehaus' boyhood adventures in Cincinnati and his student days in Europe "he could capture his attention and stop his striding about the big room." This incident illustrates the major characteristics of Niehaus, "never idle, all for action, a man of intense nature, keen of mind, and gifted with great physical endurance, with a slender and wiry frame. His life had been strenuous"; still he was busy until the very end in his eighty-first year.

This man, who was destined to become one of the foremost of American monumental sculptors, was born in Cincinnati on January 24, 1855, of an ancestry reaching far back in Germany. Both his father's and his mother's families crossed the ocean in 1814 or thereabouts, settling first in New York state, and after a few years moving West. John Conrad Niehaus was eight years of age when this migration took place, and Sophie Katherine Block was six. One family settled in Indiana and the other in southern Ohio, but the boy and girl did not forget each other, and in good time they married and moved into their first home, "a log cabin in old Cincinnati." Their only son early manifested his knack for modeling, and before reaching his majority served his time at stonecutting and woodcarving, studying meanwhile in night classes at the McMichen School of Design. With a first prize to his credit, he managed somehow, although his means were small, to go to Munich in 1876. There he entered the Royal Academy for advanced study in sculpture and allied subjects, and spent about four years in that celebrated center of art and artistic handicrafts. He was the first American to be awarded a first prize, diploma and medal. The winning composition represented "Fleeting Time," a work described as admirable in execution though obviously immature. There followed a series of journeys in Italy, France, and England; Niehaus must see the art of the Old World. In Manchester he found friends, and while in that vicinity made several portrait busts, among them one of no less a personage than Disraeli.

The ambitious young man returned to the United States in 1881. In that year President Garfield died. The State of Ohio appropriated funds for a statue of its martyred son to be placed in the Capitol at Washington, and another statue for Cincinnati was paid for by public subscription. Both these commissions were awarded to Niehaus, probably with the expectation that he would make an original and a replica. Niehaus could have no doubt that his future depended on the success with which he met this rare opportunity. He hurried back to Europe for further study, maintaining a studio for several years in Rome, where he modeled his "Garfields" and others of his best-known works. Conceiving his subject as above all an orator, and disdaining to make them simply duplicate portraits, Niehaus depicted Garfield in both statues as a public speaker, managing skillfully to convey definitely in both the impression of forensic power, although the figures are quite different, only the heads being nearly identical. In the statue in Race

Street, Cincinnati, Garfield appears as a platform speaker, wearing an unbuttoned overcoat, with one arm slightly extended. The statue in Washington, the second to be executed, is more formal in character, with a rostrum beside the speaker and the fingers of the right hand thrust inside the buttoned frock coat. In both figures the silent speaker is impressive.

These statues made the sculptor's future secure. Most of the many works that followed were distinctly successful; none was a failure. Lorado Taft wrote of "the vast array of monuments, figures, and reliefs" which came from Niehaus' hands. Among his works we note the McKinley statue at Canton, Ohio; the Harrison monument at Indianapolis; the "Moses" and the "Gibbon" in the Library of Congress; the statues of Thomas Hooker and John Davenport in the Connecticut State House; the equestrian statue of General Nathan B. Forrest at Memphis; and the monument to Francis Scott Key in Baltimore. In even an abbreviated list there should be more than a mere mention of the memorial to Samuel C. F. Hahnemann, the founder of the homeopathic school of medicine, unveiled in Washington in 1900. The figure is seated before a niche under a canopy in the middle of a large curved exedra, on which four bronze reliefs are placed. The work is universally admired.

The sculptor's daughter recalls his simple statement of the controlling purpose in whatever he did: "I only wish to erect monuments that the man with a dinner pail will understand, for he needs to understand art without too much explaining." At the end of his tribute in the Hall of American Artists, Mr. Weinman said that Niehaus "loved his art and was happiest in the doing of it." His industry was prodigious, yielding him "a vast achievement of solid worth" and an enormous array of medals. Weinman and others allude to Niehaus' hatred of injustice, his "readiness to take up the cudgels and lay about him with gusto" whenever he felt that his own rights or those of others were being violated. For years Niehaus made his home at Grantwood, New Jersey, where his workshop was known as Eagle Crest Studio.

The original of the three "Lincolns" created by Niehaus was erected in Muskegon, Michigan, in 1900. In March, 1898, Charles Henry Hackley, a wealthy resident of that city, formally asked the mayor and common council for permission to erect, at his own expense, in a public square which had been named for him, statues of Abraham Lincoln, Ulysses S. Grant, William T. Sherman, and David G. Farragut — the statues, when dedicated, to become the property of the city. There could be no doubt of the reply, for Hackley was a dominant personality in southern Michigan. According to the Hackley Memorial Association, he "had achieved a great fortune cutting the marvelous forest growth that blanketed the southern peninsula of Michigan." But "the pine vanished" and "there was othing left to cut." Muskegon had been "dependent solely on the forty-seven saw mills ringing Muskegon Lake," and, to add to its misfortunes, the city was hit in succession early in the eighteen-nineties by a sweeping conflagration and by the panic which swept the country. It was then that Hackley, with his "equally wise partner," Thomas Hume, proved himself a foresighted businessman. For when their lumber firm ceased operations in 1894, the partners served valiantly in a movement which transformed what had been an exclusively lumber-producing city into a center of diversified industries. The city has grown from a population of 21,000 in 1900 to nearly five times that size today.

With more than a little wonder one notes the series of gifts with which Mr. Hackley "endowed" Muskegon. In 1890 he bought a city block, cleared it of buildings, and placed in the center a huge soldiers' monument. On one side of this square, now named for him, stands the Hackley Public Library, and on another the Hackley Public School. He provided the city also with a manual-training school, an art gallery, and a hospital. Possibly a degree of vanity may be indicated by the prefixing of his name to his series of benefactions, but the spirit of the man is reflected in the provision for the upkeep of these institutions. All of them were handsomely endowed, his total benefactions as of July 1, 1929, being reported as nearly six million dollars. Hackley was born in Indiana in 1837, spent his boyhood in Kenosha, Wisconsin, worked his way across Lake Michigan to Muskegon, and there began his career as a plain laborer. At his death in 1905 no "blood relatives" were left to perpetuate his name, although there were two foster children.

The four Civil War statues in Hackley Park were unveiled on Memorial Day, 1900. A committee of three men, two of them Civil War veterans, chose Niehaus as the sculptor for the "Lincoln" and the "Farragut," while the "Grant" and "Sherman" were entrusted to J. Massey Rhind. The huge crowd which filled the square for the dedication watched a parade and listened to music and speeches. The statues were swathed with flags; each had a guard of honor; the daughters of deceased veterans did the unveiling. At Mr. Hackley's suggestion the ceremonies were conducted by Phil Kearny Post, Grand Army of the Republic, and the Post Commander, using a ritual prepared for the occasion, pronounced the dedication sentences. For the "Lincoln" he said: "In the name of the Grand Army of the Republic, I dedicate this statue to the memory of the great President who laid down his office to become Freedom's grandest Martyr." Cannon boomed as the flags fell.*

Within ten years Niehaus was twice called upon for duplicates of this "Lincoln." Back of the making of the first of these replicas is a story of patriotic devotion. Julius E. Francis, a Buffalo businessman, invested "time and treasure" in the accumulation of a large Civil War collection, and in "building up, equipping, and inspiring an Association that would continue his work." This was the Lincoln Birthday Association, incorporated in 1877, upon which was to devolve the supervisory control of Francis' collection, the administration of the trust fund which he provided, and "the distribution of memorial literature commemorative of the public services of President Lincoln." While this organization was making plans for a permanent home, its officers and the trustees of the Buffalo Historical Society agreed that a "room in a fire-proof building for the preservation of this memorial collection" might well be included in the plans for the beautiful marble structure overlooking Lake Erie which the Historical Society proposed to erect. Arrangements were made for the creation of a Lincoln Memorial Room for the display of the documents, autographs, and relics of the Francis Collection, and also that a statue of President Lincoln should be placed in the building, paid for by a portion of the Francis fund, the residue of which should be given to the Historical Society in consideration of its providing the Memorial Room and undertaking the custody of the collection and the statue. "A cane used by Lincoln during his tenure of office," among other association articles, is in a case made from wood "taken from Faneuil Hall, Independence Hall, the Charter Oak, the Old South Church, the frigate *Constitution* and other historic temples" in the Memorial Room. The replica of the Niehaus statue was erected in the Grand Court of the Buffalo Historical Society's building, and unveiled on September 30, 1902.

A coincidence perhaps without parallel occurred when the second

---

* There is another Niehaus statue in Muskegon, also a Hackley gift. Located in another park, it represents General Philip Kearny.

of the Niehaus replicas was unveiled in Kenosha, Wisconsin, on May 24, 1909. The statue was the gift of a self-made businessman, whose life was of the same general pattern as those of Hackley of Muskegon and Francis of Buffalo, to the city in which he had acquired a fortune. Elaborate plans had been made for the unveiling ceremonies. But, as an evening newspaper graphically describes it: "The flags which covered the bronze figure fell just as all that was mortal of the donor of the statue, a well known citizen for many years, was borne past the memorial he had erected to his last resting place in the city cemetery. The roll of musketry, the booming of cannon, the tramp of marching men, the singing of school children, which were to have made this a great day for Kenosha, were strangely absent. In place of these arrangements the city officials and the members of the Grand Army Post stood about the base of the pedestal, with heads uncovered, and as the flags fell among the flowers a hush fell upon the crowd broken only by the sound of the church bell tolling a requiem to the memory of Orla Miner Calkins. The tribute of silence lasted two minutes, and the silence was eloquent. The war veterans and the official party then joined the funeral procession."

For nearly fifty years Mr. Calkins had lived in Kenosha. His life was interwoven with the city's development. He had intended the statue to be a testamentary gift, but altered his plans a year or so before his death in the hope that he himself might participate in the dedication program. Instead, he never saw the memorial; invited to come and view it when it was set up, he preferred to wait for the unveiling, and died two days before the day assigned for the ceremony. With excellent judgment it was decided that the statue should be uncovered as the most fitting funeral tribute the city could render in his honor.

The Kenosha monument is placed in Library Park against a background of memorial trees for the soldiers who lost their lives in the first World War. The park contains also the Gilbert M. Simmons Memorial Library and a memorial to the men "who defended the Union on land and sea in the Civil War." This monument and the Library building were designed by Daniel H. Burnham.

Charles Niehaus found Abraham Lincoln a favorite subject of study. He often alluded to the fact that his father was known as "Honest John," and seemed never to tire of working on the features of "Honest Abe." For his studies Niehaus used the photographs in the War Department, the various Lincoln biographies, and the Volk life mask. Of his numerous sketch models only two remain, named by his daughter "Gettysburg" and "Emancipation." A bust in the Art Museum of Columbus, Ohio, commands the enthusiastic admiration of all who see it because of the beauty of the portraiture and the translucent quality of the Carrara marble of which it is made. In the statue the President sits in a chair of state, in an attitude of easy dignity, erect, elbows resting upon the arms of the chair, hands holding a document which he has been reading, and is now pondering, with lifted face and forward-gazing eyes. The right knee supports the left leg, with the right foot flat upon the base, while the left may have been swinging. The posture is graceful; the body is relaxed, but the man is mentally alert. The face reflects the qualities which made Lincoln a statesman; he is thinking, making up his mind, with all the elements of his problem in view. The careful observer's attention is held longest by the eyes — deep, penetrating, as of one who sees none of his immediate surroundings, but looks far into the future in full consciousness of the responsibility that rests upon him. The work grows on one who lingers in its presence, bringing home an abiding impression of the solitude, the loneliness of the man.

SOURCES: *The Sculpture of Charles Henry Niehaus*, 1900; various published obituaries and eulogies of Niehaus; Hackley Memorial Association booklet, 1929; information supplied by Miss Marie J. Niehaus, Adolph A. Weinman, the Secretary of the Hall of American Artists, the Buffalo Historical Society, the Gilbert M. Simmons Library of Kenosha, local newspaper librarians, and Mr. Niehaus.

A Briton's Concept
of the Spirit of Lincoln

ONE of the Lincoln sculptors about whom we would welcome more information than a comprehensive investigation on both sides of the ocean has brought to light is W. Granville Hastings, an Englishman who came to the United States in 1891 at the age of twenty-three and is understood to have been for some time in the employ of the Gorham Company in Providence, Rhode Island. A quarter of a century ago, in response to inquiries from Cincinnati, where his "Lincoln" had been dedicated in 1902, Providence people described him as " a picturesque character and an entertaining fireside romancer," who had done "small decorative figure work for the Gorhams" and then "went in for soldiers' monuments and the like." "In one of his seemingly flush times" he had built a studio in the garden of his house "up Benefit Street," only to remove to New York a few years later. For the Providence Art Club, of which he and Mrs. Hastings were members, he made "a bas relief frieze of festoons" for the Gallery, and "carved a lion newel post at the foot of the Gallery stairs."

Young as Hastings was when he left England, it is not strange that he should not have been an exhibitor nor a member of the art societies there. It is known, however, that at the age of seventeen he "devoted himself to the study of sculpture and art pottery," and for a time "worked for certain terra-cotta people," manifesting "great facility" in that medium. At the time his Soldiers' and Sailors' Monument in Pawtucket, Rhode Island, was dedicated in 1897, contemporary accounts noted that he had been a pupil of Jules Dalou in Paris. This bronze group, "Liberty Arming the Patriot," wherein a majestic woman in heavy draperies hands a sword to a young farmer about to leave the plough, is said to have been modeled in the Providence studio. Two years after its dedication, a tribute of the Grand Army of the Republic to the soldiers and sailors of the Civil War, also wrought by Hastings, was unveiled in Orange, New Jersey, on Memorial Day in 1899. A bronze color sergeant is making a stand at the crucial moment in a battle, with the flag in one hand and an upswung sword in the other, to rally his comrades. Hastings made some unhappy investments, and died at the early age of thirty-four, after which his "attractive widow" with her "handsome children" returned to England. Aside from the story of his Lincoln statues, this is all we have found about W. Granville Hastings.

In the grounds of a public school in Avondale, a suburb of Cincinnati, the Hastings "Lincoln" was unveiled on December 23, 1902, more than six months after the sculptor's death on June 13 at Mt. Vernon, New York. The work was given to the city by Captain Charles Clinton, who had served in the Civil War with Company B of the First Missouri Regiment of Cavalry Volunteers. The exercises were held in the Avondale Presbyterian Church, with Mayor Julius Fleischmann presiding, before an overflow audience of citizens and schoolchildren. There were addresses by General Lewis Seasongood, General Benjamin R. Cowen, the Civil War Adjutant General of Ohio, Lieutenant-Governor Harry L. Gordon, and Dr. Charles Frederic Goss, pastor of the church and in his time widely known for eloquence and as a writer on genial themes. The December weather proved unfavorable for outdoor ceremonies, but the audience, children and all, headed by two Civil War veterans, marched to the school grounds, where Mrs. Leland Banning, the donor's daughter, drew the rope which released the coverings of the monument.

The bronze figure stands in quiet dignity, with the left foot and the right hand somewhat advanced. The intention of the sculptor is well indicated by the supplementary figure of a woman half-kneeling at the base of the high pedestal. Upon a tablet carried by the pedestal she is writing an inscription, of which she has completed only four words, "With malice toward none . . .". This, then, is a Second Inaugural memorial. The manuscript is rolled in the President's left hand. He is delivering the final passage of his great appeal for unity and peace. Higher on the tablet appears the simple legend, "Lincoln — 1809–1865." The pedestal, with a rostrum and two curving stone benches each ending with a pillared lamp, after a design by Laurence Alma-Tadema, was financed by public subscription.

Of this statue three replicas were made. The first was unveiled in the little village of Bunker Hill, Illinois, on September 7, 1904, and was also a gift of Captain Clinton, who had organized a mounted company in 1861 of which many members were from this community. Clinton never lost his pride in the service performed by that company, partly among the "bushwhackers" in Missouri. After two score years the surviving "old boys" of the company were wont to declare, not without warrant, that "the First Missouri Cavalry never retreated, nor were they ever whipped." Dedication Day was a great occasion for Bunker Hill. The speakers constituted what in a now outmoded parlance would be called a galaxy — Senator Shelby M. Cullom, a personal friend of Lincoln; Richard Yates, Jr., governor of Illinois and son of the Civil War Governor Yates; General John C. Black of Danville, General Horace Clark, Benjamin Franklin Caldwell of Mattoon, and Dr. Goss from Avondale, who presented the monument in behalf of Captain Clinton. This replica is a perfect duplicate of the Avondale "Lincoln," except that the woman with the crayon is writing on the front face of the severely plain pedestal. On the back face are mounted two bronze plates, one with an inscription mentioning the captain and the soldiers of Company B.

A Hastings replica, without the writing woman, was dedicated in "an impressive setting before the beautiful court house" in Jefferson, Iowa, on September 21, 1918. A large tablet on the base is inscribed with the full sentence from the 1865 inaugural, from the opening "With malice toward none" through to the concluding "just and lasting peace among ourselves and with all nations." This statue was the gift of Mr. and Mrs. E. B. Wilson "to the people of Greene County and to the Lincoln Highway," and the donors hoped that residents and tourists would "come under the spell of that calm and dignified face and that rugged figure." The George H. Thomas Post of the Grand Army did the unveiling. Michael F. Healy, blind orator of Fort Dodge, gave the "suitable and eloquent" dedication address, holding his audience for over an hour.

The last of the Hastings "Lincolns" was accepted by the mayor and council of Sioux City, Iowa, on the morning of April 5, 1924, and unveiled that afternoon in Grandview Park. The bronze figure stands upon a base of Minnesota granite, in which is set a tablet bearing the concluding sentence of the Cooper Institute speech: "Let us have faith that right makes might, and in that faith let us to the end dare to do our duty as we understand it." Below this is the information that the statue is "a gift from John A. and Elizabeth Magoun." John Adams Magoun, named for the President, was born in 1861 in a suburb of Boston. Brought as a child to Sioux City, he was for many years president of the Sioux National Bank. The memorial stands in a lovely spot near the park entrance, surrounded by a wide sweep of lawn and beds of brilliant flowers.

Our experience in obtaining essential fundamental facts about this replica well illustrates the difficulties one sometimes encounters in tracing the history of a memorial, even one erected so recently as 1924. We had not seen the statue. Letters were not answered. Available informants differed in their statements of "facts." One news report, copied for us, affirmed the statue itself to be of granite; three other sources agreed that it is of bronze, and a colored picture tended to verify the majority statement. Our correspondents varied also in naming the sculptor; two named Hastings, but a third said that the statue "is a replica of one in the Union League Club in Philadelphia, and was made by the same man." A comparison of photographs disclosed this to be in error, and J. Otto Schweizer, the Union Club's artist, in a personal letter disavowed any connection with the Sioux City memorial. After several vexing delays, a lucky find solved both our problems. We learned from Dr. Louis A. Warren that the Jefferson replica was cast by Bureau Brothers of Philadelphia. When Bureau Brothers also appeared in information obtained by a friend in the Harvard Library as the makers of the Sioux City "Lincoln," we felt we had a sure clue. Through a Cincinnati newspaperman we learned of a scrapbook compiled in 1921 by Mr. N. D. C. Hodges, librarian of the Cincinnati Public Library, with information about Hastings. Most of the information duplicated that already on hand from Providence, but one letter from Bureau Brothers — who had not replied to our direct inquiries — declared that "if yours is the statue we cast, the sculptor's name was W. Granville Hastings . . . an Englishman by birth." This would obviously cover not only the original but the replicas — and we felt that we had arrived.

One studies the photographs of these statues, and reflects upon the short career of the sculptor who did not live to see any of them given to the public gaze. They have their faults. The chest is more massive than was Lincoln's, and the shoulders broader. Nevertheless, one thinks that the artist attained a much more than ordinary understanding of the significance of the Second Inaugural and of the character of the man. The statue has merit, and even to a casual observer it should bring a message.

SOURCES: David L. Pierson, *History of the Oranges to 1921; Journal of the Illinois State Historical Society,* October, 1930; correspondence with Senator

Robert A. Taft, Mr. Charles Ludwig of the *Cincinnati Times-Star,* the Gorham Company, Providence, R.I.; Dr. Louis A. Warren, Fort Wayne, Ind.; the Rev. Theodore G. Lilley, Cedar Rapids, Iowa; Judge James W. Bollinger, Davenport, Iowa; F. E. Gill, Esq., Sioux City, Iowa; Miss Mary Frances Sanford, Bunker Hill, Ill.; the public libraries of Cincinnati, East Orange, N.J., Pawtucket, R.I., and Sioux City, Iowa.

Edward C. Stone, Esq., of Boston, aided in obtaining information from England.

"Charley" Mulligan —
His Charm and Work

CHARLES J. MULLIGAN must have been an inspiring personality. Born in Ireland in 1866, he crossed the ocean at the age of seventeen and obtained employment as a stonecutter in Pullman, near Chicago. There Lorado Taft "discovered" him and brought him to his studio as pupil and assistant. His hands were strong and cunning. His enthusiasm, optimism, and contagious good-nature created an atmosphere of courage and good will which, according to his mentor, "henceforth became a studio habit and in time a veritable tradition of the place." Mulligan worked hard and loved hard work for its own sake. After long days in the studio he spent three evenings a week in study at the Chicago Art Institute. As student and teacher he maintained that schedule for twenty-eight years, never losing his own ardor or the power to infuse others with his own intensity and zeal. We are told that it was "a memorable experience to visit his crowded classes where a score or more of eager men and women were literally banked up against the motionless model and all working for dear life." During the great days of the building of the Chicago Exposition, Taft made Mulligan foreman of the workshop in which were massed sculptors and modelers from all over the world, many of them brilliant artists. "My first official act," said Taft in his eulogy of Mulligan, "was to put him in charge of that shop, and instantly all was peace and harmony."

All who knew "Charley" Mulligan endorse the tribute of the master who gave him his chance. His voice was big and rich; his grip was warm and powerful; his imagination was as active as his body. Every little while he would overwhelm his fellow-workers "by a cloud-burst of eloquence as he told of things he had been 'thinking up.'" Everyone loved him and wished him well, and his death in his fiftieth year was widely mourned. Lorado Taft said that his passing had given a new and poignant meaning to Daniel French's memorial to Martin Milmore, depicting the Angel of Death arresting the career of the young sculptor.

Mulligan is best remembered today for his interpretations of the lives and emotions of the working people of America. He knew how meagre were their lives, how small their pay, how they longed for better things for their children. His "Miner and Child," remarkable for its union of tenderness and strength, was shown at the Buffalo Exposition in 1901 and now stands in Humboldt Park, Chicago. To the Pan-American Exposition he sent "The Digger" and four figures of workingmen for the Illinois Building, all of which were convincing in their representation of the dignity of labor. "The Spirit of the Mines," a group for a colossal fountain, was exhibited in Chicago, but not completed in its final design at the time of his death. For the Illinois Supreme Court Building at Springfield he modeled two groups, "Justice and Power" and "Law and Knowledge." He also made the "George Rogers Clark" at Quincy, Illinois; the "Henry Clay" at Lexington, Kentucky; and the "President McKinley" in McKinley Park, Chicago. The representations of Lincoln, Grant, and Yates in the Illinois Memorial Temple in the Vicksburg National Military Park, sometimes alluded to as statues, are in fact carved relief busts of the President, the General, and the Governor.

Mulligan produced two Lincoln statues: "Lincoln the Orator," dedicated in 1903 in Rosamond Grove Cemetery, about a mile from the village of Rosamond and four miles from the city of Pana, Illinois; and "Lincoln the Railsplitter," in Garfield Park, Chicago, erected in 1911. The latter has been both derided and admired. Perhaps it should not rank as a great statue, yet it is a pleasing delineation of the Lincoln who for some fourteen years seldom missed a day in wielding what he called "that most useful instrument," the axe. He stands, a booted figure, axe in hand, young, rather slender, muscular, erect, his head high, astride a stump, resting a moment after the fall of a tree. The face is youthful, rather too smooth perhaps, the hair certainly too "nice," a young man proud of what he is doing. He can hew his own way. There is resolution, conscious power, in the countenance. The axe surely was a principal source of his mighty strength and endurance. The Chicago Municipal Reference Library has been unable to find any record of dedicatory exercises for this statue, nor do the reports of the West Chicago Park Commissioners contain any account of such a ceremony. On July 11, 1911, an engineer reported that the bronze cast had been placed "upon a permanent granite base," and on the following September 12 he reported that the statue had been "placed in the park." Apparently the Commissioners simply purchased the statue and ordered its erection.

Opinions vary also as to the Rosamond statue. It stands on a roughly-hewn granite block, at the top of a smoothly sloping hill, in the center of a circular drive, surrounded by fine trees. The pedestal is seven feet in height, and the bronze figure eleven feet. The "Orator," with the right foot well advanced and the right arm swung upward at a sharp angle, with the left hand holding a rolled manuscript and the head slightly raised, is declaiming, as we learn from the inscription, the final phrases of the Gettysburg Address. The surroundings of this statue are lovely; the cemetery is concealed from the roadway by walnut trees, and the monument stands alone upon a cleared summit, with no graves immediately around it. But the figure itself is disappointing. The face betokens the earnestness of the man, but the head is so far above the visitor that he has difficulty in obtaining a satisfactory view of it. Lincoln students are bound to be disturbed by more than a few questions. Did Lincoln gesticulate in that manner? If he had done so in the pre-presidential years, is it reasonable to assume that he would thus strive to emphasize his words in the cemetery at Gettysburg, in an address which was delivered with great deliberation, requiring only a trifle more than two minutes for its utterance? It has more than once been said that Lincoln "never in the world made a gesture like that." Sincere as the work is, somehow it falls short of the effect which we feel that such a subject, on such a scale, in such an impressive situation, ought to produce.

The village of Rosamond was settled in 1856 by Yankees from Massachusetts, who immediately on their arrival proceeded to found a church and a school. A few years later they established a permanent cemetery upon land densely covered with underbrush, which by dint of hard labor they transformed into a beautiful area. The Cemetery Association was incorporated in 1903, and among the by-laws was included the suggestive sentence, "The beauty of the entire cemetery and ground shall be considered, rather than the decoration of individual lots." In that year also, as visitors are told by the inscription on the reverse of the pedestal, the Association received the "Lincoln" as a gift from Captain John W. and Mrs. Mary F. Kitchell, "in memory of the Union soldiers and sailors and of their Commander-in-Chief." The donors also added fifty acres to the ten-acre cemetery.

The monument was dedicated on October 29. In the presentation address Captain Kitchell defended the orator's sweeping gesture. The sculptor had not been asked to present the President in the pose he held at Gettysburg, Kitchell said, but that, "preserving the form, and accustomed garb, the attitude of the speaker should be such as to emphasize in the loftiest and most impressive manner the sublime thoughts which he had uttered on that memorable occasion" — so Lincoln was depicted as "intent, strenuous, demanding." The donor, in his beautiful address, expressed the hope that "here may come youth to gather inspiration and fresh incitement to noble deeds and purposes, and that here, too, may wander age to meditate on the achievements of the past."

In 1933 this monument was rededicated with elaborate ceremonies, including a memorial tribute to the Kitchells. The Cemetery Association arranged the program, in which various Pana organizations shared. Due notice was taken of the foresight and good taste with which the cemetery had been planned, and it was truly stated that any speeding motorist might profit from a visit to that village burial ground, with its pioneer graves amid the towering trees, and the Lincoln statue high against the sky in noble solitude.

There is a replica of this statue in Chicago — but few there are who know it. The librarian of the Chicago Historical Society spent some three days in looking up the facts. It was understood to be in Oak Woods Cemetery. The cemetery officials admitted the existence of a Lincoln statue there, but no one knew how or when it got there, or who made it — "it had always been there." Newspaper files, the great city libraries, the little handful of surviving Grand Army veterans, the municipal authorities, men who had known "Charley" Mulligan, Lincoln specialists — three days in all and very little luck. Then the Historical Society, having published an amusing account of the quest, was informed that this was not another "Lincoln" by Mr. Mulligan, but the Rosamond "Lincoln" over again. Whereupon Paul M. Angle, the director of the Society, organized an expedition for the fifteen-mile trip to the cemetery to verify the facts — if facts they were. And on the front of the base was found: "Post No. 91, Department of Illinois, G.A.R. Erected June 14, 1905." And on the back: "Replica Statue of Lincoln by Permission of J. W. Kitchell, Pana, Illinois." Comparison with pictures of the Rosamond statue confirmed the inscribed statement that the Oak Woods statue is a duplicate. From a published statement of the Society we learn also of a quip alleged to have been made by one of the sculptor's former pupils, that this "Lincoln the Orator" "looked like a traffic cop stopping traffic." The witticism is not in tune with the spirit of this book, but we fancy that if "Charley" Mulligan were alive he would hail it, without a trace of resentment, with a resounding shout of laughter.

SOURCES: Lorene Martin, "The Lincoln Statue in Rosamond Grove Cemetery, Rosamond, Illinois," *Journal of the Illinois State Historical Society,* April, 1929; *Monumental News,* March, 1916; *Art and Archaelogy,* September–October, 1921; *Chicago Historical Society Quarterly,* Vol. 1, No. 5, Fall, 1946; correspondence with Chicago Municipal Reference Library, Chicago Historical Society, and Vicksburg National Military Park.

16   ILLUSTRATED PAGE 159

Franz Zelezny's LINCOLN

ONE statue of Abraham Lincoln which must be included in any comprehensive account of his sculptured memorials has a story which we approach with reluctance. High school students contributed the funds for its erection, and the unveiling took place with the usual formalities. At once there arose a storm of criticism. Condemned as "an abominable work of art," it was removed from before the high school to a less conspicuous locality in "an outlying district." The statue is of bronze, the work of a foreign sculptor, set up on a high pedestal. The figure is that of a stocky man, with wide shoulders, the right hand behind his back, the left clutching the lapel of his voluminous frock coat.

Local authorities freely express the opinion that the adverse verdict was just, and pronounce the work "a very unimportant statue." We have not seen it, but are bound to agree that in the excellent large photograph before us the word "Lincoln" inscribed on the pedestal seems necessary for its ready identification. The disposition of the hands suggests Saint-Gaudens, and the necktie and the collar are Lincolnian; but the beardless face, as a neutral scholar has said, has too much of "continental Europe" in its features to be "placed" at a glance by unsuspecting observers.

The 1908 graduating class of the Omaha High School, which raised the fund for the statue, gave the commission to an art dealer, who ordered a "Lincoln" from a Viennese sculptor named Franz Zelezny. By reason of the practically unanimous judgment of the community that both the figure and the features were "distorted" and "suggested Lincoln only slightly," the statue was quietly transferred, after the clamor had died down, to an elementary school named for Lincoln. Doubtless the members of that High School class felt most keenly the public reaction to "their 'Lincoln'" and were themselves sadly disappointed. We have not been able to ascertain the precise date of its erection, but it was dedicated in June, 1908.

Adolph Alexander Weinman

ONE day in 1908 a sculptor mounted a stepladder in his studio in New York City and demolished the full-size model of the statue on which he had been working for more than a year. It was not done on impulse in a moment of rage by a man of tempestuous temperament. The model he was destroying had been approved and accepted by his employers; the preliminary studies had been examined and admired by numerous critics. The sculptor acted deliberately, on the mature conviction that he could do better. He was also encountering increasing difficulties in obtaining satisfactory results with the material he was using. There were time limitations to be considered, however, and the model was advanced so far as to be nearly ready for casting. In this situation the sculptor sent for the secretary of the Association under whose auspices the statue was to be erected, and explained his unwillingness to allow any work to fall below his conception of what it ought to be. The secretary assured him that if a postponement in the proposed date for the dedication of the memorial proved necessary in order to allow time for the creation of a new model, he would do all in his power to procure the necessary revision in the arrangements then in progress. The sculptor knew that the secretary's influence would probably be decisive. That clinched his own decision ; he smashed the plaster model with an axe and made a new model in clay, a "more congenial material" and "for me possible of faster handling."

The result was the seated statue of Abraham Lincoln at Hodgenville, Kentucky. The secretary was Richard Lloyd Jones, appointed by the governor of the Commonwealth as commissioner for the expenditure of public funds for the memorial. The sculptor was Adolph Alexander Weinman. He never regretted what he did that day, and was the more gratified when, by extraordinary exertions, he was able to deliver the completed work on time for the original dedication date. This was not a unique incident ; many artists have abandoned once and again their incomplete works, but there are elements of drama in Mr. Weinman's act, and it is surely a shining example of the genuine artist's fidelity to the highest ideals of his calling. While the new "Lincoln" was still in clay it was pictured in various art publications, and requests for replicas poured in — from Philadelphia, Providence, and St. Louis ; from the University of Illinois and the University of Washington at Seattle. The legislature of Nebraska forthwith appropriated $25,000 for a copy. But Secretary Jones saw to it that only a single replica should be made, and that that should go to "his own university," the University of Wisconsin at Madison.

Weinman had been a favorite pupil of Saint-Gaudens, and that generous master, always willing to give a deserving man a hand up, wrote of him in his early years as an independent artist that he "had a most artistic nature," and recommended him as "the man best fitted" in the United States to design the medal for Theodore Roosevelt's inauguration in 1905. Weinman was born at Karlsruhe, Germany, in 1870, and brought to this country by his parents when he was ten years of age. He early showed his aptitude for art, and at sixteen entered the drawing and modeling evening classes at Cooper Union, having already been apprenticed to a carver in wood and ivory. After four years he became a pupil of Philip Martiny, and meanwhile continued his studies at the Art Students League, where he attracted the special notice of Saint-Gaudens, who aided and encouraged him and finally took him into his own studio as an assistant. He worked also with Charles H. Niehaus and Daniel Chester French.

Weinman began his own professional career in 1891. His first gold medal came at the Louisiana Purchase Exposition of 1904. In 1906 he won the competition for a memorial to General Alexander Macomb, which was unveiled at Detroit on September 11, 1908. "The Destiny of the Red Man," a group which won nationwide attention both for its workmanship and for its powerful dramatic appeal, depicted the migrations of the American Indian, moving slowly, ever westward, indicative of the extinction of the race. There followed the Baltimore monument for the Union soldiers and sailors, then the Lincoln statues, and after these a long succession of commissions in various fields of sculpture — independent statues, pediment sculpture for various important buildings, monumental fountains, coins, and medals. He produced the series of panels in relief for the Morgan Library in New York City, and the imaginative sculptures known as "The Rising of the Sun" and "The Coming of the Night" for the Panama-Pacific International Exposition. Throughout his long career Mr. Weinman has stood steadfastly for the high ideals of the duty of an artist which were exemplified in his destruction of the first model of his "Lincoln."

A group of eminent citizens, incorporated in New York as the Lincoln Farm Association, had set about raising funds for the transformation of the tract of ordinary Kentucky farm land on which Abraham Lincoln was born into a national shrine. Many thousands from all parts of the country responded to the Association's appeal for funds, with a maximum of twenty-five dollars and a minimum of twenty-five cents for individual contributions, and with the money thus obtained the Association bought what was said — with a very tenuous basis — to be the original log cabin in which Lincoln was born; erected it on the site of the President's birth, and built over it the Memorial Temple, whose cornerstone was laid by President Theodore Roosevelt on the centenary of Lincoln's birth, and which was dedicated following its completion on November 9, 1911, by President William Howard Taft. Having reached this point in its labors, the Association deeded to the United States its 110-acre holdings and the "improvements" thereon, and President Wilson accepted the gift in the name of the nation in an address made at the farm on September 16, 1916.

Until the Lincoln Farm Association began its campaign, Kentucky had done little if anything to honor the man who had been born on that farm. But with that campaign in progress, the legislature decided that some official action should be taken, and appropriated $2,500 for a tablet to be placed in the courthouse square in Hodgenville, which should bear, along with the seal of the Commonwealth, the statement that Abraham Lincoln was born south of the city on February 12, 1809. An appropriation was obtained from Congress, and the fund was further enlarged by private gifts, so a statue was substituted for the tablet. Various sculptors indicated their willingness to execute a suitable statue, although the amount of money on hand would not yield them any profit whatsoever. Theirs would be a labor of love and patriotism, although they did not overlook the fact that the national meaning of the work would react to the advantage of the sculptor who would receive the commission. Mr. Weinman was selected. The demolition of his first model greatly increased his financial loss, but the result was the imposing, effective, and greatly-admired seated "Lincoln" which now seems almost to overshadow the courthouse in Hodgenville.

The dedication took place on Memorial Day, 1909, which that year fell on May 31. That was the greatest day in the history of the little county seat. All morning special trains packed with visitors rolled in over the spur track from the main line from half the counties in the Commonwealth — from Frankfort, the capital; from Lexington, the "Blue Grass" center; from Louisville, the commercial metropolis. Among them were more than a few veterans who had worn the gray, and as many others who had worn the blue. Both groups looked with equal pride on the flags flying everywhere; not a star had been lost in the War between the States. All the shops and public buildings, and most of the private residences, were arrayed in bunting. The town had worked hard for that occasion, and its guests were warm in their praise of the results of its labor; many sent back thanks for the hospitality.

Near the shrouded statue a platform had been built. The massed spectators looked curiously and proudly at its occupants. Near the railing sat the man whom most of all the people wanted to see — Robert Todd Lincoln, son of Abraham Lincoln and Mary Todd, now in his sixty-sixth year, ten years older than his father had been on the night of his martyrdom. Near him sat Mrs. Ben Hardin Helm, a half-sister of Mary Lincoln, well beyond three score years and ten; her husband, the Confederate general to whom President Lincoln offered a Union colonelcy in 1861, had fallen at Chickamauga almost half a century before. There as a matter of course sat the governor, Augustus E. Willson, whose duty it would be to accept the statue in the name of the Commonwealth. The sculptor, following the exercises with pride, was

126

compelled several times to bow in response to the applause which hailed the mention of his name. Prominent among the local men sat Otis M. Mather, chairman of the Monument Commission. And there was "Marse Henry" Watterson, editor of the *Louisville Courier-Journal,* who had fought for the Confederacy and had long been famous as a warrior of the pen. Volley upon volley of cheers saluted the editor as he mounted the stand. Hodgenville was small, but the occasion was great, and the community rose to it in genuine Kentucky style.

The chairman, known for many years as "Judge" Mather, introduced John M. Atherton of Louisville as master of ceremonies. He in turn presented a former Chief Justice of the Kentucky Court of Appeals, who invoked the pride of his auditors by an address on "The Kentucky Pioneer." There were moist eyes when a young woman, Miss Florence Howard of Hodgenville, read the familiar poem by Francis Miles Finch. Mrs. Helm sent a special message of thanks for Miss Howard's rendering of the famous lines:

> Under the sod and the dew,
> Waiting the judgment day;
> Under the laurel, the Blue,
> Under the willow, the Gray.

There followed the high moment of the day, the unveiling of the statue. A woman appeared at the railing and with a gentle pull of the confining cord broke apart the flags, which as they fell about the base were received by four schoolgirls. And there sat Abraham Lincoln of Kentucky, the man who had defeated disunion. With perfect comprehension of the beauty of the gesture, the committee had chosen Mrs. Helm to uncover the bronze figure. A daughter of the Commonwealth, the favorite sister of Mary Todd, an ardent patriot in her devotion to the South and then to the North, what an emotional tide must have flooded her heart as she looked upon that portrait of her brother-in-law! Did she recall how she had first seen him in Lexington in 1847, when he lifted her in his arms and said, "So this is Little Sister?" Perhaps she remembered how the President had intervened in her behalf when she was stopped at Fortress Monroe on her return from her husband's funeral in Atlanta, and how "Mary" and "Abe" had met her "with warmest affection" on her arrival at the White House. And there beside her sat her nephew, who, then Captain Robert Lincoln, had in 1865 rendered her a service in Richmond.

Henry Watterson, orator of the day, did what was expected of him. His brilliant speech, somewhat rhetorical, in the old-fashioned style of eloquence, containing an abundance of ideas, was a Union, not a Confederate, address. No one in his time soared higher in eulogizing Abraham Lincoln than did "Marse Henry" on this and other occasions, and he was cheered to the echo. "If the wise and good men who made the Republic," he began, "and the brave but helpless men who fell on both sides in the War of Sections, could have survived to this day, they would feel that they had not lived and died in vain; they would realize that they had builded wiser than they knew; beholding a reason for their sacrifice and travail in the fruition of a huddle of petty sovereignties held together by a rope of sand into an Empire as splendid and as solid as England and a World Power strong enough to stand against the Universe."

From this exordium he went on to picture in broad strokes the founding of the Republic and the conditions which provoked the war in which Abraham Lincoln appeared as a world figure. While the throng packed into the little square listened intently, he declared, "I grew to manhood in the mid-period of the Republic. The keynote of the popular aspiration was love for the Union. It was intense, over-mastering, all-pervasive. The merest handful of the North, scarcely more than a group at the South, ventured a discord. But when the final trial came the one American who held to the keynote was Abraham Lincoln. He could not be diverted from it. He stood Doric, the embodiment of the Union. We owe its preservation to his wisdom, to his integrity, to his firmness and his courage. As none other than Washington could have led the Armies of the Revolution from Valley Forge to Yorktown, none other than Lincoln could have maintained the Government from Sumter to Appomattox. All of us now are Unionists; and though upon the south side of the schoolroom the educational process was somewhat warming, seemed extra-disciplinary, partaking overmuch, as some of us thought, of birch and ferrule, we are none the less Unionists though we ranged ourselves in Confederate ranks and made faces at the school-master."

From this foundation the speaker launched upon his long and elaborate encomium of the Civil War President. "God rules the world, the winds and the waves. He raises mortals to the skies and He casts them down beneath the surface of the earth. In Abraham Lincoln He gave us a symbol of American liberty and a type of American manhood which might be marked and known of all men and seen from afar, gnarled of bark, fine of grain, of fiber solid and of texture rare, adapted to all uses and capable of exquisite polish. In his career we may learn what an American partisan ought to be as distinguished from what he ought not to be. We only need to read the documentary history of his Administration to discover that he was not merely in intellect the foremost man of his time but that in character he ranks with the few great men of all time. In collision with him the rest appear as pasteboard men. He grows in length, breadth and thickness the longer we survey him. . . .

"Where did Shakespeare get his genius?" asked Watterson. "Where did Mozart get his music? Whose hand smote the lyre of the Scottish plowman and stayed the life of the German priest? God, God, and God alone; and as surely as these were raised up by God, inspired by God was Abraham Lincoln; and a thousand years hence no drama, no tragedy, no epic poem, will be filled with greater wonder, or be followed by mankind with greater feeling than that which tells the story of his life and death."

A rousing ovation followed that peroration. With tact and skill the orator had dealt with the delicate questions which arose in many minds that day, for Kentucky in 1861 had tried to be a "neutral" state. The popularity of the speaker, fairly earned by many years of hard hitting from his editorial chair, helped him to put over his ideas. And the warm-hearted men and women of that border state which had fathered both Abraham Lincoln and Jefferson Davis were prepared by the years of fratricidal strife to be generous in their judgments.

A wave of admiration for the Weinman statue swept over the country. President Charles R. Van Hise of the University of Wisconsin ratified the proposal for a replica with enthusiasm. The chairman of the University's Board of Visitors, Mr. Thomas Evans Brittingham, a Madison businessman, clinched the project by offering to pay the cost of bringing the statue to the campus, provided the state would furnish a suitable site for it. It was also necessary to obtain the approval of the Commonwealth of Kentucky, for the law vested the ownership of the original in that State. The legislature was not then in session, but the indefatigable Richard Lloyd Jones, commissioner in charge of the erection of the Kentucky statue, visited many of the members and obtained an understanding that a grant of the right for the casting of one, and only one, replica would be given to the sculptor, to be disposed of as he might direct. Weinman agreed that the University of Wisconsin might have this duplicate upon payment of the cost of casting, he himself receiving no financial reward. An exceedingly rare brochure issued by the University recognized the sculptor's "personal sacrifice and noble generosity."

The replica was dedicated on Alumni Day, June 22, 1909, three weeks after the unveiling at Hodgenville. In his letter of presentation Mr. Brittingham expressed the hope "that this monument, erected to one of the world's greatest benefactors, placed where it will be seen by countless thousands of young men and women at a most impressionable age, may be a constant inspiration to them." President Van Hise doubted not that the bronze face of Abraham Lincoln would "modify the spiritual faces of the students of the University who are to view daily the sad, calm, sagacious, determined and rugged face of our great President of the Civil War."

For many, perhaps for all, who were present that day, the crowning feature of the program was the Ode written for the occasion by Dr. William Ellery Leonard, distinguished faculty member, noted as a writer of verse and prose. This notable poem, outstanding among thousands of tributes in the Lincoln centenary year, but strangely enough not well known among Lincolnians, was read by its author. Among the lines most worthy of quotation are:

> There runs a simple argument
> That, with the power to give a great man birth,
> The insight and the exaltation
> To judge him at his splendid worth
> Best proves the vigor of a continent—
> The blood that pulses in a nation.

By this test the poet proceeds to judge whether the people of the Great Republic of the New World walk alone by "that iron faith" whose works are found in "prairies sown," "factories aflame," mountain mines, "victorious battle fleets and towering cities." He answers "No"; the American people are wiser than they think —

> God and the west wind and the morning star
> And manhood still are more than steel or stone!

He hears Stanton's prophetic cry when "the gaunt form lay dead." He marks how the people whisper, and "look in each other's faces and grow dumb," while Lincoln crosses "the valleys to the muffled drum."

Ships and mountains and our children have been named for the martyred chief; his words are treasured, and often we linger best

> Around the little things he did or said,
> The quaint and kindly shift, the homespun jest,
> Dear random memories of a father dead. . . .

His picture hangs on cottage walls, and his birthplace has been
made a shrine: he has become the

> Folk-hero of the last among the races,
> As elemental as the rocks and trees;
> One of the world's old legendary faces,
> Moving amid Earth's unknown destinies.

On that day sculptor and poet fairly matched each other in their delineation of Abraham Lincoln.

After an interval of ten years the statue was moved to a new site
on what was then named Lincoln Terrace, and another and more
elaborate ceremony took place. On that day, June 24, 1919, the University paid tribute to its students and alumni who had served in the
World War. Medals were awarded, the Gold Star roll was read, Richard Lloyd Jones made the address in memory of Lincoln, and Dr.
Leonard's ode was read again.

No more lovely situation for the statue could be imagined. It is
placed directly in front of Bascom Hall, the main building of the
University, containing the president's and deans' offices as well as
numerous classrooms and lecture halls. The building stands atop the
highest hill on the campus, with commanding views of the lakes and
the city. Later buildings have shut off some of the views, but "Bascom" still dominates the campus. There Lincoln sits, gazing eastward
toward the state Capitol a mile away. Stone benches about the monument and the steps of the building invite students to loiter in that
green-clad area. They cannot ignore the presence of the statue, and
most of them must in some measure come under its spell.

While only one replica of the Weinman statue exists, there are, in
a sense, two "originals." The casting of the Hodgenville original and
of the Wisconsin duplicate having been completed, Mr. Weinman presented his model to the St. Louis Art Museum, where it was given "a
bronze finish" with what are described as "very pleasing results."

Less than thirty months after the dedication at Hodgenville, Kentucky came into possession of another Lincoln statue, also the creation of Mr. Weinman. This was the gift of James Breckinridge Speed, son of William Pope Speed and nephew of Joshua and James Speed, a Louisville businessman and philanthropist, whose name recalls Lincoln's most intimate friendships. "Josh" Speed had befriended "Abe" Lincoln when he left New Salem to make his home in Springfield. He had taken to the strapping and practically penniless young man on sight. With him, at a critical period in his life, Lincoln had maintained more confidential relations than ever with any other man. When Speed went back to Louisville, Lincoln wrote that without him Springfield would be a very lonesome place. After Lincoln had broken his engagement to Mary Todd, and while he was still oppressed by the ailment he called "the hypo," he went to Louisville for a visit with Speed at the home of his mother, and always remembered gratefully the welcome he received and the healing influence of those surroundings. After twenty years Lincoln sent an inscribed portrait to Speed's mother from the White House. James Speed became Lincoln's Attorney-General in 1864.

James Breckinridge Speed's gift, a standing "Lincoln," was erected in the Capitol at Frankfort and dedicated on November 8, 1911 — a gala day, because, for the first time in almost a hundred years, a President of the United States was coming to Frankfort. As a matter of course the city was gay with flags and bunting, and the new Capitol, which had been occupied only a short time, "was almost completely swathed with banners." One special train brought five hundred guests from Louisville, among them "Marse Henry" Watterson, again the orator of the day. A train from Cincinnati had on board President William Howard Taft, his half-brother Charles P. Taft, and scores of public men from outside the Commonwealth. Only a handful of Kentucky counties failed to send a delegation.

The exercises were conducted under difficult conditions, owing to the design of the handsome building. The statue was placed in the "Hall of Fame" on the first floor, beneath the massive dome, at the foot of a rotunda surrounded by balconies. The first floor; the second-floor galleries, reserved for the official party; the next balcony above, a portion of which was "set aside for colored persons"; and the various hallways converging upon the rotunda were all filled. Governor Willson again served as master of ceremonies. A male chorus sang "My Old Kentucky Home" and "Dixie." Alice Speed, a granddaughter of the donor of the statue, three years of age, and her cousin John, not much older, were brought forward for the unveiling. With the releasing of the flags which concealed the statue "there was a long moment of silence" and then "the murmur of many voices."

In introducing President Taft, Governor Willson referred to President Monroe's visit to Frankfort in 1819. The President's remarks were necessarily brief, for he was due to make the address the following day at the Lincoln Farm near Hodgenville. A letter from Robert T. Lincoln declared, "How happy my father would have been if he could have foreknown this splendid act of the nephew of the absolutely dearest friend he ever had in the world, and of its reception by Kentucky." Thereupon the governor introduced that nephew, and then the sculptor, both men receiving ovations. Farther along, in accepting the statue, Willson alluded to the gift's coming from a Union soldier and the presentation speech of Watterson, who had worn the Confederate gray.

Everybody knew what to expect of "Marse Henry," and got it. The orator that day appeared at his Wattersonian best. He began with a tribute to James Breckinridge Speed, "lover of books, of pictures, and of music," continued with an account of Lincoln's attachment for Joshua Speed, and how "Conscience and Destiny had joined their hands to write a drama such as may not be found elsewhere outside the pages of romance," then "paused" to speak "with some particularity . . . of the parentage and especially the maternity" of Lincoln. "No falser, fouler story ever gained currency," said Watterson, "than that which impeached the character of the mother of Abraham Lincoln." With obvious relish the speaker lingered upon some of his personal contacts with the President, telling how he had obtained a copy of the Inaugural Address in 1861, and certified his faith in a well-known and cherished incident by declaring that "Judge Douglas . . . reached over my arm" to take Lincoln's hat during the delivery of the address. The incoming President's "self-possession was perfect that day. . . . He delivered that address as though he had been delivering inaugural addresses all his life."

The way ahead was "made" for Lincoln, Watterson declared. The Democratic Party had committed hara-kiri betimes. Through the breach effected by Douglas, his lifelong rival, in the wall of Democracy, Lincoln, at the head of the Republicans, marched in triumph. And again: "Happily, there remain no more hidden chapters, not even any more disputed passages, in Lincoln's life. His was the genius of common sense. He possessed all the distinguishing characteristics of the politicians of the middle period of the last century: their craft, plausibility and cleanliness; their inclination toward doctrinal and dogmatic discussion; their loyalty to political organization and engagement; their vital love of their country and their pride in its institutions. A 'Conscience Whig' he began, and a 'Conscience Whig' he continued to the end." Contrasting Lincoln with Douglas, Watterson found that with Lincoln "intellectual dignity was paramount"; it "shone even through the uncouth youth who studied law by the firelight." In turn Lincoln brought Seward and Chase to understand his intellectual superiority, and even Stanton, surly though he was, and in spite of his "sometimes trying virtues."

Lincoln was a Southern man. "All his people were Southerners. . . . Not less than the North has the South reason to canonize Lincoln; for he was the one friend we had at court. . . . If he had lived there would have been no Era of Reconstruction, with its mistaken theories, repressive agencies and oppressive legislation. . . . For Lincoln entertained with respect to the rehabilitation of the Union the single wish that the Southern States — to use his homely phraseology — 'should come back home and behave themselves,' and if he had lived he would have made this wish effectual. . . . The Declaration of Independence was his Confession of Faith, the Constitution of the United States his Ark and Covenant of Liberty, the Union his redoubt, the flag his shibboleth."

With a tribute to the Commonwealth that had given to the war both the chieftains, Abraham Lincoln and Jefferson Davis, and "to each of the contending armies a quota of fighting men equal to that contributed by any other State singly to either army," and having invoked the memory of Henry Clay and of John J. Crittenden, the orator called upon all Kentuckians, whether they called themselves Democrats or Republicans, to renew their "allegiance to the constitution of the Republic and the perpetuity of the Union." A former Confederate soldier pronounced the benediction.

The bronze "Lincoln" unveiled at this ceremony stands in the place of honor in the circle at the foot of the rotunda of the Kentucky Capitol, and not far removed, although off-center, is a statue of Jefferson Davis, by Frederick C. Hibbard, who was in time to mould a statue of Lincoln with Mrs. Lincoln standing beside him. It is difficult to find a vantage point for any patient examination of this "Lincoln." The figure is nine feet in height, and stands on a five-foot pedestal, so that unless one stands at some distance in a hallway one must look either up at a sharp angle or down from a balcony. But despite these difficulties, the impression of beauty, dignity, virility is instant.

There are many things in common between this standing "Lincoln" and the sculptor's seated "Lincoln." Both the Weinman statues deserve their popularity. About both there is a noble dignity, as of a man conscious of his powers — self-possessed, determined. At Hodgenville the President sits at ease in the wide curve of the chair, one hand gripping its arm, the other clasping a folded document. The folds in the coat and the creases in the vest are not smoothed out, as though Lincoln, indifferent to all such minor matters as personal appearance, had dropped into a chair with a problem in hand for consideration. The face is serious; no twinkle betokens the imminence of a neighborly salutation, but the countenance is sympathetic, not so worn as in the final months of his life. Kindly, almost benign, a thoughtful, earnest man, silent, still, the President must determine a policy, alone with his conscience and his knowledge of the complex elements that strive for mastery in the welter of war. The standing "Lincoln" at Frankfort is this same man, erect, with undrooping head, his right hand at his side, the left curved about the top of the chair back, over which a coat is thrown. The chair is the same. The same wrinkles are in the vest. The man has risen, moved round to the side of the chair, and lifted himself to his full height. The sculptor has not tried to make a different portrait.

Weinman once said that while he had read books, studied photographs, and used the Volk life-mask, he had avoided the heads other artists had carved. So he found his Lincoln. One feels that these portraits are of the same man at the same time, with only an alteration of attitude. In the seated "Lincoln" there is the suggestion of mental activity and physical repose; the standing "Lincoln" suggests action of both mind and body. Has his problem been solved? Has he made his decision? Is he about to put his conclusion into effect? Only a slight and subtle variance in the expression of the face, and the change in the physical position, indicate the alteration in the mood of the man. One should see these statues, as did the writer, on consecutive days, and study their differences and likenesses. One student at least numbers them among the "Lincolns" to which he returns again and again with gratitude for their artistry and for their portrayal of the most magnanimous of Americans.

SOURCES: University of Wisconsin, *Memorial Statue of Abraham Lincoln,* 1909; Arthur Krock, ed., *Editorials of Henry Watterson,* 1923; Henry Watterson, *"Marse Henry," an Autobiography,* 1919; contemporary press reports of the Watterson addresses, portions of which may be found in the *Cosmopolitan,* March, 1909; correspondence with Adolph A. Weinman and with Dr. Julius E. Olson, Madison, Wisconsin.

18 ILLUSTRATED PAGE 162

John Rogers —
His "Groups" and His LINCOLN

THAT antislavery and highly influential "religious newspaper," *The Independent,* published early in 1860 an article from "a special correspondent" entitled "A Contrast — Demonology of the Nineteenth Century." The article, signed only "C" — it is a fair guess that the writer was the Rev. George B. Cheever, pastor of the Church of the Puritans in New York City, and one of the relatively few metropolitan clergymen who boldly denounced slavery — dealt with "a couple of sculptures by a young artist, now of this city, presenting the extremes of slavery and freedom." One of these works was a group depicting the family of a New England farmer, the "hearty, happy father," his day's work done, resting by the fireside, playing with his children, while the mother sits nearby, her face "bespeaking the very perfection of household contentment." The contrast was provided by a group portraying the sale of a slave family on the auction block; the auctioneer bending forward "with his leering, demoniac face into which the artist has conveyed to an intense degree the despicable and diabolic character produced by the infinite debasement, villainy and cruelty of his employment"; the black father's face "impressive in the silent expression it conveys of the sense of his misery," while on the other side of the trader stands the anguished mother with her children, "who are trying to hide themselves in the folds of her clothing that they may not be torn away from her."

"C" proceeds to use this contrast as a text for a denunciation of the "peculiar institution" which the commercial metropolis feared almost to the point of cowardice. This is "a devil's trade. . . . And to think of such a social condition being vaunted as the climax and perfection, not of human luxury and affluence merely, but of the divine benevolence. And yet, to think that here in New York men stand in such horror and dread of the symbols and description of this heavenly institution, that our young artist can not find a shop-window in Broadway in which the owners or occupants will permit him to introduce his studies in this line to the admiration of our citizens! If slavery is so divine a state, the gift and appointment of our Maker, and slave-holding the attribute of legislators, an employment, dignity and policy worthy of the gods, how happens it that this group-symbol of that state, or of the ministering spirits as essential to it as the guardian angels at the gates of Paradise, or the forms of the cherubim before the Holy of Holies, should be abhorred of men and dreadful even to the shop-keepers?" At the end of his second column "C" suggests that "if any of our readers desire to see or to purchase these admirable groups, which are among the first works of the young artist of whom we have spoken, they can do it by calling at 599 Broadway, and inquiring for Mr. Rogers up-stairs."

This "young artist" was John Rogers. These were almost the first of his famous "groups." He needed money, and the dealers in art and in practically all other goods refused to display his wares, so in his thirty-first year he arranged to have the "Slave Auction" peddled from door to door. In a letter of January 19, 1860, Rogers informed his mother's sister, Mrs. Ephraim Peabody of Boston, that the stores "were afraid of offending their southern customers," but two weeks later he sent her word that "the 'Slave Auction' is beginning to go like hot cakes." Rogers found a backer in Lewis Tappan, who had retired from business in 1849 to devote himself to humanitarian labors, and the abolitionists practically annexed the group for propaganda purposes: Rogers had been selling copies for $1.50, but now informed his aunt that "the abolitionists here all have advised me to put the 'Slave Auction' at three dollars, although many think that is too high." This was the artist's first success. By the end of the war in 1865 his precarious financial situation had been transformed to a well-established prosperity.

Rogers was born in Salem, Massachusetts, in 1829, and educated in the Boston public schools. He had in mind the profession of an engineer, but eye trouble intervened, and a lucky chance one day led him through a Boston street where, seeing a man moulding figures in clay, the idea flashed upon him that such work would not be so much of a strain on his eyes. During the years that he worked as a machinist in Manchester, New Hampshire, he devoted much of his free time to modeling, displaying the results in neighborhood fairs. He traveled to Spain for his health, then migrated to the West and became the head of a railroad shop in Hannibal, Missouri. Somehow the persistent young man managed to spend a year in Europe studying art, and came home with the resolution that whatever sculptural work he might do should be American in theme rather than imitative of the traditional classicism of the studios abroad.

Rogers found a job in the Chicago city surveyor's office, and a "group," winning acclaim at a charity fair there, determined his future career. "Checkers at the Farm" has always been one of the most popular of the Rogers "groups." The checkerboard rests on a flour barrel, and the booted New England farmer sits on an upturned bushel basket. The city man, who wears spats, strokes his chin and studies the board with an expression of surprise and chagrin. The lady from the city stands between the players and prevents the child she holds from upsetting the board. All the "properties" are correct. It is an amusing incident told in plaster.

Rogers decided to try his fortune in New York, arriving there late in 1859, about the time that the discovery of the process of casting in gelatin enabled him to multiply his groups inexpensively. He produced them in rapid succession, never seeming to be at a loss for subjects. Homely anecdotes, amusing or pathetic incidents, readily recognizable as facets of human life, became his stock in trade. Whether Rogers was or was not an abolitionist, the theme of the "Slave Auction" and the contrast with the simple homes of New England would naturally appeal to one of his antecedents, and it can hardly have surprised him that the antislavery crusaders boomed such groups. Of the Rogers war series probably the most popular was "One More Shot."

Versatile and imaginative, Rogers successfully modeled Shakespearean scenes and a series representing Joe Jefferson in *Rip Van Winkle*. Similar to "Checkers" are such groups as "The Charity Patient" and "Coming to the Parson." In all, John Rogers is said to have produced eighty-seven groups, of which a hundred thousand were sold during his lifetime, and in 1876 his catalog prices ranged from five to fifty dollars. A "nervous affection of his hands" compelled him to give up modelling in 1894, but he lived on at his Connecticut home until 1904.

There was a period not so long ago when the well-appointed American home, especially in the country and the smaller cities, displayed chromos on the parlor walls, plush albums on the center table, iron deer on the lawn, and one or more Rogers "groups" in the bay window. A writer in *Farm and Fireside* in 1874 declared that "what Hogarth was in pencil, Canova and Michelangelo in marble, Reynolds and Landseer on canvas — all the excellencies of these masters of art have their illustration in the plaster of John Rogers." Other writers near the end of the century, with more information and better judgment, deprecated comparisons of Rogers' "groups" with those of the sculptors of Greece or of the Renaissance, representing Rogers as having provided the American people with "the homely tales to tally with homely lives" which they demanded in his time.

Rogers was forgotten practically by common consent not many years after his passing. Now comes a gratifying renewal of affection for his work. For Rogers did much for American art; copying no one, he hoed his own row. No other American has better portrayed the life of the plain people of his time.

None of Rogers' "groups" is more treasured than "The Council of War." In the more familiar of two versions, Lincoln sits in a chair studying a large map of the campaign proposed by Grant in 1864. Behind the chair stands Secretary of War Stanton, while at Lincoln's right the Union commander points with one hand to a place on the map, while he explains his plans. The portraits are good, the attitudes natural, and the arrangement excellent. William Ordway Partridge, himself a sculptor, considers this Rogers' best portrait group, and a high achievement. At least one of Partridge's readers would subscribe to his opinion that if the "Council" had been carried out in heroic size, it would have been Rogers' happiest monumental work.

Rogers did work of heroic size, though in no instance do his "groups" appear to have exceeded two feet in height; his bronze equestrian statue of General John F. Reynolds, who fell on the first day of the battle of Gettysburg, is at the Philadelphia City Hall, and his bronze "Lincoln," a third larger than life-size, is in Manchester, New Hampshire. This "Lincoln," in plaster, had won a gold medal at the Chicago World's Fair, and was also exhibited in New York. Although Rogers had not visited Manchester in many years, he now proposed to present this statue to that city in remembrance of his residence there. The local art association welcomed him "home" with an exhibition of his work, including, it is reported, over seventy pieces. This collection was understood to be the most nearly complete in existence; unfortunately it was destroyed by fire in January, 1902. Today there are large collections of Rogers' works at the New York Historical Society and in the Essex Institute in Salem.

The Lincoln statue was placed in the public library of Manchester, and Mayor William C. Clarke accepted it in the name of the city. Rogers himself undertook to supervise its erection, but his health was so poor that he found it necessary to invoke the help of his lifelong friend, Henry W. Herrick, well known in his day as an artist and designer, who was born in the Granite State. Presently the plaster figure was removed to a corridor in the high school, but it is said to have sustained some damage in the moving and additional damage from "other causes" — specifically the pranks of students — so that its survival was in peril. Louis Bell Post of the Grand Army of the Republic, determined to preserve the statue, came to the rescue, and Edward P. Richardson, a member of the Post, led a movement for casting it in bronze. As this occurred in the Lincoln centenary year, public reaction was favorable. The city government granted the use of the model for the casting. The Manchester organization adopted the plan used in 1820 by the Bunker Hill Monument Association, whereby every contributor of one dollar or more received a membership certificate, and the money required for the bronze and the base was raised without outside help. The total of the contracts was $4,680. The city government appropriated $2,500, and after all bills had been paid the treasurer still had $199 on hand. These facts are worthy of mention as a rare example of the right way to do such things.

The municipal authorities gave permission for the placing of the monument on the lawn before the high school, and an admirable dedication program was carried out on Memorial Day, May 30, 1910. The G.A.R. Departmental Commander and his staff had charge of the ceremonies, and Mrs. Minnie R. Bryant, Patriotic Instructor of the Daughters of Veterans, did the unveiling.

The orator of the day, Sherman E. Burroughs, recalled "the weird combination of qualities that made up the personality of Abraham Lincoln, and the startling contrasts in his strange career." Lincoln was "fast becoming a half-mystical figure. In the haze of historic distance its outlines fade away and become less and less distinct and definite, but its proportions become more and more heroic with the passing years." Yet the man was "as simple and unaffected as a child. No man better knew the worth of substance and the mockery of show. . . . Genius has no sire but God. Its lineage and the process of its growth alike defy all laws of man's discovery." Lincoln was "not an enthusiast, an extremist, nor an agitator. His mind was essentially conservative and constructive. He invaded no field until he had surveyed its confines and approaches with the greatest caution. He looked far ahead and all around, but once he had a situation well in mind his action was bold, prompt, and decisive. He foresaw with unerring vision that the conflict with slavery was inevitable. A policy of compromise, pursued for a half-century, had failed of substantial results." The speaker evinced a real acquaintance with the spirit and practice of the man whom the sculptor had portrayed.

There before the assemblage, during the delivery of the oration, sat the Civil War President in bronze, in an attitude of listening to the speaker. The artist had seated him in a wide chair, with his knees crossed, his right arm resting on the chair back. The left hand holds one end of an unrolled map, which reaches over the chair arm to the floor. The President's head is slightly bowed and tilted a little to one side; he has raised his eyes from the map to look off into space. The face is earnest and meditative, the face of a man in thought. The entire effect is pleasing. The work is a real achievement for a relatively self-taught sculptor. Four bronze tablets are set into the stone of the pedestal, carrying suitable records of the origin of the work and a few of the moving words of the Second Inaugural Address.

SOURCES: *The Independent* [New York], February 16, 1860; George Rockwood Cheever, *Lincoln and the Causes of the Civil War*, 1936; Mr. & Mrs. Chetwood Smith, *Rogers Groups*, 1934; Ashton Thorp, *Manchester of Yesterday*, 1939; *New York Historical Society Quarterly Bulletin*, April, 1937; *Amoskeag Bulletin*, May 1, 1916.

Elwell's Baffling Statue

ON LINCOLN's birthday in 1912 President William Howard Taft placed a wreath before a statue of the Civil War President at East Orange, New Jersey, while a battery fired a salute in honor of the distinguished visitor. Among the thousands of spectators who witnessed the tribute were three local leaders who had served the city well. At the close of the ceremony these three exchanged pledges to hold each year until the end of their lives a memorial service for the great American whom above all others they admired. Frederick Danby was the first of the trio to pass away; Lincoln E. Rowley, who served for many years as city clerk, died in 1933; David Lawrence Pierson, who had spent nearly half his long life in writing a history of the group of cities known as "the Oranges," survived until 1938, and until the end kept faith with his departed comrades. In 1934 there was published an account of the observance of the anniversary in the City Hall council chamber, with veterans of the Spanish-American War and World War I present and Mr. Pierson presiding, at the end of which a group of Boy Scouts marched to the Lincoln statue to deposit a wreath for themselves and in the names of the trio who had kept the faith so long.

It was Mr. Pierson who fathered the project for the erection of a Lincoln statue in the city. Late in 1908 he appeared before the City Council to urge the prompt initiation of the project. The centenary year of Lincoln's birth was at hand; books, pamphlets, magazine articles, orations, and poems had directed the attention of the whole nation to the significance of the approaching anniversary; thousands had contributed for the purchase and preservation of the birthplace farm in Kentucky. It was too late for East Orange to set up a permanent memorial for the birthday, but it was not too late to arrange for appropriate ceremonies, and formal exercises were held, with Governor John Franklin Fort of New Jersey presiding. A decision was taken to inaugurate a movement for a bronze statue to be placed on a commanding site on the North Parkway. Francis Edwin Elwell was commissioned to create the memorial, the cost to be eight thousand dollars.

On the anniversary of the Gettysburg Address in 1910, while "cold

By A. Frilli.
Memorial Museum,
San Francisco, Calif., 1915

By Pietro Mezzara. Lincoln School,
San Francisco, Calif., 1866

143

By Lot Flannery.
Judiciary Square,
Washington, D.C., 1868

By Henry K. Brown.
Union Square,
New York City, 1870

144

By Henry K. Brown. Prospect Park, Brooklyn, N.Y., 1869

By Vinnie Ream. Capitol, Washington, D.C., 1871

146

By Randolph Rogers. Fairmount Park, Philadelphia, Pa., 1871

By Larkin G. Mead. Oak Ridge Cemetery, Springfield, Ill., 1874

148

By Thomas Ball. Lincoln Park, Washington, D.C., 1876.
(Replica, Park Square, Boston, Mass., 1879)

By Augustus Saint-Gaudens. Lincoln Park, Chicago, Ill., 1887.
(Replica, Parliament Square, London, England, 1920)

By Augustus Saint-Gaudens. Grant Park, Chicago, Ill., 1926

152

By George E. Bissell. Edinburgh, Scotland, 1893.
(Replica, Clermont, Iowa, 1903)

<small>OPPOSITE:</small> *By Leonard Volk. Rochester, N.Y., 1892*

153

By William R. O'Donovan and Thomas Eakins.
Prospect Park, Brooklyn, N.Y., 1895 (?)

By Alfonso Pelzer. Lincoln, N.J., 1898.
(Duplicates at Detroit, Mich.; Wooster, Ohio;
Boise, Idaho; Wilkinsburg, Pa.; Fremont, Neb.)

*By Charles H. Niehaus. Hackley Park, Muskegon, Mich., 1900.
(Replicas, Buffalo Hist. Soc., Buffalo, N.Y., 1902;
Library Park, Kenosha, Wis., 1909)*

By W. Granville Hastings. Cincinnati, Ohio, 1902.
(Replicas, Bunker Hill, Ill., 1904; Jefferson, Iowa,
1918; Sioux City, Iowa, 1924)

157

By Charles J. Mulligan.
Garfield Park, Chicago, Ill., 1911

y Franz Zelezny.
incoln School,
maha, Neb., c. 1908

By Charles J. Mulligan. Rosamond Grove Ceme-
tery, Rosamond, Ill., 1903. (Replica, Oak Woods
Cemetery, Chicago, Ill., 1905)

159

By Adolph A. Weinman. Hodgenville, Ky., 1909.
(Replica, University of Wisconsin, Madison, Wis., 1909)

By Adolph A. Weinman. Capitol, Frankfort, Ky., 1911

By John Rogers. Central High School, Manchester, N.H., 1910

By Francis E. Elwell. East Orange, N.J., 1911

By Gutzon Borglum. Court House, Newark, N.J., 1911

By George E. Ganiere.
Webster City, Iowa, 1913

By George E. Ganiere.
Burlington, Wis., 1913

By J. Otto Schweizer. Gettysburg, Pa., 1913

By J. Otto Schweizer.
Union League,
Philadelphia, Pa., 1917

OLD GLORY

LET US HAVE PEACE

1861–1865

DEDICATED TO THE VETE... OF THE CIVIL WAR

168

By an unknown. Moberly, Mo., 1914 (?)

OPPOSITE: *By Peter Bisson. Pacific Park, Long Beach, Calif., 1915*

By George G. Barnard. Cincinnati, Ohio, 1917.
(Replicas, Manchester, England, 1919;
Louisville, Ky., 1922)

170

By Merrell Gage. State House, Topeka, Kans., 1918

By Alonzo V. Lewis. Tacoma, Wash., 1918

By Alonzo V. Lewis. Spokane, Wash., 1930

By Andrew O'Connor. Capitol, Springfield, Ill., 1918

By Andrew O'Connor. Fort Lincoln Cemetery, Md., 1922

175

By Ira A. Correll. Odon, Ind., 1922

By A. L. Van den Bergen. Racine, Wis., 1924.
(Replica, Clinton, Ill., 1931)

ERECTED
MAY 30, 1915
TO THE MEMORY
OF OUR HEROES.

178

By Bartoli. San Juan, Puerto Rico, 1926

OPPOSITE: *By Steven A. Rebeck. Alliance, Ohio, 1924*

179

By Lorado Taft. Urbana, Ill., 1927

180

By Haig Patigian. City Hall, San Francisco, Calif., 1928

By George F. Waters. Portland, Ore., 1928

By Isidore Konti.
Memorial Park,
Yonkers, N.Y., 1929

By Leonard Crunelle. Freeport, Ill., 1929

By Leonard Crunelle. Dixon, Ill., 1930

By Max Bachman. Minneapolis, Minn., 1930

y James E. Fraser. Lincoln Park, Jersey City, N.J., 1930

By Max Kalish. Cleveland, Ohio, 1932

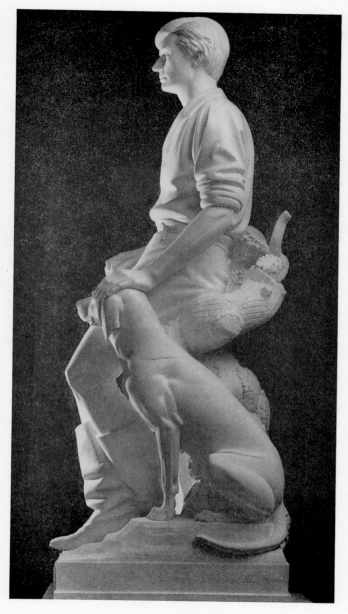

By Paul Manship. Fort Wayne, Ind., 1932

By Charles Keck. Wabash, Ind., 1932.
(Replica, Hingham, Mass., 1939)

By Charles Keck. New York City, 1949

By Gaetano Cecere. Milwaukee, Wis., 1934

By Henry Hering. Indianapolis, Ind., 1935

193

By Bryant Baker. Buffalo, N.Y., 1935

By Samuel Cashwan. Ypsilanti, Mich., 1938

By Nellie V. Walker. Lincoln Memorial Bridge, Lawrence Co., Ill., 1938

By Clarence A. Shaler.
Ripon College, Ripon, Wis., 1939

*By Louis Slobodkin. Interior Building,
Washington, D.C., 1939*

198

By Clyde Du Vernet Hunt.
Historical Museum,
Bennington, Vt., 1939

199

By Frederick C. Hibbard. Racine, Wis., 1943

By Avard Fairbanks. Ewa, Hawaii, 1944

By Boris Lovet-Lorski.
Macon County Building,
Decatur, Ill., 1946

202

By Fred M. Torrey. James Millikin University, Decatur, Ill., 1948

By Daniel C. French. Capitol, Lincoln, Neb., 1912

By Daniel C. French.
Lincoln Memorial,
Washington, D.C., 1922

By Henry J. Ellicott. c. 1867 (?)

winds swept the valley," ground was broken for the base of the monument, and Mr. Pierson read Lincoln's famous speech. The statue was dedicated on the following Flag Day, June 14, 1911, one of the three members of the Committee on the Statue, Captain John H. Palmer, conducting the ceremonies. Almost exactly three years after its appointment, the Centenary Committee rendered its final report; the funds had all been raised by "subscriptions from among the people," and the "first statuary erected in East Orange" was the result of their generosity and of the untiring labors of the committee.

They had chosen their sculptor on his record. One of his best works — the "Dispatch Rider of the Revolution," dedicated in 1907 — was available for their inspection in the neighboring city of Orange. Elwell probably never did a better piece of work. The bronze horseman, cloaked and spurred, is dismounting, yet the group conveys clearly the spirit of his mission. He is not riding, but he is in action, and his duty is urgent.

Elwell had served for a time as a curator at the Metropolitan Museum, and a succession of distinguished achievements had marked his career. Left an orphan, his boyhood was spent among the inspiring surroundings of Concord, Massachusetts. His grandfather, Elisha Farrar, the village blacksmith, a man whom everyone knew and respected, a thinker, and a comrade of Thoreau, became like a father to the lad. Young Elwell worked at the forge, did chores for the neighbors, and went along with his grandfather and Thoreau on their tramps over the countryside. Listening to their talk was in itself an education. The Alcott family liked him. He looked almost with awe upon Emerson. Just as he finished high school, his grandfather died, and a relative obtained employment for him with a firm of Boston surgical instrument manufacturers — excellent training in expert use of the hands and the eyes.

Elwell had decided what he wanted to do with his life. The Alcotts noticed his knack for drawing; Abba May Alcott, who had founded an Art Center in Concord, befriended him in various ways. As early as 1876, in his eighteenth year, Elwell was coming to "the Center" for plaster to experiment in modeling a bust he hoped to cast. "Dan" French, eight years older, also in Concord, expressed his faith in the future of "Frank" Elwell. The upshot was that Elwell's Concord friends loaned him money to cross the ocean. He studied in Paris, in Ghent, and elsewhere; and when he returned in 1885, after a seven-year absence, he could point to his successes as an exhibitor in the

Paris Salon, in Brussels, and in London. Presently there came to him a commission from the city of Edam in Holland, the outcome of which was what is said to be the first statue modeled in America by an American artist to be erected in Europe. His next work of importance was a group portraying Charles Dickens and "Little Nell," which earned him a higher measure of popularity, perhaps, than he enjoyed at any other time. The multitudes who flocked to the Columbian Exposition in 1893 were unanimous in their enthusiasm for this work, which had the same appealing qualities as the Rogers "groups," recalling a story which everyone had read and no one had forgotten. In 1896 Elwell exhibited at the Salon an idealistic and impressive work which was at once acquired by a Parisian and kept in the city. Elwell's long-time interest in Egyptian history and art found expression in "Egypt's Awakening." The seated figure, partly clad in priestly robes, aroused from slumber, seems to come to life, the body stretching upward, the arms uplifted, the face kindling with newly aroused aspirations. He had produced the Winfield Scott Hancock monument for the Gettysburg battleground, an original fountain with figures of an Egyptian character for the Pan-American Exposition, numerous portraits — among them a bust of Thoreau — and several memorials, including the "Edwin Booth" at Mount Auburn in Cambridge. With these and many other works attesting Elwell's versatility, the tide seemed to be at the crest when, at the age of fifty-three, his "Lincoln" was unveiled.

Yet it is a baffling and somewhat disappointing figure. The President is posed upon a simple pedestal, with a long cloak spread across his shoulders, both arms hanging at full length, one hand holding the inevitable high hat. The head is erect, the eyes are level. A regiment might be passing before him in salute: he might have risen to address an outdoor audience and be waiting for the applause to subside: there is no consensus of opinion as to its merit and purpose, nor is the sculptor known to have left any memorandum before his death in 1922 stating the meaning of the statue. It is an original. None other is like it.

SOURCES: Charles E. Fairman, *Works of Art in the National Capitol,* 1913; Michigan State Library, *Biographical Sketches of American Artists,* 1924; David Lawrence Pierson, *History of the Oranges,* 1922; Caroline Ticknor, *May Alcott,* 1922.

Several newspapers have stated in later years that President Taft came to East Orange "to unveil a monument to Lincoln." The contemporary newspapers record no such visit, while Pierson's *History* definitely states that the wreath was placed at the base of the statue on February 12, 1912.

Gutzon Borglum

FEW of the Lincoln sculptors have equalled, and probably none has surpassed, Gutzon Borglum in the ability to put ideas into words. Often his ideas were original, sometimes unorthodox, but most of the many things he had to say were worth saying; he never hesitated to express his views, always in a manner that professional writers might have envied. While the Lincoln Memorial was under construction in Washington he answered a question one day by asking, "What would you think of taking Mr. Lincoln or Mr. Bryan over to the Acropolis and putting them there in bronze?" Borglum had little patience with the placing of the Prairie President in a Greek temple. At Springfield, Illinois, in 1915, he described an artist as "simply a man whose heart beats a little quicker than those of the rest of you. It is because he gathers a little more of the struggles, of pathos, of sweetness, of desires, that come to man during the twenty-four hours; and he must express it, he must write it, he must sing it, he must paint it, he must model it." In at least three of these mediums Borglum excelled; he wrote well, although often at odds with the literary mentors of his day; he painted well; and as a sculptor he achieved eminence.

The "musts" that burned in his heart made him something of a "stormy petrel," it has been said, and compelled him to strive with unending energy to use his wings. He once defined the purpose of art as "to drop a plumb line into the depths of life, to find thereby the great emotions that are common to all mankind, and to express them so that all mankind will understand the expression." His statue of Lincoln at Newark, New Jersey, and the colossal marble head of Lincoln in the Capitol at Washington fall definitely within the bounds of this statement. At another time he said that "there is something in sheer volume that awes and terrifies, lifts us out of ourselves." The project for the transformation of a mountainside into a memorial to the Confederacy, and the carving of the heads of four Presidents at the summit of Mount Rushmore in South Dakota, stand for his conviction that there are multitudes of people who only thus can be shocked into some appreciation of greatness.

John Gutzon de la Mothe Borglum, using for once the full name which his Danish parents entrusted to him, was born in Idaho. The month and day of his birth — March 25 — have gone through many editions of *Who's Who* without change, but the year, after being recorded for over a decade as 1867, was altered in 1932 to 1871. Borglum's father was a pioneer of artistic temperament, who for several years made woodcarving his trade. The family changed its residence from time to time; another son, Solon Hannibal Borglum, also a sculptor of distinction, was born in Ogden, Utah, in 1868. The father established himself as a physician at Fremont, Nebraska — just when, we do not know — and in time acquired a large ranch. Gutzon went to school in Fremont and in Omaha, but he loved the outdoors more than books. There were plenty of horses on the ranch for him to ride, and with the eyes of an artist he studied them in repose and in action.

As a boy he had begun to carve. At nineteen he was off to Paris, his aim in life decided upon. Already Americanism had become a kind of religion with him. After only a half-year in France, he sent a painting to the Old Salon, and a bit of sculpture to the New. Both were accepted.

On his return to the United States, Gutzon found that his brother Solon had been living for months at a time as a cowboy, and at intervals with the Indians, intent upon the mastery of the life of the West. Each brother inspired the other. Gutzon insisted that Solon should study art as a profession, and for several months acted as his instructor. Gutzon joined Solon in the Sierras, and was brought into contact with many phases of Western life that he had not known. Many of his works reveal what his familiarity with the mountains and the prairies did for him. At his one-man, all-American exhibition in London near the end of the century, he presented numerous novel themes: a stagecoach rocking through a mountain pass, a herd of wild horses on the gallop over the prairie, Indian riders displaying their skill. He once explained that his celebrated work "The Mares of Diomedes" was based on the method by which horse thieves operated in the West — a skilled and brawny horseman, mounted on a tractable steed, would cut out several horses from a herd, and by his "lone will and strength guide them in a wild stampede." Borglum gave the work an air of antiquity by leaving the rider unclad, and named it for one of the labors of Hercules.

At the end of this second stay in Europe, the sculptor established himself in New York, with a studio at Stamford, Connecticut. The descriptive folder issued there in connection with a memorial exhibition of his work informed the visitor that in the forty years preceding his death on March 6, 1941, he had created one hundred seventy public monuments.

It was in 1916 that Borglum began work on the mass of granite a few miles from Atlanta. The Daughters of the Confederacy had asked him to consider the carving of a memorial to the Confederate Army on the side of Stone Mountain. In 1927, at the unveiling of his statue of Alexander H. Stephens in the national capitol, the sculptor affirmed his conviction that "the War between the States was a necessary tragedy for the founding of a greater Union." An agreement having been made, the sculptor attacked his Stone Mountain task with enthusiasm. The committee had in mind only the carving of a figure of General Robert E. Lee, but Borglum insisted on a supporting cast of many hundreds of figures: he would have a long column of Confederate soldiers marching across the almost perpendicular face of the mountain, headed by Lee, surrounded by his generals. The work must be a tribute to American valor, a Memorial to the Lost Cause. By means of a projecting lantern throwing enlarged pictures on the cliff, the outlines of the figures were marked out. America's entrance into the first World War interrupted the chiseling for a time, but with the arrival of peace Borglum took up the work again with no diminution of his irresistible ardor. This is not the place to tell the story of the troubles that ensued. According to the press reports, the sculptor was dismissed, and with the aid of an assistant he smashed his models, holding them to be his own property.

Still the craving to produce something gigantic endured, and it found fruition in the enormous heads of Washington, Jefferson, Lincoln, and Theodore Roosevelt in the Black Hills, not far from Custer's battleground. The first granite was blasted from the face of Mount Rushmore in 1927. The sculptor himself located the cliff, developed the design, and directed the carving. At threescore and ten he swung like any young man on a swaying seat at the end of a cable, four hundred feet above the valley. Drilling, dynamiting, and chiseling continued until the full realization of Gutzon Borglum's vision was at hand. The sculptor passed away with the tremendous job nearing its triumphant consummation, but his son, who had been his chief assistant, continued the work, and eight months later Lincoln Borglum announced the finishing of what his father had called "the Shrine of Democracy." The heads had been made in the dimensions of men nearly five hundred feet in height, at an expenditure of $836,000 of Federal funds.

In a newspaper article published in 1927, Gutzon Borglum declared that for twenty years he had been reading the life of Abraham Lincoln, and studying especially the conditions of his boyhood. He was well within the mark in that statement, for in 1910 he had told in a magazine that he had read nearly everything Lincoln had written. He had taken the Volk life-mask, measuring it in every possible way, and learned it by heart. At Springfield, in a 1915 address, he spoke in rhapsodical terms of Lincoln's face. "No man," he said, "has been more ridiculed about his face, his figure, his manners. Yet there never was a kinder man, a more just man, and I ask of you could he have been all these things and not have some evidence of it in his face, in his manners, in his general appearance? . . . Lincoln had a head and a face . . . that was almost Greek in its construction. I have never found a better head than his, and I have never seen a face that was so mature, so developed, in its use of his expression; and I say this after an exhaustive study of all photographs extant."

In a long essay on the physical aspects of Lincoln, Borglum spoke of the high and regular forehead as "ideal in shape"; of the brow that "projected like a cliff," of the eyes that "seemed to be in a kind of ravine." He located "the storm centre" of the face in the right eye, and "the mirth centre also." The left eye was "dreamy." We may not follow him all the way in his ramble over that face, with his comments on the wrinkles, the month, the nose which "yielded to the constant activity of the right side of his face." About that face he said: "You see half-smile, half sadness; half anger, half forgiveness; half determination, half pause; a mixture of expression that drew accurately the middle course he would follow — read wrongly by both sides." Lincoln's face was described in somewhat similar terms by George Grey Barnard, and one is also reminded of Robert G. Ingersoll's remarkable apostrophe: "Abraham Lincoln, strange mingling of mirth and tears, of the tragic and grotesque, of cap and crown, of Socrates and Democritus, of Aesop and Marcus Aurelius, of all that is gentle and just, humorous and honest, merciful, wise, laughable, lovable, and divine; and all consecrated to the use of man; while through all, and over all, were an overwhelming sense of obligation, of chivalric loyalty to truth, and upon all the shadow of the tragic end."

Borglum originally intended his huge marble head of Lincoln simply as a study, based on his examination of the life-mask and of a large collection of photographs. He told how he had cut and cut again that head, experimenting with indications of grief, pleasure, surprise, anger, and mixtures of those moods. The modeling was done in scale for a figure twenty-eight feet in height.

Eugene Meyer, Jr., acquired the work, and in April, 1908, he offered it as a gift to the United States. No Congressional action was necessary; a law dating back to 1831 authorized the Library Committee to accept such works of art as might be considered worthy, and to assign places for their installation in the Capitol. The Joint Committee on the Library formally took action on Mr. Meyer's proposal on May 7, and chose the Rotunda as the appropriate place for the head. The action and the location assigned were right; President Lincoln belonged, not to any one state, but to all the states, and this colossal portrait is so placed as to compel the attention of even the most casual visitors to the great building on Capitol Hill.

One lingers long in the contemplation of this head and of the excellent photographs which are now widely distributed. He sees in its features the reflection of a mighty soul, the soul of a Man, sombre and meditative, remote and isolated, as he surveys the duty to which destiny has assigned him, a strong face softened with sympathy, a man "brooding above the tempest and the fray."

That a bronze replica of this remarkable portrait is handsomely mounted at the entrance to the Lincoln Monument in Oak Ridge Cemetery in Springfield, Illinois, so placed that no tourist can overlook it, is well known. There is also a replica in a foreign capital, which relatively few Americans have seen or heard of. It may be seen upon a white marble pedestal in a public park in Oslo, Norway, where it was unveiled in connection with the Exhibition held in the summer of 1914 in commemoration of the separation of Norway from Denmark a century earlier. To that northern land it was sent as a gift from the Norwegian citizens of North Dakota. Fifty counties of that state each contributed a hundred dollars to purchase the replica, and a large deputation of North Dakota citizens, headed by Governor Louis Benjamin Hanna, crossed the ocean, bringing with them the bronze reproduction of the marble head as a souvenir of their devotion both to their ancestral land and to their adopted country. They were welcomed in the name of the Norwegian people by the President of the Storthing, and their gift was received by King Haakon in a ceremony described by one American witness as "moving in its spontaneity and simplicity." Truman H. Bartlett, Boston sculptor and Lincoln authority, pointed out in commenting on this incident that Borglum himself was a Danish-American. Bartlett went on to say that Borglum was "the only sculptor who has really studied the life mask of Lincoln."

Theodore Roosevelt is said to have surveyed Borglum's Newark statue of Lincoln from all sides, and at length to have exclaimed: "This doesn't look like a monument at all!" The sculptor accepted that as the greatest compliment ever bestowed on his work. He said of this creation that, "so far as sculpture permits, I have tried to give to posterity, in a true, unstudied picture of this great human being, a glimpse of possibly the best loved man in our national history, as he might sit, quite alone, unposed by artist or sculptor, free from the artifice with which art too often falsely clothes our great characters, and thereby fails to give that personal note of manner, attitude, and movement — the only means an artist has of conveying the soul of a man."

The statue is placed in front of the courthouse, not upon a pedestal, but on a low platform on the margin of the sidewalk, at the foot of the steps leading to the entrance of the big building. The bearded Lincoln sits on a plain, unbacked bench. His feet are solidly planted on the platform. The knees jut forward a long way into space. The right hand rests on the bench; the left crosses the body and droops from the right leg just back of the knee. The body is tilted forward and leans a little to the right. Beside him rests the familiar old-fashioned stovepipe hat — we wonder if any documents are filed in it. The man is weary and relaxed. He has been mopping his brow. The head is nobly carved. The eyes look out in a street crowded with people, but Lincoln is resting and thinking. It is hard for him in these presidential years to find a retreat where he can meditate in solitude. Patience sits upon that face — and care. The man is utterly still. The hint of a smile lurks about one corner of the mouth. This is the Lincoln whom the people loved of old, and whom they revere and love today.

This beautiful creation was given to the city of Newark by Amos Hoagland Van Horn. He began a commercial career in Newark in 1860 on a borrowed capital of five dollars, with which he opened a little furniture repair shop. He soon sold out for $25.00 and entered the Civil War as a volunteer. After two years' service he started in business again, in a basement, with a capital of two hundred dollars. Over

214

the years he expanded to become a wholesale and retail furniture dealer, and conducted a storage and warehouse business besides. His unostentatious benefactions in his lifetime were numerous. His will provided $25,000 for "a suitable monument of Lincoln," and $100,000 for "a monument for the soldiers and sailors who served their country in the Civil War," to be erected in Military Park. This memorial also was done by Borglum, who created a crowded group, symbolizing the whole military history of the nation, with forty figures and two horses; this work was dedicated in 1926.

The "Lincoln" was unveiled on Memorial Day, 1911. In fulfilment of the will of Mr. Van Horn, the trustees presented the statue to Lincoln Post of the Grand Army of the Republic, which in turn gave it into the permanent care of the mayor and common council of the city. Former President Roosevelt received the deed for the statue in behalf of the Post, and it was accepted in behalf of the city by Mayor Jacob Haussling. The dedication address was made by Mahlon Pitney, Chancellor of New Jersey, who later became an Associate Justice of the United States Supreme Court. Pitney described "the great President" as "alone with his thoughts, not far removed from the hurry and bustle of his environment, but for a moment undisturbed. . . . Manifold duties of office obtrude themselves; the sense of care, of responsibility, of burden, comes back; . . . the lines upon the face deepen, the pensive look comes into the cavernous eyes; the rapt spirit, oblivious of the wearied frame, searches for the proper solution; as yet no satisfactory answer has been found; but the face manifests a serene confidence in the ultimate triumph of the cause to which his life is dedicated."

There Abraham Lincoln sits for all time in Market Street, where the human tides ebb and flow day after day. A feature so rare as to be almost unique is that the figure, which is one and a half times life size, is so placed that the face is on a level with the eyes of passers-by. And another fleck of genius is that the President sits not in the middle, but at the end of the bench. Anyone who chooses may sit in neighborly relations with him. They might swap stories. All manner of people sit upon that bronze bench, cast in one piece with the statue. Tired beggars sit there; there are verses which tell of "a toiler" who, "with broken gait and hands in clench," one "bereft of hope," sinks "beside him" there.

In a very special sense this is the children's Lincoln. They play about that unmoving bronze as with a friend in life. That left arm makes a nestling place into which they like to climb. Many children have been photographed, singly or in groups, with this great man. Women and men loiter about the bench waiting for a company of children to come for play about their steadfast Friend. It is a lovely sight. Few men are so dull as not to be moved thereby. Justice Wendell Phillips Stafford, of the Supreme Court of the District of Columbia, has written verses in which these lines occur:

> The great form leans so friendly father-like,
> It is a call to children. I have watched
> Eight at a time swarming upon him there,
> All clinging to him — riding upon his knees,
> Cuddling between his arms, clasping his neck,
> Perched on his shoulders, even on his head;
> And one small, play-stained hand I saw reach up
> And laid most softly on the kind bronze lips
> As if it claimed them. They were children of —
> Of foreigners we call them, but not so
> They call themselves; for when we asked of one,
> A restless, dark-eyed girl, who this man was,
> She answered straight, 'One of our Presidents.'
> 'Let all the winds of hell blow in our sails,'
> I thought, 'thank God, thank God, the ship rides true!'

SOURCES: *The Newark Lincoln,* published by the Free Public Library for the Trustees of the Van Horn Trust, 1912; Charles E. Fairman, *Works of Art in the United States Capitol Building,* 1913; Gutzon Borglum, "The Beauty of Lincoln and His Place in Art," *Lincoln Centennial Association Addresses,* 1915; catalogue of the Stamford exhibition of the works of Gutzon Borglum; Robert G. Ingersoll, *Abraham Lincoln,* 1907; Gutzon Borglum, "Address at the Unveiling of the Statue of Alexander H. Stephens in Statuary Hall in the Capitol in Washington," *Senate Document No. 179,* 70th Cong., 2 Sess.; correspondence of Truman H. Bartlett with the *Boston Herald,* 1917.

Ganiere's LINCOLNS

GEORGE ETIENNE GANIERE is the only sculptor to have two Lincoln statues, both originals, dedicated in the same year. He was born in Chicago and trained in the Art Institute in that city, where he served for some time as an instructor. Having removed to Florida, he became the Director of the Department of Sculpture at the John B. Stetson University in DeLand, and of a similar department at Rollins College in Winter Park. Besides the "Lincolns," he was the sculptor of the equestrian statue of General Anthony Wayne in Fort Wayne, Indiana, and of the Gunsaulus Memorial for the Armour Institute in Chicago. He was an exhibitor at Buffalo in 1901, at St. Louis in 1904, and at San Francisco in 1915, and served as the official sculptor for the State of Florida at the Century of Progress Exposition at Chicago in 1933. He died in 1935.

The first of Ganiere's statues of Lincoln stands in the high school at Webster City, in central Iowa. The pedestal records the facts of its origin: "In memory of Harry Groves. Graduated with the Class of 1895. Died on March 4, 1909. Presented to the Lincoln High School by his Father, Alexander Groves." Harry Groves was born on an Iowa farm; he attended in succession a district school, the high school, Iowa State University for a year, and the University of Michigan for nearly five years, half the time as a law student. He practiced for six years in Montana, undermining his health by too intensive application to his profession, and went — too late — to Arizona to recover his vitality.

The dedication addresses on April 9, 1913, indicate that the statue was well chosen as a memorial for that young man. The speakers dwelt upon the traits which "justified the belief that Lincoln was his ideal" — his rugged honesty, how he hated shams, pretense, and ostentation, his faculty for self-expression in clear and simple words. Even in his physical proportions Groves resembled Lincoln.

Accepting the statue in behalf of the Board of Education, Jesse W. Lee alluded to "the large public usefulness" of such a memorial, under the eyes day by day of young men and young women "just beginning to get a glimpse of the larger things of life." While "they were forming ideas, planning careers, selecting heroes and heroines, for generations to come there would ever be present before their growing minds that lifelike image of Abraham Lincoln." They would know his story, and "how when the opportunity of great service came to him he was prepared." An eminently suitable address that must have been. A member of the class of 1914, Harry Miller, accepted the gift in a simple speech in the name of the school.

Although this is a beardless "Lincoln," he holds in his right hand a scroll so unrolled that observers may easily read from it the well-known closing passage of the Second Inaugural. The face is almost stern in expression, the head high, the left foot well forward. Lincoln might be saying: "This is what I stand for."

Ganiere's other "Lincoln" was presented by Dr. Francis Meinhardt to the little city of Burlington, in southeastern Wisconsin. Meinhardt, by profession a dentist, was interested in all forms of beauty, and had learned woodcarving while at college. He traveled extensively, and always returned with renewed enthusiasm for works of art. The plans for the Lincoln statue for his home town were completed before Dr. Meinhardt's death, but unhappily he passed away without witnessing the consummation of his long-cherished desire.

Ganiere was recommended by his mentor, Lorado Taft, for the making of the statue; the original model is in the possession of the Meinhardt family. Few "Lincolns" are so simple in design. The bearded President stands on a roughly-hewn pedestal, the left knee slightly bent, the hands folded behind his back, and his head slanted downward. The figure stands amid the trees in a triangular space at the junction of three streets. On dedication day, October 13, 1913, a brother of the donor, Albert Meinhardt, presented the work to the city, and a distinguished Congregational clergyman from Milwaukee made the principal address. There was an understanding between the sculptor and the donor that this "Lincoln" should not be duplicated.

SOURCES: *In Memoriam of Harry A. Groves,* booklet loaned by Professor R. Gerald McMurtry; courtesy of Mr. F. R. Starbuck, of the *Racine Journal-Times,* and Mr. O. C. Hulett, of its Burlington bureau; correspondence of Mrs. William Andrew Fulton, a sister of Dr. Meinhardt.

Schweizer's
Pennsylvania LINCOLNS

BY FAR the most imposing of the hundreds of monuments on the field of Gettysburg is the huge structure erected by the Commonwealth of Pennsylvania in recognition of "her warrior sons" who fought there. The single possible exception to this statement might be the Eternal Light Peace Memorial, erected by the Federal Government in 1938. This simple tower, topped by an undying flame, stands on the other side of the town from the main battlefield.

Pennsylvania's huge granite structure is located on the battle ground. It is surmounted by a dome on which a "Winged Victory" is perched, and pierced by archways above which are reliefs representing battle scenes. More than eighty bronze tablets, arranged in panels around the base of the monument, bear the names of thirty-five thousand officers and men who fought in that famous contest. The Memorial Commission, in the circular letter inviting architects and artists to offer competitive designs for the monument, included several interesting reservations. A "monument of earth like the imposing and simple pyramid at Waterloo would not be considered on account of duplication," and "the Commission would like to get away from the common tombstone or the common shaft style as a basis of design." These men, more than forty years after the battle, were cognizant of the standardized appearance of most of the Civil War memorials put up in the years immediately following the war. They stipulated that "the structure must be suitable for the purpose, . . . unique, chaste, and in good architecture."

The Commission suggested that "for two possible statues or bas-reliefs . . . President Lincoln and Governor Curtin should be the subjects." The fifth of a series of appropriation acts, approved in June, 1911, provided for the expenditure of $40,000 for not two, but "eight bronze statues," one each of Lincoln, Curtin, and Generals Meade, Reynolds, Hancock, Birney, Pleasanton, and Gregg. The architectural design offered by W. Liance Cottrell was accepted. W. Clark Noble was chosen as sculptor for the "Curtin," Cyrus E. Dallin for the "Hancock," and Lee O. Lawrie for the "Meade," the "Birney," and the "Reynolds." And for the "Lincoln," the "Pleasanton," and the "Gregg" the Commission selected J. Otto Schweizer, of Philadelphia, who was also awarded the contract for statues of Generals Geary, Hays, and Humphreys, to be placed in other situations on the field.

The monument was dedicated on September 27, 1910, with addresses by H. S. Huidekoper, chairman of the Commission; Edwin S. Stuart, governor of the Commonwealth; James W. Latta, for the infantry; General David McM. Gregg, for the cavalry; and James A. Gardner, for the artillery. By that date the original plans had been fulfilled, except that no statues were in place. Colonel John P. Nicholson's report for 1913 as Chairman of the National Park Commission lists the eight bronze statues and their several sculptors, and adds that the statues were "mounted" on April 23, 1913. No local newspaper contains any hint of unveiling exercises. The *Gettysburg Times* simply noted that the statues had been placed in position; the *Star and Sentinel* and the *Gettysburg Compiler* expressed deprecatory opinions of their craftsmanship, with the former adding that "the memorial job" on the monument itself "had been disappointing in construction."

The Schweizer statues, however, did receive favorable comment from the *Star and Sentinel*. The sculptor himself, writing in later years about this "Lincoln," said that several members of the Commission who had known the President personally had been much pleased with the facial expression of the portrait, but added that he himself was no longer satisfied with it, and that, although the head had been highly praised, he "would do it differently today." More than one modern critic, nevertheless, has extolled warmly the "Lincoln" as grouped with "the admirable portraits of Pleasanton and Gregg," and Lincoln students are likely to be impressed by the delineation of the President's features, especially when viewed in profile.

Born in Switzerland in 1863, Mr. Schweizer studied art in Zurich, Dresden, and Florence before coming to the United States in 1894. His versatility and industry are exemplified in the great number of busts, statues, medals, and medallions which he has produced in his long career in this country. A complete list is practically unobtainable; the sculptor refers sometimes to the mass of papers and "hundreds and hundreds" of pictures from which a more or less comprehensive catalogue might be compiled. Many of his subjects have been of a military character — state memorials, battle monuments, portraits of soldiers. Of unusual interest are his "Mother of the South" in Little Rock,

Arkansas, and his Colored Soldiers' State Memorial in Fairmount Park, Philadelphia. He has modeled three statues of Frederick W. von Steuben: one at Valley Forge, Pennsylvania; another at Utica, New York; and the third, an equestrian statue, at Milwaukee, Wisconsin. His "Molly Pitcher" is in Carlisle, Pennsylvania, and at the Philadelphia City Hall one finds his universally admired "Peter Muhlenberg."

Schweizer is also the creator of the notable "Lincoln" in the clubhouse of the Union League in Philadelphia. This work was dedicated with ceremonies worthy of the fame of the League and of the nobility of the statue. The speaker of the evening, William Renwick Riddell, Justice of the Supreme Court of Ontario, gave an address of unusual charm and power, packed with ideas rarely brought forward on such occasions. "Democracy was not born on July 4, 1776," he said, nor is democracy a form of government. "Republics in form may be autocracies or oligarchies in fact." Because a form of government is monarchical or even autocratic, it is not necessarily undemocratic. Democracy is "a manner of thought, a bent of the mind and soul."

"In that great war for freedom, for democracy, for civilization," continued the Canadian jurist, "there stood at the front the great man whom you commemorate today. . . . Abraham Lincoln, sir, was the beau ideal of democracy. He was the first true, fully democratic President. . . . There is no other President who is worth mentioning in any way near the same category as your great President Lincoln. . . . He was born amongst the people, he was one of them, and there never was a finer saying, or one that better indicates the humanity of his heart, than his saying that 'God must love the common people; He has made so many of them.' One of the common people himself, he loved them as his own . . . and because he knew that the future of the world depends, not upon King or Kaiser, or philosopher or man of high station, but upon the common man, I say to you that Lincoln whom you celebrate today is the greatest democrat the world has ever seen, in the true sense of the word." Going on to deal with the situation in 1914, Justice Riddell told how "Canada hesitated not a moment, and was bewildered by the course of the United States, until it flashed upon us like a vision that your President had brought you into the war not as a divided nation, but as a nation united in soul in a passionate and insistent demand for justice and right." And he ended as he began, by contrasting again democracy and autocracy.

Former Governor Edwin S. Stuart described the room which the

League was dedicating that night, as the members viewed it for the first time. Created "as a perpetual memorial to those who offered their services to their country during the great crisis of 1861–1865," it had been aptly called a "Hall of Fame." Stuart felt that "it might well be called a Temple of Inspiration." On the walls "in enduring bronze" were the names of all League members, officers and privates, who had entered the services. The room was "hallowed by the statue of the man whom they upheld and sustained, and whose ideals brought this League into being." There were present veterans, members of the League, who had seen and talked with Lincoln, and two "who were at his side at Fort Stevens. . . . They stood with him on the parapet of the fort on the only occasion when a President of the United States was under fire in actual battle."

The statue was unveiled by Mr. George P. Morgan, "the patriotic saint of the Union League," acting in place of General R. Dale Benson, who had fallen ill. The work was accepted as "the sign and symbol of our mission and our enduring ideal." And the League guaranteed its support of the President in the war then going on, "in the spirit of the immortal words carved above the memorial tablets that popular government should not 'perish from the earth.'"

That must have been a happy evening for the sculptor. He was surrounded by his creations, for his medallion portraits of Grant and seven other Union generals upon the walls of the paneled room complemented the "Lincoln" standing in a white marble niche in the middle of one wall. Schweizer regrets that the indirect lighting of the room shadows the eyes and chin and disfigures somewhat the facial impression of the statue. Nevertheless, the work is enthusiastically admired. The illustration used in this volume was made before the statue was installed in its niche. It well suggests the intent and resolute attitude with which the Gettysburg Address is conceived to have been delivered. The bent left arm and the clenched fist are enormously more expressive than any sweeping gesture. One reads in the face the lofty idealism and stern devotion of the man giving utterance to the fundamental convictions with which he carried on the War for the Union. Here he is every inch a leader of men.

SOURCES: Union League, *Founders' Day, 1917, Dedication of Memorial Room,* 1917; Report of Gettysburg Battlefield Memorial Commission, 1914; correspondence with Frederick Tilberg, Gettysburg National Park historian; letters from Mr. Schweizer, and material loaned by him.

Bisson's LINCOLN — *in Granite*

THERE is at least one Lincoln monument in the United States for which Confederate veterans cheerfully contributed. The Blue and the Gray of Long Beach, California, a veterans' union, proudly proclaimed itself "the only known organization of the kind in existence" in the official history of the movement which brought about the erection of this memorial, and this group is included in the list of organizations which helped raise the necessary funds, along with the Grand Army of the Republic, the Sons of Veterans, the Woman's Relief Corps, and similar associations. The insigne of membership is described as "an enameled stick-pin button, one and a half inches in diameter, containing cuts of a 'Johnnie' and a 'Yank,' each waving the Stars and Stripes in colors over the other's head."

The memorial is known, however, as the Abraham Lincoln Grand Army of the Republic Memorial Monument, and its erection was essentially an enterprise of Northern veterans and related groups. In 1906 the president of the Auxiliary to the Sons of Veterans, Mrs. Carrie Drake, initiated a movement for "a monument consisting of a heroic soldier figure mounted on a granite pedestal." We have been unable to ascertain just when the statue of Lincoln was substituted for the figure of the soldier. After the beginning in 1906, an interval of nine years ensued before the plan was revived by Mrs. L. W. Archer, the wife of a Past Chaplain of the Grand Army. Mrs. Archer obtained the cooperation of Major John S. Hair, a member of a Chicago Grand Army Post, who consulted with various leaders among the local veterans, and with their aid formed the Citizens' Monument Association, which carried the movement to success. Major Hair became the general manager and Colonel George W. Wilcox the chairman. In a formal statement the manager said: "We were comparative strangers, and not members of the local G.A.R. Post, . . . but there are more veterans in Long Beach out of than in the Post, all comrades under the same flag." Comrades and other citizens united in the cause. Financial aid was obtained from both the state and the city, as well as from business houses, churches, and hundreds of individuals. In the enthusiasm aroused by the successful consummation of their undertaking, a double celebration was arranged: thousands attended the laying of the cornerstone of the monument on June 29, 1915, and still more thousands came to witness the dedicatory ceremonies on the following July 3.

The cornerstone was laid with an adaptation of the Grand Army ritual. The Rev. Hugh K. Walker, for many years a noted Presbyterian clergyman, and at the time pastor of the First Church in Long Beach, delivered the principal address. He believed Long Beach had "never done anything half so much to her credit as is the erection of this monument to Abraham Lincoln," whom he pronounced "the foremost citizen of the United States, . . . the typical American, truly a product of this country, while George Washington, from whose place in the hearts of the American people I would not detract, spent a part of his life under another flag." Dr. Walker, himself a Southerner born in Tennessee, dwelt on "the great esteem in which Lincoln is held today among citizens of the South as well as of the North."

The unveiling was done on July 3 by Master John W. Hair, a grandson of Major Hair. Colonel James M. Emery, also a member of a Chicago G.A.R. post, as secretary of the Association, presented the monument to the municipality. At the moment of the unveiling a salute of twenty-one guns thundered from the United States cruiser *Chattanooga,* sent by the Secretary of the Navy for the occasion. The spirit of the day is well reflected in the rhetorical exuberance of the descriptions of the exercises: "When the flag was flung to the breeze and the cannon barked the Presidential salute from the cruiser lying at anchor in the offing, the Stars and Stripes were thrown back gracefully from the figure of our martyred President, and a cry went up from the vast throng of people assembled in the park, moving picture artists frantically operated their machines mounted on the housetops, and the irresistible young American, short of stature but long in enterprise, climbed a telephone pole in order that he might see it all."

This monument, statue and all, is made of California granite of two beautiful varieties. The statue, seven feet in height, was carved by Peter Bisson, who had come from the great granite center at Quincy, Massachusetts, to carve a statue of Junípero Serra for Mrs. Leland Stanford. Bisson remained in California and became well known for his execution of many commissions. The statue is designed to be a duplicate of Saint-Gaudens' standing "Lincoln." A description in a local newspaper states that "several photographs of that statue were secured and from them the plaster of Paris model was made by Charles Gruenfeld, of Los Angeles, a graduate of the Institute of Fine Arts in Chicago, and a student under the famous sculptor, Charles Mulligan." On each of three faces of the pedestal appear the names of Civil War generals and admirals, with their battles; the front face carries a full-spread flag with Grant's famous sentiment, "Let us have peace." The total height of base, pedestal, and statue is nearly twenty-three feet. In 1915 the park in which the monument stands was called Pacific Park; the name has since been changed to Lincoln Park.

SOURCES: Transcripts from the Long Beach Public Library; correspondence with Ralph G. Lindstrom of Los Angeles; *Souvenir of the Unveiling, Dedication and Presentation of the Abraham Lincoln G.A.R. Memorial Monument,* Long Beach, 1915.

24   ILLUSTRATED PAGE 169

The Lincoln Statue in "Little Dixie"

IN THE county named for "Old John" Randolph of Virginia, and the county-seat named for Colonel William Moberly, the one-time president of the Chariton and Randolph County Railroad Company, stands the only statue of Abraham Lincoln in Missouri. For many years the people of the state were unaware of its existence, and today the great majority of the residents of that highly industrialized community are either entirely ignorant of the fact or prefer to ignore it. In Kansas City, a relatively short distance from Moberly, an organization known as the Patriots and Pioneers Memorial Foundation accumulated several thousand dollars a few years ago "towards the erection of a Lincoln statue which would be the first in Missouri," before the promoters of that enterprise encountered the undeniable priority of the marble "Lincoln" which had been on display in a conspicuous position in a Moberly cemetery for a third of a century. The Foundation's funds were insufficient for an outdoor statue of heroic size, and a portion was used to purchase a Lincoln head, moulded by Paul Manship, for the Western Gallery of Art in Kansas City.

The surprising indifference of Moberly's citizens to their statue is a reflection of the historical background of the city. Moberly is in the midst of a region long known as "Little Dixie," where Southern sympathies are still so strong that the grandchildren of soldiers who fought for the Union are advised that they will get along better with their comrades in the public schools if they say little or nothing about such matters. Missouri in Civil War times was a border state. Heavy fighting determined its destiny. The Confederate government accepted as valid the action of an irregular meeting of the General Assembly purporting to have dissolved the state's allegiance to the Union, and formally admitted Missouri to the new fraternity of states. After the bitter battles of 1861 and '62 the state was the scene of numerous daring raids. Bands of "bushwhackers" destroyed and plundered property. Roving groups of hard-riding horsemen terrorized many communities, paying little attention to the recognized laws of war. Randolph County's population in those years was predominantly "secesh" in sentiment. The first lot sales in Moberly took place within a year after the ending of the war, and the village was incorporated as a city in 1873. At the time of the "golden jubilee" local newspapers described the war years as a period of disorder "when everything was wide open and everything went," and told how men strode about in that "frolicsome town" with revolvers in their belts and knives in their boot-legs.

Today Moberly is a "railroad town." The Wabash shops are the dominating industry. With a population approximating twelve thousand, the town has tree-lined residential streets, handsome modern homes, and more than a few "terrific Victorian houses," offering "examples of gingerbread unlimited." It boasts public parks, a Carnegie library, and a handsome auditorium. Not long ago, when a large portrait of Lincoln was wanted for a Lincoln birthday ceremony in the American Legion Hall, the only one to be found was in the Negro school named for the Emancipator. Possibly the situation here described on apparently competent authority can be duplicated in many other cities in which only small groups hold the memory of Lincoln in affectionate reverence.

It happened that on the day in 1866 when the first sale of lots took place in Moberly there was a wedding at "the old McKinsey homestead" south of the village, by which Mary Ann, the daughter of that home, became the wife of Enoch G. Deskin, who had served in the war with the Illinois volunteer regiment named for their governor "the

Yates Sharpshooters." Deskin became a leader among Moberly veterans, and, as a mail carrier of many years' service and a member of the municipal government, he knew everyone and was a man of influence in the community. The daughters of that marriage, Misses Nora, Belle, and Nell Deskin, are one of the few sources of information about the Lincoln statue. For their family, Memorial Day was a great day of the year. Abraham Lincoln Post of the Grand Army of the Republic, whose membership list at one time contained 150 names, including veterans from neighboring communities, paraded year after year to Oakland Cemetery, headed by a band playing "Onward, Christian Soldiers," and heard an address and decorated both the Union and the Confederate graves there. For a long time Enoch Deskin was Commander of the Post and his wife president of the Woman's Relief Corps. The Post and the Corps raised $525.00 to buy the Lincoln statue; the Deskin sisters report that it was no easy task to raise that sum by direct gifts and such indirect means as "ice cream socials, bunco parties, and other entertainments."

The statue, ordered from Italy through the president of a local monument company, was shipped to New York aboard the last freighter to leave that country before hostilities began in 1914. The name of the sculptor is unknown. The City Council granted permission to erect the statue in the cemetery, on a site not easy to overlook. For the dedication the hard-working veterans were fortunate in obtaining the services of two speakers of high reputation, Rabbi Leon Harrison and Judge Lee Rassieur, both of St. Louis. No programs are available, nor have we discovered any newspaper accounts of the ceremony; the local newspaper files are incomplete for the years preceding 1923. There are discrepancies among the available sources of information as to the actual day and year of the unveiling. One authority gives the date as May 30, 1916; the simple inscription on the pedestal reads "erected May 15, 1914." We are informed that there were delays owing to difficulties in getting the speakers on "the same Memorial Day." While complete certainty is impossible, we accept Memorial Day, 1916, as the correct date, for the pedestal is known to have been ready some time in advance of the dedication, perhaps with the inscription already cut.

Diligent delving has revealed nothing to invalidate the claim that this statue of Italian marble, surmounting a base of Vermont granite, is the only Lincoln statue in Missouri. It is an indubitable fact also that on the dedication day Miss Nell Deskin unveiled the statue, and her father, Enoch Deskin, read the Gettysburg Address.

SOURCES: Newspaper clippings loaned by, and correspondence with, the Deskin sisters, Mrs. John J. Gasparotti, and other residents of Moberly; letters from Edward M. Stayton, of Independence, Missouri.

25   ILLUSTRATED PAGE 170

George Grey Barnard

ON THE Sunday nearest Lincoln's birthday in 1932 a sculptor occupied the pulpit of All Souls Universalist Church in Brooklyn. George Grey Barnard spoke that day by invitation of the minister, Dr. Cornelius Greenway. They were old friends. The clergyman had come to the aid of the artist when Barnard was notified that he must vacate the Washington Heights studio in New York City in which for many years he had sought to embody his dreams in marble and bronze. For that Sunday service in February, 1932, Barnard had loaned the church his massive head of Abraham Lincoln, a work so large that six men were needed to place it in the chancel. In his address Barnard told of the infinite pains he had taken in the creation of his statue of Lincoln. For a hundred days he had sought the secret of that face. Explaining his conception of an artist's duty, Barnard maintained that retouching pictures and carving imaginary portraits of our great men was "a thwarting of democracy."

Many of Barnard's hearers must have been reminded of the controversy attending the exhibition of his "Lincoln" fifteen years before, when the question of its merits and demerits became not only a national mêlée but attained almost the dimensions of an international "incident." Critics and art-lovers flailed each other with unbecoming violence. That redoubtable Irish pamphleteer and playwright, George Bernard Shaw, exchanged polite but emphatic letters on the subject with Judd Stewart, one of the most widely known of American Lincolnians, to whom the Barnard figure was "the stomach ache statue." The echoes of that lively wrangle have long since died away. The statue stands in Cincinnati, and replicas in Manchester, England, and Louisville, Kentucky. Today it is accepted as an extraordinary work of art, but opinions still differ as to its value as a delineation of Abraham Lincoln.

That stormy discussion in the latter half of 1917 degenerated to the level of the ranting of demagogues in the fury of a political campaign. The editor of an art magazine printed several screeds, of which the following is the choicest specimen: "The statue suggests that even in its greatest hero democracy breeds nothing but a stoop-shouldered, consumptive-chested, chimpanzee-headed, lumpy-footed, giraffe-necked, grimy-fingered clod-hopper, wearing his clothes in a way to disgust a rag-man." The first of the series of condemnatory articles in *The Art World* appeared in June. The editor allowed that Lincoln's "slouchiness" was an "absurd myth," that while the President was not an Adonis nor a matinee idol, he was not an ugly man. He may have been rugged, but he was not a roughneck. His hands and feet were "small for so large a man." Sometimes he was careless in dress, but he wore good clothes and he dressed for occasions. Those awful trousers! Those deformed feet! That utterly untrue face! The statue was "a mistake in bronze."

Robert Todd Lincoln sent his thanks to Editor F. Wellington Ruckstuhl for taking up the cudgels so vigorously to castigate this sculptor, and told of the horror with which he contemplated the project of sending to London a replica of this statue, already erected in Cincinnati. By November, 1917, the work had become for *The Art World* "a calamity in bronze." The magazine berated Theodore Roosevelt for saying that we had at last the Lincoln of the debates with Douglas. Not so, thundered Ruckstuhl. No one ever saw Lincoln's hands clasped in that disgusting manner across his body. The statue was an atrocity; it ought to be finished — with dynamite! Its erection in London would be an international disaster. In at least five articles of this character the magazine argued that art and craftsmanship are not the same thing; that any "Lincoln" in London must represent the bearded President, and that "a sculptor should serve his country as the President serves the nation, expressing the mind and feeling of the people and only in forms that please, not himself, but the public." Barnard challenged that sentiment. The great majority of the people, however, were emphatic in their repudiation of his statue, basing their views in the main on newspaper and magazine articles and pictures. There was much criticism of Mr. Ruckstuhl. The Teutonic cast of his name brought charges that he was a German — and we were at war with Germany. Ruckstuhl replied that he was born in France, an Alsatian, and was brought to America in 1855; and his magazine continued its campaign against the statue as "something the cat brought in on a wet night."

Other periodicals and the press in general mixed in the altercation. It was "good stuff." The *Milwaukee Sentinel* offered the widely-quoted suggestion that with a few alterations the figure might do duty for Ichabod Crane. *The Independent* conducted a referendum, naming six statues for the balloting; the Saint-Gaudens standing "Lincoln" led in the returns with 9,820 votes, and Barnard's with 1,207 stood at the foot of the poll. *The Nation* wondered about the probable American reaction to "a realistic Disraeli, of his curled and florid period," while *Life* pictured John Bull gazing askance at Barnard's effigy, and asking how Uncle Sam would like "one of Lord Nelson made by Barnard."

The minority opinions included those of many artists of the highest rank. The *North American Review* presented the reasoned judgments of Frederick MacMonnies, sculptor, Thomas Hastings, architect, and Richard Fletcher, art critic, all of whom found much to praise and little to condemn in the statue.

A writer on art subjects in the *Sun* descanted on "the comedy" of the situation, with its overseas complications. It was "obviously Shavian," precisely the sort of thing such a satirist as G. B. S. would clutch. Perhaps he would "fire off" an opinion "as to whether the children of great men are to be accepted an infallible judges of their parents." Whether or not the *Sun's* correspondent knew about it, Shaw, in correspondence with Judd Stewart, had written that "the current criticisms of the Lincoln statue have convinced me that it is either a monstrosity or a masterpiece." In December, 1917, Stewart mailed Shaw a half-dozen photographs of Lincoln, three showing him as the beardless candidate of 1860 and three as the bearded President of 1863 and '64, declaring in an accompanying letter that the sculptor had "made an impossible monstrosity out of President Lincoln's figure." Stewart also informed his famous correspondent of a vote taken by the *Philadelphia Evening Telegraph* on the proposal to send a copy of the "stomach ache statue" to London. Out of 167,079 replies to the questionnaire, 98,112 favored sending a replica of the Saint-Gaudens statue, and only 2,016 stood for Barnard's. Zealous for Lincoln's fame and anxious that London should see him correctly dressed as a statesman and looking the part, Stewart was doing his bit to prevent the installation of Barnard's work at the focal point of a world empire.

But for Stewart to send these figures to Shaw was a mistake. The iconoclastic G. B. S. enjoyed being a heretic; he liked to consort with minorities and to expose the inconsistencies of popular emotional reactions. Fundamentally sincere he may have been, but he never saw the harm in "spoofing" when there hove in sight a subject seemingly made to order for the play of his wit. The Stewart photographs had not reached him when he wrote his long statement of January 11, 1918, and Shaw proceeded to judgment on the basis of the quarter-length portrait of Lincoln published in Lord Charnwood's biography in 1916. There are striking similarities between this profile, taken in 1860 by Alexander Hesler, and the bronze face of the statue, but in 1860 Lincoln was better dressed and managed his hands quite "properly." At any rate the unpredictable commentator recorded his impression that Barnard had "somehow hit off the right conception for a statue of Lincoln for London."

Offering the opinion that Saint-Gaudens had raised himself "to an eminence that can fairly be called illustrious by his commanding talent," Shaw declared that he had never heard of Barnard until the controversy over his statue arose. To be sure, Saint-Gaudens' standing "Lincoln" was "in the right place — in America." Its merits "jump" at the spectator at once. It is a brilliantly clever typification, in the person of Lincoln, of the popular President, the successful politician, the genial humorist. It is agreeably tailored, like a favorite actor on the first night of a fashionable comedy.

But things were different in London. The man who succeeds in politics in England is not like the typical successful American politician, and he is very unlike Lincoln. Even Lincoln's humor "does not touch us." English statesmen "make a point of being the worst-dressed men in the country," and "the Saint-Gaudens suit of clothes, on which so much stress is laid on your side, would remind everybody here of Sir Charles Wyndham at his gayest on the stage." The Lincoln cult in England had received an impulse from Charnwood's penetrating book, and, though it might seem ridiculous to those seeing Lincoln as Saint-Gaudens saw him, "we perceive here that Lincoln was essentially a saint," and "that is the only interest he had for us or for any nation outside the United States." Shaw believed that Lincoln "was a man of genius of the kind that crosses frontiers and takes its vessel far above and beyond the common political categories into the region which belongs, like the sky, to all mankind."

So, continued Shaw, anyone who grasps these ideas must see that the Saint-Gaudens work is "impossible." But Barnard's statue is "the image of a saint," and the head is "something like a mirror of Lincoln's soul." The work was "not faultless." Whereas "saints tread the earth lightly and are generally alive to the tips of their toes, the lower half of the Barnard figure seems springless and dead, and the feet are of clay." Lincoln was "rather given to dancing before the ark," and Barnard "has made a digression from the son of the morning to the son of the soil." And in this there appears a confusion of motive. "The feet are used to suggest that Lincoln trudged through ploughed-up fields as a boy, and the hands to shew that he wielded an axe and split rails." Saint-Gaudens gave "inhumanly wide shoulders" to Lincoln; Barnard "swung over a little too much to the champagne bottle build." But Barnard had "the deeper insight." He escapes from "the clever superficiality" of Saint-Gaudens. "I can see the worst of his work as clearly as the best — he cannot throw any dust in my eyes."

Shaw concluded that he must give his verdict for Mr. Barnard. British connoisseurs would shrug their shoulders over the Saint-Gaudens. It would be just the kind of thing Americans would think first-rate. Set up the Barnard statue in London, "and no doubt some foolish remarks will be made about him . . . but the connoisseurs will have to stop and look, to hum and haw, to admit that there is an idea there, to point out that there is a lot of real execution in that head, to ask who did it, and on being told that it is by an American, to exclaim 'Nonsense! No American could possibly do work of that class.'" To those who professed to know little about art, and feared that an American statue might cut a poor figure in London, Shaw could only say, "You should see most of the others!"

G. B. S. must have enjoyed writing that letter. Probably he grinned over his gibes. One who lets Shaw's sentiments simmer in his mind is bound to feel that some of his "digs" are just. Great as we think the Saint-Gaudens statue to be, it is nevertheless true that many unthinking persons who gush over it have little conception of its value as a portrait, or of its artistry. They see the man whom all Americans love, the martyr whom all revere. Informed observers, however, have little difficulty in defending their admiration for that statue. After sixty years it holds well its original place in the affection of all classes of people.

Shaw saw at once what it was that rasped the sensibilities of the average American in the Barnard statue. Not the face; that head could stand, and has stood, the scrutiny of critics of all grades of competency. But the hands and their position, the feet, the clothes! The sculptor had modeled the body of the Lincoln of the New Salem days, and the head of the mature man of the years when he was nearing the presidency. That is the major fault of the work — what Shaw called a "digression," amounting in sculpture to what composers call a "dissonance" in music. The wandering photographs reached Shaw at last, but the Englishman refused to recant. Both sculptors had exaggerated Lincoln's shoulders, in opposite directions, and Barnard had stayed within possible limits. Neither had said the last word in sculpture about Lincoln; "only Rodin at his best could have done that." Stewart considered that G. B. S. had based his judgment on "very incomplete evidence," and sent more photographs. Surely Shaw would modify his views, at least as to Barnard, whose statue "all too closely approaches the cubistic art of these latter days." Shaw welcomed the pictures — indeed, nothing could induce him to give them up, although friends begged him to spare a few. But he adhered to his opinions.

Shaw's "verdict" certainly was founded on insufficient evidence. Small wonder that Judd Stewart felt amazed at his opinion. Remembering that Shaw was a professional purveyor of paradoxes, who liked to shock people, we may well believe that there was a sly gleam in his eyes as he rounded his periods to Stewart. But only George Bernard Shaw knew — and he never told.

At the time of George Grey Barnard's death, it was said of him that "between his early interest in mediaeval art and his later project for a war memorial his career developed on a stormy path that led from the pure art of portraying beauty to the allegorical expression of human destiny." No one today questions the astounding ability of the man, the grandeur of his ideas, or the sincerity with which he wrought, with the veritable fury of a fanatic, to make those ideas real to all who might see his work. He was extremely temperamental. Such men are apt to encounter storms. He would not compromise one jot on a point of artistic integrity. How he managed to live for a full year in Chicago, and study at the Art Institute, on a capital of eighty-nine dollars, passes comprehension. He found ways to exist in Paris for two years, while working at the Beaux Arts and other schools, on three hundred dollars. All one winter he slept in his overcoat, under a roof that let rain and snow fall on his bed. Many such stories, essentially true, are told of his years of privation.

At the time of Barnard's birth, on May 24, 1863, his father, Joseph H. Barnard, was pastor of a Presbyterian church in Bellefonte, Pennsylvania. It was in Illinois and Iowa that the youth disclosed his talent, experimenting with the mounting and modeling of birds, and while still a boy acquiring a high degree of skill as a taxidermist. One day a discerning visitor saw his collection of casts, and told his father that the lad was a "born sculptor." So he left school to learn engraving as a trade on which he might depend for a livelihood. The sale of a portrait bust of a child provided him with the money to go to Paris. He toiled from dawn to midnight, weeks at a stretch, mixing little, if at all, with the Bohemian life of the city, conscious of his powers and interested only in their development.

In 1894, at the Salon, a conspicuous position was given to several works by an unknown artist upon which the official jury bestowed high praise. These sculptures included, among other pieces, a beautiful bit called simply "Boy," a group showing two young men groping in the darkness of eternity for each other's hands, called "Brotherly Love," and a colossal group, recognized instantly as a masterpiece, for which the title is said to have been taken from a line in a poem by Victor Hugo, translated as "I feel two natures struggling within me." The work stands for the war within the human soul. Perhaps the title traces back to the days when the boy sat under his father's preaching, for the idea is of the essence of Calvinism.

The enthusiastic Parisians demanded the name of the unknown exhibitor. The young American was promptly made an associate member of the Société des Beaux Arts. His famous group for many years held such a commanding position in the Metropolitan Museum in New York City that no visitor could avoid seeing it. It was so placed not only in recognition of its worth as a work of art, but also as a symbol of the purpose for which such institutions are maintained. The Museum still considers it a very important work; it stands now in a gallery known as "The Park Entrance."

That group laid the foundation for Barnard's reputation. Yet when he returned to the United States commissions were slow in coming, and he was contemplating a return to France when a telegram from the architect of the new Pennsylvania Capitol summoned him to Harrisburg. Barnard obtained the contract for sculptural work, in the amount of $700,000! It was a dazzling triumph. Barnard hurried to Paris, where skilled labor could readily be had, and leased a huge studio. But no money came from Harrisburg. He paid his fifteen assistants out of his own pocket, and carried on, his mind intent on the grandiose projects he had conceived. The mildest statement which can be made is that there were "misunderstandings." The amount of the contract was cut in half, halved again, and then reduced to $100,000! Barnard found himself the victim of what has been denounced as "a great scandal." But his name was not besmirched, and he never lost his courage. His workmen stood by him. The story, with its charges of malversation and of plain graft, is hard to trail through its devious meanderings. Many felt that Barnard had been "shamelessly defrauded." Private parties came to his rescue. Only two of his projected groups could be completed for the amount to which his contract had dwindled. Two members of the faculty of Columbia University saw and liked his work, and associated with themselves a group of men of means, including Archer Huntington, Robert C. Ogden, and Walter H. Page, who financed Barnard in his predicament. In the end they were reimbursed by the state.

The dedication was a great day for Barnard. Many eminent men attended. Among the guests of honor were the sculptor's aged father and mother. The newspapers described his "magnificent groups," depicting "The Burden of Life" and "Labor and Brotherhood." These are huge compositions, containing thirty-two figures of heroic size. They stand today atop the wide steps leading to the Capitol, so mounted as to flank its triple-arched entrance. Fellow sculptors have unanimously extolled them as masterly in craftsmanship.

In the midst of his disheartening difficulties in Paris, Barnard mounted a bicycle and began an exploration of the remote corners and byways of France, searching for old statues and remnants of Romanesque and Gothic art. He found an astonishing number of fine things, of which the local peasantry had not understood the significance. Some of these he sold to reduce his debts; others he kept to form the nucleus of a valuable collection, now housed in the splendid group of buildings known as the Cloisters, which serves as the medieval branch of the Metropolitan Museum.

In his later years Barnard was haunted by an idea, said to have flashed upon him on Armistice Night in 1918. Why not a colossal monument to Peace, which should rival in size and in its appeal to the hearts of men the war memorials erected through the ages in the capitals of the world? Barnard took over a building, old and huge, near the Cloisters site, and established a studio in which he worked for years on his Rainbow Arch, to be a hundred feet high and sixty feet wide. In the sixth and seventh decades of his life he was as rapt in his devotion to this exalted idea, and as tireless in his concentration on the labor of its realization in stone, as he had been forty years earlier in his struggles for recognition in Paris. On this Arch would be mounted scores of heroic figures. It must serve as a rebuke to mankind for the folly of war, and expound the tragedy of the sacrifice of the young and the strong, and the survival of women, old men, and children who live on only because of their unfitness for war.

With Barnard, lofty and far-visioned idealist that he was, this project became practically an obsession. Nothing else mattered. Vandals smashed the product of several years of toil — he began again. The land on which his studio stood was made over to the city — he managed to move his huge model to an abandoned Edison Company powerhouse, and carried on. In 1935, for the first time in twenty years, he gave an exhibition of his work in an art gallery in the city. Visitors noticed the religious slant of his mind, the originality of his productions, the statue of Christ for which a football player had posed. Those who sought out the sculptor in his studio found themselves in the atmosphere of a shrine. Abraham Lincoln was always there. Then, in the spring of 1938, Barnard had to leave the unfinished Arch and the studio. He died on April 24. Had he survived fifteen days longer, he might have been present at the opening of the Cloisters to the public.

Such was the man whose "Lincoln" caused so much commotion in 1917 — a man of unsurpassed devotion to his art, loyal to the noblest standards of truth and duty, whose ideas and visions, as he once said, seemed to lift him as upon wings for flight. His work, like that of any other man, must be examined and estimated without regard to the labor it may have cost or the sincerity with which it was wrought, but the career and character of such a man should at least deliver him from sneers and vituperation.

Barnard's "Lincoln" was unveiled in Cincinnati on March 31, 1917. It was a gift to the city by Charles Phelps Taft, a half-brother of President William Howard Taft, and his wife Annie Sinton Taft. A five-man committee, including Mr. Taft, had awarded the commission to the sculptor on December 10, 1910. The total amount invested by Mr. and Mrs. Taft in their gift was $100,000.

Never was a commission taken more seriously. The sculptor told the story of the creation of the statue several times — once early in 1917, to a Cincinnati newspaper reporter, while the statue was on exhibition in the grounds of Union Theological Seminary in New York City; again in 1930 to the artist Samuel J. Woolf for *The New York Times;* and in the account under his own signature, included in the brochure published in Cincinnati in the dedication year. These statements are almost identical. Barnard as a boy had heard his grandfather talk of Douglas and Lincoln; he had made himself familiar with the life of the Railsplitter. His portrait must reveal the real man, the leader who had stood by and for the plain people among whom he had been reared. It must not be only a statue of a President. Barnard tried to fathom the soul of the man whom everyone addressed as "Mr. Lincoln" while calling him "Abe" at all other times.

He got the face from Volk's life mask. He made a Lincoln head twelve feet high with the eyes closed, not an exact copy of the mask although derived from it. The study of the eyes came later. For two years Barnard hunted for a model, and found one at last in Kentucky, a man half an inch taller than Lincoln, born only fifteen miles from "Tom" Lincoln's farm, who had split rails all his life. This man, surnamed Thomas, produced his father's old broadcloth coat and boots, dating back to 1858, and posed in them. He had worn the trousers at his work in the woods. Lincoln's hands were big and hard from toil. Barnard carved them big, and folded them patiently across each other. He made the feet big and the shoes coarse. He said to Mr. Woolf, "I saw in Lincoln the beauty of mankind and I saw in him the man of sorrows. It was this beauty that I endeavored to depict."

For the dedication ceremony Dr. Lyman Whitney Allen, a widely known Presbyterian clergyman, wrote and read a poem of unusual power. Once more the clay had "found a dowered hand to shape a wonder." The statue was

> Great history featured by great artistry,
> A poet's allegory wrought in bronze.

The presentation speech by former President Taft is one of the most attractive and thoughtful of Lincoln addresses, and also contains some passages which seem to anticipate the resentment with which many Lincoln lovers would regard this statue. Lincoln and his parents were "the plainest of the plain people," and "he lived and dressed and ate and spoke as they did." Beyond all other men he educated himself. He loved politics, but never allowed politics to impair his mental honesty. Unlike most men who confront great issues in politics or in religion, he sat as a judge upon his own views, weighed all opposing arguments, and was ready when the great storm burst upon the nation. His criticism of the Dred Scott decision was "eminently just and fair." He was a great lawyer and would have made a great chief justice. His war years disclosed a "sinking of the personal equation that we find nowhere else in our history." With "wonderful political genius he held the union sentiment united for the war." No one thinks of national wealth when he is named. His story vindicates the rule of the people. The sculptor here "portrays the unusual height, the sturdy frame, the lack of care in dress, the homely but strong face, the sad but sweet features, the intelligence and vision of our greatest American." And in that crisis year of 1917, in the nation's "impending struggle for the right of the peoples of the world against wrong," the memory of Lincoln was "a living force, an anchor of hope, an inspiration to highest effort, an earnest of victory."

The statue stands upon a small boulder in Lytle Park, a clear space in the center of the city, surrounded by trees and shrubbery. The park is named for William A. Lytle, a member of a well-known family of the city, who served in the Mexican War, entered the Civil War in 1861 as a colonel of volunteers, became a brigadier general, and was killed at Chickamauga. Lytle wrote the poem, "I am dying, Egypt, dying."

Remarkable as is this statue, we think the Saint-Gaudens "Lincoln" was more suitable for display in the heart of London. There should stand the bearded President rather than the Lincoln of the prairies. Fortunately, a more appropriate site was found for the replica of Barnard's creation. The facts are outlined in the inscription on its base: "This monument of Abraham Lincoln, / the work of George Grey Barnard, / was through the friendly offices of the Sulgrave Institution / and the Anglo-American Society, given to the city of Manchester / by Mr. and Mrs. Charles Phelps Taft, of Cincinnati, Ohio, U.S.A., / in commemoration of Lancashire's friendship to the cause for / which Lincoln lived and died, and of the century of peace / among English-speaking peoples. 1919."

Any complete account of the manner in which the Barnard and the Saint-Gaudens statues came into competition for erection in London, and of the way the resultant embarrassing problem was solved, would require more space than is here available. The facts may be summarized. Committees had been organized in the United States and in Great Britain to celebrate the century of peace. Their activities were suspended, but not abandoned, on the outbreak of the World War in 1914. A proposal to place a replica of the Saint-Gaudens "Lincoln" in London had already been made. After the unveiling of the Barnard statue in Cincinnati, members of the American committee approached Mr. Taft in behalf of the centenary celebration, and he offered to pay the cost of a Barnard replica for London. Supposing that this offer came from the entire American committee instead of a fraction of its membership, the British committee accepted the offer and obtained an official designation of the Westminster site. The subsequent publicity precipitated or intensified the storm in America, to the bewilderment of the English promoters of the celebration.

On the day of the dedication of the Barnard replica, the *Manchester Guardian* said: "London, in possessing Saint-Gaudens' statue, will have Lincoln, the President; Manchester has Lincoln, the Man — a better possession for the country of the Cotton Famine, — and in the great rugged head of the new Statue it has something to touch the spirit of the children of future generations like the Great Stone Face of another American's imagination."

The dedication took place on September 15, 1919, nearly a year before the similar ceremony for the London Saint-Gaudens. Barnard's work stands on a wide expanse of greensward in Platt Fields Park. The press noted that any such work "of overpowering height, springing from a short base two feet from the ground," must have "space and amplitude." The day was beautiful, bringing out clearly the details of the statue's modeling "against a soft autumn sky." The city made an occasion of the event. There were speeches and toasts at a luncheon provided by the Lord Mayor. John W. Davis, American ambassador, referred fittingly to the valor with which the two nations fought and won the Great War, and went on, amid cheers, to extol the two men "who stood out prominently among those who prevented a rupture" between England and America at the time of our Civil War. To one of them, Abraham Lincoln, they were raising a monument that day; the other, John Bright, a citizen of Manchester, already had a monument in the public square.

At the unveiling in the early afternoon, Judge Alton B. Parker, Chancellor of the Sulgrave Institution, made the presentation speech.

Dwelling on Lincoln's policies, he declared that "the hateful Reconstruction Period's history would never have been written had the broadminded, warm-hearted, forgiving Lincoln escaped the assassin's bullet." Applause greeted his grateful references to Richard Cobden and John Bright. Cheers sounded when he paid tribute to the cotton spinners who sustained Lincoln at the time of the cotton famine in Lancashire.

The English newspapers declared their inability to understand the excitement in America over Barnard's work of art. Why should it be called "horrible," "grotesque," "defamatory?" On the contrary, it had "the transcendent qualities that make it so fine a piece of art and so wonderful a revelation of character." The work must be seen many times, in solitude, in order to appreciate it. Then one would note "the strength and serenity of the look, the line of the lip, the set of the chin, the modeling of the cheek, the expressiveness of the hands."

A third Barnard "Lincoln" stands on the lawn beside the public library of Louisville, facing one of the principal streets of the city. At the time of its unveiling, this statue was said to be more than a replica of the Cincinnati original; the pose is the same, but the sculptor had telegraphed from New York shortly before the dedication that "no work leaves my hand for bronze that is not developed and redeveloped in the surface of a wax figure." Barnard had also said in a letter that "he had remodeled all details to give the most lifelike touches possible." Presumably the casual observer would notice no difference. Members of the Louisville committee expressed the opinion that "the changes were chiefly in softening of lines around the head and the lower parts of the figure."

The unveiling exercises took place on October 26, 1922. Lieutenant Governor S. Thruston Ballard made the address of presentation in behalf of the donors, Mr. and Mrs. I. W. Bernheim of Louisville. A little granddaughter of the Bernheims pulled the cord that released the shroud. Mayor Huston Quinn accepted the statue in behalf of the city. Seated among the guests of honor were Miss Ida Tarbell and several Lincolnians of lesser fame. Louisville proudly welcomed the Barnard "Lincoln."

Probably there will never be unity of opinion about this work. But calm has succeeded clamor; it is appraised in these days, when discussed at all, in tones of friendly debate. It no longer seems necessary to anyone to pelt it with verbal brickbats. Many who do not like it agree that it is the work of an earnest and reverent artist, an achievement so impressive that it cannot be ignored. In size it challenges attention, towering more than thirteen feet in height.

George Grey Barnard turned away from the nice, smooth, smug idealizations which misrepresent so many public men. Probably he did exaggerate the backwoodsy aspect of the giant from the West; doubtless the feet are too big; but the stance is right. The sculptor could not demonstrate that Lincoln folded his hands over his stomach in the way they are disposed in the statue — but neither could any of the critics prove that he did not. We ourselves have seen more than a few old men of the Middle West stand, intently listening, in that posture. We question the correctness of Theodore Roosevelt's assertion that this is the man who debated with Douglas. No, this Lincoln is closer to New Salem than to Galesburg and Freeport. The Adam's apple is too conspicuous. The hair is unkempt, swept as it was by the prairie winds and habitually tousled by Lincoln's fingers. The serious observer is drawn away from the hands, the feet, the clothes, to that face. Photographs can be taken from such a level and at such an angle as to make it ugly, almost hideous, devoid of the sadness, tenderness, and friendliness which we associate with Lincoln. But after all discounts have been levied, Barnard's "Lincoln" remains a work of remarkable power. That face! We forget the pose and the suit, and return to the eyes, studious and foreboding, to the cheeks lean with toil, to the chin set and solid. That delineation of the thinking, growing, impenetrable Lincoln fascinates the open-minded student. This work, of right, must have a place among the great statues of Abraham Lincoln.

SOURCES: *Barnard's Lincoln*, Cincinnati, 1917; Nicholas Murray Butler, *Across the Busy Years*, 1939; Charles F. Goss, *Cincinnati, the Queen City*, 1912; Burton J. Hendrick, *Life and Letters of Walter H. Page*, 1922; William Webster Ellsworth, *A Golden Age of Authors*, 1919; Cornelius Greenway, article in *The Christian Leader*, May 7, 1938.

The correspondence between Judd Stewart and George Bernard Shaw is used with the permission of the owners of the letters, the son of Mr. Stewart, and Mr. Shaw, and of Dr. Robert L. Kincaid, who obtained copies of the originals.

A Kansas LINCOLN
the Children Love

THE seated "Lincoln" in the State House grounds at Topeka is the first statue produced in Kansas, and, as the *Official State Directory* proudly proclaims, is "the work of a native Kansan, born in 1892." This "Lincoln" happens also to be the result of the first public commission entrusted to Merrell Gage; it was executed by him almost immediately following the completion of his art studies, and dedicated on Lincoln's birthday in 1918. At the time of the unveiling the young sculptor was a sergeant in the Medical Corps of the United States Army, due to entrain in a few days for duty overseas; he came in khaki on special leave from Camp Doniphan for the dedication.

While Gage attended Washburn College School of Art, the director, Mrs. L. D. Whittemore, advised him to adopt sculpture as a profession. In New York he studied in the Art Students League, the Robert Henri School, and the School of Beaux Arts, and served for some time as an assistant to Gutzon Borglum. Returning to his home town, he set up a studio in a roomy barn on the family property, and started work on several projects, with a "Lincoln" as his major interest. At this period he taught sculpture in Washburn College and in the Kansas City Art Institute. About fifteen years ago he went to California, and now maintains a studio in Santa Monica.

Kansas has his "Pioneer Women's Memorial," also erected on the State House grounds; his busts of John Brown and Walt Whitman are in the Mulvane Museum at Topeka, where his "Flight," an aviation memorial in honor of Captain "Phil" Billard, stands in the memorial building. In the California State Exposition Building at Los Angeles one finds his "Ranch Girl" and his "Steel Worker." For the walls of the Edison Building he carved a series of panels, and also three panels high on the walls of the *Times* building, symbolizing "The Written Word," "The Printed Word," and "Journalism." For the Scientific Laboratory on the campus of the University of Southern California he produced a comprehensive series of sculptured decorations, which "were poured in concrete as an integral part of the walls."

These are carvings of prehistoric animals, for which the artist had to satisfy both his own standards of execution and the demands of scientists that the creatures of the far-gone Pleistocene Age should be accurately represented. The sculptor was busy for a long time in measuring bones in museums, watching the descendants of long-vanished animals in zoological gardens, and examining documentary sources in libraries. During his California years Gage has been a teacher of art in the University, and has specialized in lecturing on the face of Lincoln. His devotion to that theme has not ebbed with the passing years. He chats with his auditors about the prairie lawyer and his development into the great President, modeling from a bucket of clay the changes which experience and age made in the rugged countenance of the man.

In his address at the dedication of the Topeka "Lincoln," Sergeant Gage explained that his work was dominated by the humanitarianism of his subject's character. On that morning, while he was busy with the details of the arrangements for the ceremony, two elderly women seized the opportunity for a long look at the work. Gage heard one of them ask, "Why doesn't Lincoln sit up like a regular statue?" The other replied, "Why, he's listening to what the people are saying." And the sculptor said to them, "That was my very idea in sculpturing Lincoln. I wanted to portray the thoughtful friendliness of the man. This was the key idea of the whole interpretation." He explained also that the place for the statue in the State House grounds had been selected because this was intended to be an unconventional statue. A position against the tall columns of the building would have demanded a standing figure, whereas "there was nothing architectural about my 'Lincoln.'"

In after years Gage was happy to learn that many thousands of children had been attracted by his "Lincoln," and that hundreds of them had "climbed into his massive lap" to be photographed. A Topeka newspaper recalled Merrell Gage's association with Gutzon Borglum in New York, his months of study of the life and looks of the man Lincoln, and how later he had given "three months of mechanical planning and nine months of clay modeling" to the making of the statue, with a life mask and sixty different photographs about him. Gage's model was placed on a revolving table, so that he might study his work in varied lights and shadows. Even in the somewhat crouching position, the bronze "Lincoln" is six feet in height.

The preliminary exercises of dedication were held in Memorial Hall, with bugle calls, addresses, and songs. The assemblage then marched to the State House grounds, where the Art Department of the Woman's Club, whose efforts had initiated the movement for the erection of the statue, took charge of the ceremonies. The unveiling was done by Mary Ruth and "Bob" Larimer, niece and nephew of the sculptor, respectively four and a half and three and a half years of age. Governor Arthur Capper, later senator, accepted the statue for the state.

SOURCES: *Official Directory of Kansas;* information furnished by the Kansas State Library; correspondence with Mr. Merrell Gage.

27 ILLUSTRATED PAGES 172 AND 173

The "Sculptor Laureate" of a State

IN THE Northwest they called Alonzo Victor Lewis "the Sculptor Laureate of the State of Washington." His passing in November, 1946, was much lamented, for he had produced most of the memorial statues in the State. Of these the most widely known was his "Doughboy," standing before the Civic Auditorium in Seattle — a work which produced a good deal of controversy, not so much as to its artistic merit, but more on account of the alleged enigmatic smile on the face of the young soldier. Among Lewis' other commemorative productions in Washington state are the American Legion Memorial at Centralia, the Memorial to the World Flight Aviators at Seattle, and the official State War Memorial on the Capitol grounds at Olympia. Perhaps his most popular work is the statue of Ezra Meeker, "the beloved pioneer," at Puyallup. He moulded many portrait busts, among them a notable likeness of Dr. Mark A. Matthews, a celebrated Presbyterian clergyman of Seattle. Lewis worked with pigments and canvas as well as with clay and plaster, although he will be most widely remembered for his sculptures. Born in Utah, he studied in Chicago, New York, and Paris, and after living about twenty years in Spokane established himself in Seattle, where he died at the age of sixty.

There are two bronze "Lincolns" by this sculptor in the state, one set up at Tacoma in 1918, the other at Spokane in 1930. The suggestion for a Tacoma statue of the Civil War President is understood to have originated with Mr. W. H. Gilstrap, a former secretary of the Washington State Historical Society. The idea was promptly taken up by men and women representing various patriotic organizations. The deaths of Mr. Gilstrap and several other principal promoters of the project, together with a change in economic conditions, relegated the movement to the background. A contract had meanwhile been made by the Managing Committee of the Lincoln Memorial Association for a monument to cost between five and seven thousand dollars, but an insufficient amount of money had been raised. For about a year a big plaster figure had stood in the sculptor's studio, wrapped in dampened blankets at night to keep the plaster from drying out, and protected with fires in winter to prevent freezing.

A letter to a newspaper and an editorial appeal rescued the plan from oblivion. The schoolchildren swung into action. An eighth-grade girl in the Grant School, named Marian Richardson, became interested. She wrote the letter and gave the first dollar for the new crusade. The Board of Education authorized the Superintendent of Schools to allow the pupils in all grades to give and collect money for the cause. The twelve hundred students in the high school named for Lincoln "entered into this enterprise with unequaled enthusiasm," one of them said, and "in one month of activities raised eleven hundred and thirty dollars in actual cash." The school historian records that the students of another high school and the pupils of all the grade schools worked with earnestness in the campaign, although they lacked the special incentive of the students of the Lincoln School, on whose grounds the statue was to be placed. The pride with which these boys and girls looked back on their whirlwind of activities is readily perceptible between the lines of their reports. One boy raised $60.00 and one girl $71.00, while the Camera Club of "the other high school" sold over two thousand post cards at a dime each. In all, the schools raised $4,089, and outside donors, individuals and societies, gave $725.00 more. These funds were intended in the main for casting the figure.

The sculptor's struggles first to conceive and then to produce a worthy "Lincoln" are indicated in the published accounts of his labors. For a long time he had "thought and dreamed about Abraham Lincoln." He had "almost memorized Herndon," and had read many other works that might help him to portray the man. He made numerous sketches in clay, and experimented with several armatures. He advertised for men of Lincoln's dimensions to serve as models. Somehow he obtained the measurements of a Lincoln suit of clothes, from which a tailor made the garments the statue was to wear. The model completed, the sculptor turned to its preservation, and when at last the money was provided it was sent to New York for casting.

In January, 1918, the bronze figure arrived in Tacoma. The dedication provided a great day for the city and for the sculptor. Lincoln's birthday was chosen for the ceremonies. The United States was at war, and the Tacoma men in training at Fort Flagler made their last formal appearance in the city before going overseas. From Camp Lewis came a group of French officers as guests of the municipality. Governor Ernest Lister made the dedicatory address. Marian Richardson, assisted by Harry Osborn of the Willard School, released the flag which had covered the statue.

This "Lincoln," nine feet in height, stands on a seven-foot base carved from British Columbia granite, on which are inscribed the concluding phrases of the Gettysburg Address. The figure has been described as "faithfully depicting the long, lank, shambling Lincoln, . . . with the huge flat feet that had followed the furrows, the gnarly hands bred to the ax, and yet which held the pen whose English is the wonder of literature, and that signed the freedom of a race." The figure and the clothing had been wrought with "unpicturesque fidelity" to the facts. The eyes travel upward "and rivet themselves upon the face," which is "bent just enough to reach us with his benevolent gaze as we walk below on our common path."

The story of the Spokane "Lincoln" is comparatively simple. The Clara Barton Fortress of the Daughters of the Grand Army of the Republic made plans for a memorial in 1912. Ten years later Mr. Enoch Sears and Judge C. B. Dunning, of the Department of Washington and Alaska of the Grand Army, proposed that a heroic statue of Lincoln in bronze be erected in the city. A Lincoln Memorial Association was organized by merging several plans and agencies. A base for the monument was dedicated at the 1923 annual encampment of the Grand Army, and in the same year a commission for the creation of the statue was given to Mr. Lewis. The outcome was a pedestal ten feet high and a twelve-foot bronze "Lincoln," in which the sculptor, accepting a suggestion of the veterans, depicted the President as Commander-in-Chief of the Union forces in the war against secession.

This statue stands in a triangular parkway near many important buildings, in an area known as the Civic Center. The Commander of

246

the Union forces stands at his full stature, his feet together, arms hanging at his side, the left hand holding his high hat, with a military cape draped over the right shoulder. The head is held high. The artist visualized Lincoln looking across a great battlefield. The usual photographs of this statue produce erroneous notions of its merit; the head is too far above the observer to convey all the emotional intensity depicted in the face. The eyes are narrowed for far vision, and shadowed by the heavy brows. The countenance is worn, the muscles are taut; the man is thinking of "what they did here"; he is counting the awful cost of saving the Union.

The dedication on Armistice Day brought to the Center an enormous crowd, estimated at forty thousand, including veterans of three wars. Senator Clarence C. Dill presided; Samuel P. Weaver, president of the Association, presented the memorial to the city, and it was accepted once by Commander W. W. Work of the Washington-Alaska Department of the G.A.R., and again by Mayor Leonard Funk. The principal address was delivered by Dr. Ernest O. Holland, president of Washingon State College, who recalled how, at the World Parliament of Religions at the Columbian Exposition of 1893, the vast audience on the opening day, having heard tributes to religious leaders of all ages and all faiths, "arose and applauded and continued to applaud" the name of Abraham Lincoln. How much Lincoln had done for the West! One day he signed the charter of the transcontinental railroad, and the very next day signed the act which founded the Land-Grant colleges.

The moment for the uncovering of the bronze figure arrived. The multitude had waited with keen expectancy. President Hoover pressed a telegraph key in the White House, and a balloon was liberated, lifting an American flag which had veiled the figure of the former President. As the people watched and applauded, "a shower of American flags from aerial bombs dropped by planes drifted down while the massed bands played the National Anthem." No other unveiling of any of our scores of Lincoln statues has been more spectacular or better devised for awakening popular enthusiasm.

SOURCES: Correspondence with Spokane Chamber of Commerce, Dr. Ernest O. Holland, Samuel P. Weaver, Senator Clarence C. Dill, the Spokane Public Library, the Lincoln High School of Tacoma, the librarian of the *Seattle Post-Intelligencer,* and Alonzo Victor Lewis; official program of the Spokane dedication.

The LINCOLN *of*
the Farewell Address

ILLINOIS celebrated the centenary of her admission to the sisterhood of states in 1918. On October 5 of that year the cornerstone of the beautiful Centennial Memorial Building was laid, and on the same day were dedicated two statues of the sons whom the state most desired to honor. Both of these statues stand before the State House between the walks leading to the East entrance, the statue of Lincoln at the head of a flight of steps leading from the street, with the statue of Stephen A. Douglas standing some fifty yards behind and directly in front of the portico. From the street both statues are flanked by the colonnade and wings of the great building, with its imposing dome rising three hundred sixty feet above the lawn. Atop the dome at four hundred feet the flag of the Union spreads to the breeze.

The statue of Lincoln first commands our attention, depicting a lean man of inordinate height, with long legs and arms, a small chest, downcast face, and sombre eyes; the attitude is that of a man deeply moved, as though conscious of the solemnity of the experience through which he is passing.

The statue of Douglas produces by contrast an impression of tremendous force and power. It almost seems alive in its virility; the short legs, the square block of the torso, the huge head with compressed lips, the defiant gaze, the mass of hair — this man is responding to a challenge.

Nothing could be finer than the manner in which Illinois thus proudly proclaims her love and admiration for Stephen A. Douglas and Abraham Lincoln. These bronze effigies flash to the mind the dramatic contrasts of the looks and the careers of the men they represent. Douglas is in the midst of a thrilling speech; Lincoln is saying good-bye to his neighbors as he starts for Washington to assume the office which has been denied to his great rival. He is standing on the rear platform of the railroad car. Behind him, accentuating the lines of his figure, is a plain granite slab, on the back of which are inscribed the words of his beautiful sentences of farewell.

It was an impromptu speech; his heart was in it. He said: "My friends: No one, not in my situation, can appreciate my feeling of sadness at this parting. To this place, and the kindness of these people, I owe everything. Here I have lived a quarter of a century, and have passed from a young to an old man. Here my children have been born, and one is buried. I now leave, not knowing when or whether ever I may return, with a task before me greater than that which rested upon Washington. Without the assistance of that Divine Being who ever attended him, I cannot succeed. With that assistance, I cannot fail. Trusting in Him who can go with me, and remain with you, and be everywhere for good, let us confidently hope that all will yet be well. To His care commending you, as I hope in your prayers you will commend me, I bid you an affectionate farewell."

This statue was produced by Andrew O'Connor, who was born on June 7, 1874, in Worcester, Massachusetts. His father was a sculptor, who made cemetery designs and monuments, and taught his son to use the chisel. The ambitious youth left his home at the age of sixteen, and spent several years wandering about the United States and Europe. We hear of his having been employed in the studio of William Ordway Partridge, of his having studied for a time with Daniel Chester French, of his working with various painters and sculptors in London between 1895 and 1898, and that it was while he was employed in the studio of John Singer Sargent that he made a definite decision to embark on an art career.

For many years O'Connor lived in Paris, making numerous trips to America in connection with his commissions. He was greatly influenced by Rodin, with whom he spent some time as a pupil. In 1906 the Salon awarded him its second medal, and in 1928 he won its first prize with a "Tristan and Isolde" done in limestone. His "Mother of Sorrows," a heroic bronze figure of a kneeling woman, originally intended to become a part of a colossal war memorial, was accepted for the Tate Gallery in London in 1931.

When Augustus Saint-Gaudens early in the century saw O'Connor's designs for the ornamentation of the central portal of the entrance to St. Bartholomew's Church in New York, he is said to have called a cab and hurried to MacDougal Alley in Greenwich Village to congratulate the startled artist whom he found at work there. Stanford White also became interested in O'Connor in the early period of his career through his design for a relief panel for the bronze door of a tomb. White was instrumental in obtaining several commissions for

249

O'Connor, among them a bas-relief for the J. P. Morgan Library in New York. Suggestive of the Rodin influence are the reliefs and the eleven heroic statues which adorn the Essex County Court House in Newark, New Jersey. The bronze statue of General Henry W. Lawton, a man of almost exactly Lincoln's height, was completed in Paris and erected in Indianapolis. An attractive and popular work is the memorial to Theodore Roosevelt, in the form of a Boy Scout group, for a fountain at the Glen Ridge Golf Club in Chicago. The four boys in this group are said to have been modeled by the sculptor's sons; they stand with their dog on a pedestal at the head of a pool.

At the Louisiana Purchase Exposition in St. Louis in 1904, O'Connor was represented by an allegorical study entitled "Inspiration." His "Lafayette" is in Baltimore; his monument for the tomb of General Emerson Liscum in the Arlington National Cemetery; his marble statue of General Lew Wallace in the Capitol at Washington, and a bronze duplicate in Crawfordsville, Indiana. O'Connor was a gifted artist, of high competence in an extensive range of subjects and styles. It has been said that "his work often is conceived in the most exquisite elegance and again he creates subjects shrouded in a phenomenal and impressive gloom."

O'Connor created two Lincoln statues of heroic size, and also modeled a portrait bust which is in the Royal Exchange in London. One of the statues was to have been unveiled on the lawn of the State House in Providence, Rhode Island, on Lincoln's birthday in 1931. A movement for the erection of such a memorial had been under occasional discussion for years, but no commission was appointed until 1930, when O'Connor was chosen to make a model. The total cost was expected to be about $20,000; schoolchildren contributed pennies and dimes, and the State appropriated several thousand dollars. But financial complications prevented the consummation of the plans, and the statue remained in the yard of the Gorham Manufacturing Company in Providence. After about fifteen years this "Lincoln" was purchased by a corporation owning a Maryland area, just over the District of Columbia line, including the fort named for the Civil War President. This area is often called Fort Lincoln Memorial Park, but Fort Lincoln Cemetery would be a more accurate title; officially it is The Capitol Cemetery of Prince Georges County, Maryland. Here in 1814 was fought the unhappy battle of Bladensburg, and nearby is the old dueling ground where Commodore James Barron killed Commodore Stephen Decatur. At this writing it has not been determined just when or where on these grounds the Lincoln statue will be permanently placed. It is now mounted on a temporary site where it is seen to great advantage. Wherever placed, it will surely attract the attention of all, and the study of many, who visit the cemetery. The President sits in a big chair made of plain blocks of timber, with a shawl thrown back from his shoulders and drawn between his knees, his bared head looking downward as though brooding over problems he must solve.

Of the Springfield "Lincoln," those of the neighbors and friends to whom he addressed his feeling words of farewell who still survived the lapse of over half a century were wont to say, "That is the man I remember." The statue has been criticized and occasionally ridiculed. The adverse comments are, in substance, that the face is not a faithful portrait, the attitude is slouchy, the dress is that of a man who does not in the least understand the altitude of the office for which he has been chosen, and the contrast with the brilliant masterpiece of Douglas discredits the judgment of the committee which selected this model. Some of these opinions contain elements of truth; but let it be remembered that this choice was not the hasty decision of an incompetent jury. The Illinois Art Commission reached their decision by progressive eliminations. Fifty-two designs were submitted for their consideration, forty-nine in a general competition and three by invitation. The three designs submitted by invitation were the work of Albert Jaegers and Herman A. MacNeil of New York, and of Andrew O'Connor. Each received an award of $500.00. There were also prizes for the best three models in the general competition: one of these went to Gilbert Riswold of Chicago, who won the separate competition for the Douglas statue; another to Charles Keck of New York; and the third award was divided between Paul Jennewein of New York, and Mrs. Gail Sherman Corbett. None of these seven was unknown to fame. The Commission, keeping strictly within the bounds prescribed for its work, selected four competitors — Jaegers, MacNeil, Riswold, and O'Connor — to receive an additional $500.00 each for enlarged models of their designs. After several months the ultimate choice was made.

O'Connor called his design "The Lincoln of the Farewell Address," a title which provides a key for the refutation of some of the unfavorable views of the work. The portrait is faulty, however, because it depicts a beardless Lincoln, whereas the President-elect had grown a set of whiskers — still ragged — during the four months preceding his departure from Springfield. We venture the suggestion that the sculptor, who was described at the time as "an American studying in

Paris," may not have known of this alteration in Lincoln's looks, and that in their pleasure with the theme and the design the Commission ignored this deviation from photographic accuracy. For O'Connor has caught Lincoln's mood.

The departing President-elect was profoundly moved. Standing on the platform of an old-fashioned passenger coach, he may have leaned forward at the rail, looking down through the mists of a rainy morning into the faces of people who had known him intimately for years. Elected to the Presidency, he is still the simple man who lived and worked among them day by day. Did they, we wonder, catch the new throb in his voice, or the new cadence in his style? "Not knowing when or whether ever I many return" — the Gettysburg Address and the Second Inaugural are forecast in that phrase. Lincoln has spent wearing hours contemplating the future. His loneliness in the crisis confronting the nation accounts for the droop of the shoulders, the tired arms, the mournful face. There is no lack of dignity in that face. The countenance is strong, although the eyes suggest the imminence of tears. The Lincoln of the debates with Douglas was another man. The sculptor might have shown him then as the orator, with blazing eyes, erect and dominant. The contrast is right; both the statues are right, when one considers them with due regard for the meaning their makers sought to convey.

The address of dedication was made by Godfrey Rathbone Benson, Lord Charnwood, the English writer, whose biography of Lincoln had been published in 1916. Speaking at a time when the first World War had reached the highest tension of the desperate fighting, Charnwood told his auditors that there was no statesman whose example was so often cited in Great Britain as that of Abraham Lincoln. He reminded them that men were dying for Lincolnian ideas "of democracy, of freedom, of equality," though often baffled by the assertion of equality "when in certain obvious ways Nature herself has fashioned them so unequal."

With a reference to Douglas and the debates of 1858, Charnwood declared: "There is no statesman, no poet, no philosopher, whose thoughts on these deep matters are at once so profound and far-reaching, and put in language so transparently simple, as was the case with Abraham Lincoln." Beyond Lincoln's statecraft and the poetry of his language there "was something interwoven in his genius" which brings him "singularly near to the hearts of men of all conditions and characters and kinds." In some ways "Lincoln resembled the Old World idea of the chivalrous knight, but his simplictiy, humility, commonness, and readiness to take life on the amusing side, set him apart." In him were met and fused the idealist and the practical man, "a union without which practical qualities and idealism are alike — vanity." It seemed to Lincoln that God had a work for him to do, and for that, in his manly humility — "the most uncommon of all the Christian graces" — he believed himself to be ready.

America and England, each in its own way, said Charnwood, were striving to achieve Lincoln's ideals of human progress. What Lincoln accomplished in saving the Union, "we and our sons have set our hearts to do today." The English biographer of the American President referred to the young men — French, English, American — sacrificed in the war. His nephews had fallen; perhaps his son would fall. "We here highly resolve that these dead shall not have died in vain." The occasion invited eloquence, and Lord Charnwood rose to a lofty level of ideas and expression.

SOURCES: Charles F. Fairman, *Works of Art in the National Capitol;* Michigan State Library, *Biographical Sketches of American Artists,* 1924; *Journal of the Illinois State Historical Society,* October, 1914, January, 1920; correspondence with Gorham Manufacturing Company, Providence, R.I.

29 ILLUSTRATED PAGE 176

A Limestone LINCOLN

ANOTHER of the few Lincoln statues which just comes within the definition of heroic statues was made from a single block of Indiana limestone. It stands in the town of Odon, in the public park commonly called "The Old Settlers' Grounds," which serves as a suitable place for the annual meetings of those pioneers. The sculptor of this "Lincoln" was Ira A. Correll. He proudly recalls his share in causing an area in his native town to be set aside for public use; as an uncommissioned Committee of One he designed, executed, and presented to the town the only statue of Lincoln erected in the neighborhood of the Indiana family home.

Odon, with a population of about two thousand, is fifty miles north of the site of "Tom" Lincoln's farm, where the future President spent the fourteen years before the family removed to Illinois. The town was originally named Clarksburg, commemorative of the historic exploit of George Rogers Clark in the conquest of "the Illinois country," but so many Midwestern towns had chosen that name that this one, some thirty miles from Vincennes, decided to change its designation. Odon is just on the margin of the Indiana limestone region.

Ira Correll's father was a workman in stone and marble, who modeled in clay and carved his designs; "some of them were beautiful and are admired today," his son declares. By the time young Correll was eighteen years of age, in 1891, he had learned all that his father and an old Welsh sculptor named David Richards, who had studied abroad, could teach him. He went on to Chicago, where, as he explains carefully in view of numerous misleading newspaper reports, he studied "under the direction of Lorado Taft" but never as a student in the Art Institute. For a full half-century he has practiced his art. He did carvings in stone for such buildings as the Masonic Temple in Detroit, the Hotel Stevens in Chicago, the Sterling Library at Yale, and the British Embassy in Washington. He also produced the Pearl Harbor Memorial in bas-reliefs in Dallas, Texas, and a reproduction in stone of Leonardo da Vinci's "Last Supper." For several years he has been a member of the Texas School of Fine Arts at Austin, where he teaches sculpture, wood carving, and clay modeling, and still carries on, in association with his son who is also a sculptor, as an independent professional. He maintains an Indiana home, though his headquarters are at Austin.

The Odon statue was unveiled on the first day of the Old Setters' meeting, August 17, 1922. No organized group and no individual other than the sculptor having had any part in financing the work, the ceremonies were simple. The unveiling was done by Correll's daughter Helen. "My purpose," says the sculptor, "was to present Lincoln in the most natural and simple manner, with no attempt at drama or allegory." For the head he depended on the Volk life-mask. The right hand resting on a book symbolizes Lincoln's "early struggle for knowledge"; a tree trunk with an axe leaning against it suggests "how he made his living in his youth." The figure, standing on a four-foot pedestal, is one inch taller than Lincoln's actual height.

SOURCES: Mr. J. W. Fesler and Dr. Robert M. Dearmin of Indianapolis; Mr. Fred Dearmin and Miss Ethel Williams of Odon; Mr. W. R. Correll of St. Petersburg, Florida; Mr. Ira A. Correll of Austin, Texas.

This Statue Attests
an Epigram

OF ONE Lincoln statue it may fairly be said that its replica is far better known, even among Lincoln scholars, than the original. This statue was the work of a "Belgian sculptor," so-called, of whom hardly more is known than his name, A. L. Van den Bergen. A plate on the base of the original in Racine, Wisconsin, bears the single word "Volk," but how this name came to be on the plate is an unsolved mystery; the bronze casting was done by the American Art and Bronze Company of Chicago, which firm is known to have named Van den Bergen as the sculptor. We think, while reserving the right to alter our opinion on the appearance of evidence to the contrary, that the "Lincoln" in Clinton, Illinois, is a replica of the Racine statue. Comparison of photographs provides a basis for this conclusion, and at least one reference work states that view to be correct. The Clinton statue is "signed" "Van den Bergen, Sc." Although the Illinois replica is more widely known, due in part to its connection with one of Lincoln's most famous epigrams, the Racine original must have the right of way in our account of Van den Bergen's work.

The *Racine Journal-News,* today the *Journal-Times,* carried this paragraph about the statue on Lincoln's birthday, 1924: ". . . The Ninth Ward Booster Club, its officials and members, should receive the congratulations of every Racine citizen for its labors in raising the fund necessary to provide this lasting tribute. And thanks should be extended to those whose contributions made it possible. The school children can well take pride in this statue and feel an ownership in it because of their pennies, nickels and dimes contributed for it."

That in brief is the story of this memorial. The movement for its acquisition was fathered by an aggressive promotional organization having one city ward for its field of operations, although gifts were received from citizens residing elsewhere. The statue was erected on a triangular plot where three streets intersect. It stands on a granite base. The inscription is not the closing words of the Gettysburg Address, so often encountered in connection with our "Lincolns," but the opening sentence: ". . . Our fathers brought forth on this continent a new nation, conceived in liberty and dedicated to the proposition that all men are created equal." The dedication exercises were conducted in the evening in the auditorium of the Lincoln High School. Spotlights focused on the statue as "little Charles Davies, Jr., pulled the cords" to unfurl the flag that wrapped the figure.

After an interval of seven years the replica was put up at Clinton on Armistice Day in 1931. Lincoln was as well acquainted with this locality, in Salt Creek valley in central Illinois, as with the valley of the Sangamon. In his dedicatory address that day, Judge Lawrence B. Stringer of Lincoln said: "From 1839 to the very year in which Mr. Lincoln was elected President of the United States, DeWitt County was continuously a part of the old Eighth Judicial District which he traveled and in which he practiced law. . . . In the old brick court house which occupied the Clinton public square, for nearly two decades Mr. Lincoln was present at substantially every term of the DeWitt Circuit Court." It was at Clinton, the speaker might have added, that Lincoln and Stephen A. Douglas appeared in the only murder trial in which they were on the same side. This was in 1840, when Spencer Turner was charged with the murder of Matthew K. Martin. Lincoln and Douglas convinced the jury of Turner's innocence. At Clinton, also, in a campaign for another term in the United States Senate, Douglas spoke one day in 1858 for three hours, with Lincoln among his auditors. Two days later they arranged for their series of joint debates.

The leader in the movement to obtain a Lincoln statue for the Clinton courthouse yard was L. O. Williams, a local attorney and Lincoln enthusiast. The ceremonies for the unveiling were held in the afternoon in the First Methodist Church, owing to the unobliging disposition of "the weather man," but the unveiling was managed in advance of the speaking program. Judge Stringer's address enumerated the chief attributes which had "made Lincoln great." Honesty, "not merely legal honesty" or "conventional honesty," as "the best policy" with "accent on the word 'policy,'" but that "honesty which is absolute and fundamental." There were his humility, his humanity, his sense of justice, "his devotion to the cause of the common people and his optimistic belief in the ultimate triumph of the eternal truth" — that was "our Lincoln of central Illinois."

This is not an inspired statue, but it looks more like the man than do many other statues with their padded chests and broadened shoulders, and it expresses the patriotic sentiments of the community. On the back of the pedestal we read: "That it may not be forgotten that here for nineteen years as a Lawyer and Friend he was Counselor and Teacher of our Forefathers, this Statue is erected by the Citizens of DeWitt County to the Memory of Abraham Lincoln." On the front are two statements of Lincoln's: "I must stand with anybody that stands right; stand with him while he is right, and part with him when he goes wrong"; and the famous epigram: "You can fool all the people part of the time, and part of the people all the time, but you cannot fool all the people all the time."* Below this appears the attestation, "Spoken in an address at Clinton, July 27, 1858, by Abraham Lincoln."

SOURCES: Correspondence of Emil C. Wiegand and F. R. Starbuck, Racine, Wisconsin; courtesies by M. L. Houser and Ernest E. East, Peoria, Illinois; the Racine Public Library, and the Vespasian Warner Public Library of Clinton; *Clinton Centennial*, 1935; Lawrence B. Stringer, "Abraham Lincoln," *Journal of the Illinois State Historical Society*, January, 1932; Harry E. Pratt, *Lincoln 1840–1846*.

For the Veterans of Three Wars

THE city of Alliance, Ohio, proudly claims to possess the first joint memorial ever erected in honor of the veterans of three wars of the United States — the Civil War, the War with Spain, and the first World War. This claim is probably justified, for this memorial was dedicated in 1924, while the colossal monument by Gutzon Borglum in Newark, New Jersey, with forty-two figures representing the entire military history of the country, was dedicated in 1926. President Lincoln, as the Commander-in-Chief of the Union forces in the Civil War, represents the veterans of that conflict; plain soldiers in uniform, one

* The authenticity of this saying has been challenged, and it has been attributed to Phineas T. Barnum, Robert G. Ingersoll, and others. The trend of scholarly opinion favors Lincoln's authorship. Joseph W. Fifer, held by many to be a competent witness despite his years, stood for it on the authority of his informant, Milton Hay (James O'Donnell Bennett, *Private "Joe" Fifer*, 1936, p. 22). See also Richard Price Morgan in *Abraham Lincoln by Some Men Who Knew Him*, essays assembled by Isaac Newton Phillips, 1910, p. 102, and Isaac Newton Phillips, *Lincoln*, 1910, pp. 108f.

with a musket, the other with a sword, stand for the veterans of the later wars. The figure of Lincoln rises high in air; the others are on bases projecting from the lower section of the central shaft. The "Lincoln" is bulky. He stands with a scroll in his left hand, and with the right hand swung slightly forward, palm open and fingers curled. Below on the face of the shaft are crossed flags in bronze. The memorial is the work of Steven A. Rebeck, who was born in Cleveland in 1891 and practices his profession in that city.

An unusual and possibly unique feature of the dedication ceremony was the arrangement for unveiling the three statues. The figures were draped in large flags hung from a high staff just back of the central shaft. At the proper moment, while a band played a patriotic air, the enveloping cords were cut and the colors were hoisted by ropes to the top of the staff, well above the head of the towering "Lincoln." The Lincoln statue was unveiled by Miss Blanche Greenwalt. This ritual was repeated for each of the other statues.

Colonel C. W. Blodgett, of Cincinnati, a past Commander-in-Chief of the Grand Army of the Republic, one of the volunteers of 1861, who had known Lincoln personally, was the speaker. His reminiscences delighted a group of veterans for whom that dedication day, July 4, 1924, was a great occasion.

The original scheme had been to erect three separate memorials in different sections of the public square; the grouping came about through the advice of the Cleveland bronze founders who did the casting. This does not seem to account, however, for a curious difference in dates, the explanation of which has eluded our inquiries: on the base of the central shaft one reads, "Erected May 30, 1915, to the memory of our heroes."

SOURCES: Secretary of Mount Union College, and the Carnegie Free Library, Alliance, Ohio; Carl W. Schaefer, Esq., Cleveland.

The Puerto Rico LINCOLN

A HEROIC statue of Abraham Lincoln is on view in San Juan, Puerto Rico, where it was erected a quarter-century ago. For some years we were confident of its existence because two persons connected with the United States Army reported that they had seen it, but three years of letter writing failed to establish any contact with residents, tourists, or officials who knew anything about it. All, from a former governor down, doubted that in Puerto Rico such a work could be found, and many said outright that nothing of the kind ever had been set up in the island. Many letters of inquiry went unanswered.

A photograph eventually came to us in 1951, however, from the Government of Puerto Rico, through Gustavo Agrait, executive assistant to the present governor, who gave the date of erection as 1926, and the sculptor as an Italian named Bartoli. Sculptured in marble, this seated "Lincoln" is placed on a pedestal in the grounds of the Abraham Lincoln Elementary School, in Sol Street, San Juan. The President is seated in a large, highly ornamented chair, in a formal pose. Everything about the sculpture is "elegant." This "Lincoln" might be in attendance on a ceremony of some kind. The right hand holds a document bearing the inscription "EMANCIPATION PROCLAMATION."

In 1922 Mrs. Rosario Timothée, principal of the Lincoln School, began raising funds for execution of the statue through contributions from alumni who had started attendance since 1901, the year in which her husband, Pedro Timothée, had become principal of the school. An inscription on the pedestal of the statue reads as follows:

A INICIATIVA Y ESFUERZOS DE
ROSARIO ANDRACA DE TIMOTHEE
CON EL CONCURSO DE
LOS PROFESORES Y ALUMNOS DE
ESTA ESCUELA SE EREGIO
ESTE MONUMENTO 1926

SOURCE: Correspondence with Gustavo Agrait, Executive Assistant to the Governor of Puerto Rico.

Lorado Taft

JOHN MILTON GREGORY, the first regent of Illinois Industrial University — now the University of Illinois — was determined that the institution should become "a true university," not limited, like most Western land-grant colleges, to "practical" instruction for farmers and mechanics. The change of the name of the institution in 1885, five years after his resignation, was in large part the result of his service in enlarging the curriculum well beyond the bounds of that of a vocational school.

In 1873 Gregory had served as a United States commissioner to the International Exposition in Vienna. That tour gave him the opportunity to buy, chiefly in Paris, what proved to be the largest collection of art objects in the Western States, acquired by means of a fund of several thousand dollars raised by local subscription. The resultant exhibition was something of a wonder in its day; out of it the University's art gallery was developed. In the collection shipped from France were about a score of full-sized statues, including a Laocoön and a Venus de Milo, more than two score statues reduced in size, a hundred busts, and many photographs and lithographs. President Gregory and Don Carlos Taft, professor of geology, supervised the unpacking of the boxes when they arrived in Urbana in 1874. But in many of the cases they found only a mass of fragments. The plaster casts were so badly broken that one of the school's trustees "allowed" that the stuff would make good fertilizer.

The stricken president and professor undertook to fit the pieces together, but failed. Taft's fourteen-year-old son was allowed to try his luck, and with keen eyes and nimble fingers, he found where almost every splinter belonged. He also found his vocation. "I'm going to be a sculptor," he declared — and he never changed his mind. Lorado Taft became not only a sculptor of high distinction, but an inspiring teacher of art as well; his pupils loved him and revere his memory.

The Middle West owes Taft a special debt for expanding its appreciation of beauty in human life, of the message of art in a democracy. He invested his great natural gifts in the creation of enduring beauty and in numerous crusades to educate the public taste. Attendance at his free lectures in Chicago multiplied from scores to hundreds, then to thousands. He led caravans of motor pilgrims all over Illinois, awakening their pride and that of his local auditors in the manifold scenic beauties of their state. In France, in 1918, as a Y.M.C.A. lecturer to the "doughboys," Taft was quite overwhelmed by their interest while he explained, with lantern-slides, the art and architecture all about them. A great personage was Lorado Taft, with his big voice, quick wit, engaging manner, and his immense and always available store of interesting and authentic information.

Taft's father was a New Hampshire farmer who became a Congregational minister and educator. His mother was a dauntless woman who faced poverty with a smile and encouraged her son to make the most of his endowments. Lorado was born in Elmwood, Illinois, in 1860. His parents were his only instructors until he entered the new college where his father taught, from which he was graduated in 1879.

With an abundance of faith and courage, but very little money, Taft started for Paris the night after he obtained his master's degree in 1880. For three years he studied under Augustin Dumont, and after a short visit to America returned to Paris for three years more. Several times fortunate things happened when he got down to his last sou.

Ready to set up for himself, he decided to make his home in Chicago — a fortunate decision. While there were many sculptors in the East, only a few worked in Chicago, and there Taft found opportunities at once. The building of the White City for the famous Fair of 1893 provided a thrilling experience. He became the superintendent of all sculpture for the Exposition, and for months worked in intimacy with artists of established fame and others who dreamed of fame ahead, artists from all over the United States and from foreign lands as well.

From 1886 to 1907 Taft was an instructor at the Chicago Art Institute, and a lecturer there until 1929. He also lectured at the University of Chicago and served as non-resident professor of art at the University of Illinois. His *History of American Sculpture* was published in 1903, and his *Recent Tendencies in American Sculpture* in 1921. He died in 1936.

When Taft had been only a year in Paris he earned a Premier Mention in the annual display of the École des Beaux Arts. An order for a statue of Schuyler Colfax, now standing in Indianapolis, brought him back to America in 1886. Three years later his statue of General Grant was erected in Leavenworth, Kansas. While waiting for larger commissions during his early Chicago years, he did numerous odd jobs. One of his students remembers his laughing remark that he made few soldiers' monuments, and was thankful he did not sign them. The Columbian Exposition enabled him to give transitory materialization to two dreams. His "The Sleep of the Flowers" and "The Awakening of the Flowers," standing at the entrance to the Horticultural Building, were much admired, but both perished when the building was destroyed.

Taft's heroic group known as "The Solitude of the Soul," a poetical interpretation of the manner in which friendships are made, depicts two men and two women, groping their way out of a central block of marble somehow finding each other's hands. This work won a gold medal, and many today regard it as Taft's finest achievement. It was acquired by the Art Institute. It was after reading Maeterlinck's drama *Les Aveugles,* which he described as "that wonderful tragedy whose symbolism expressed the great longing of all humanity for light in life," that Taft conceived the idea of indicating in sculpture the emotions of a company of the blind, young and old, sane and insane, men and women — with only a little child to see.

Taft's beautiful "Alma Mater," a group of three figures, is at the University of Illinois; the monument "to the Pioneers who bridged the streams, subdued the soil, and founded a State," stands in the town where he was born. His colossal "Washington" is in Seattle, his "Admiral Porter" in Vicksburg, and "The Crusader," a memorial to Victor Lawson, in Graceland Cemetery, Chicago.

A selected list of Taft's "important sculptural works" compiled by Mrs. Taft, contains forty-one titles. Probably the most widely known are the Fountain Groups and the colossal Indian statue popularly known as "Black Hawk." "The Fountain of the Great Lakes," erected in Chicago, shows five nymphs arranged upon a pyramid of rocks, pouring water into a series of shells, with "Superior" at the top and "Ontario" at the base. Half the population of the United States may have seen the "Columbus Fountain" in front of the Union Station in Washington, with a world globe surmounting a high central shaft, before which stands Columbus with folded arms at the prow of a ship.

The sculptor has told the origin of "The Fountain of Time." The idea came from the lines of Austin Dobson:

> Time goes, you say? Ah, no!
> Alas, Time stays: We go!

And Taft "saw the mighty crag-like figure of Time, mantled like one of Sargent's prophets, leaning upon his staff, his chin upon his hands, and watching with a cynical, inscrutable gaze, the endless march of humanity . . . swinging in a wide circle around the form of the one sentinel and made up of the shapes of hurrying men and women and children in endless procession, ever impelled by the winds of destiny in the inexorable lock-step of the ages." Among the hundred figures the sculptor unobtrusively included himself. This work also is in Chicago.

Without mentioning others of the Fountains, we glance at the so-called "Black Hawk" — the name was repudiated by Taft himself — looming above the forests from a high bluff that the Indians of Illinois liked to visit. There, with folded arms, in what is now a state park, the sculptor's idealized red man stands, fifty feet in height, and surveys the valley. To make that statue, in a place so difficult of access, was a tremendous undertaking; a big crew worked night and day for ten days to "pour" it in concrete.

Such a man as Taft, intensely artistic, deeply emotional, highly imaginative, must have dreamed many dreams that could never be realized in one lifetime. He thought constantly of new sculptures, and of new methods for bringing home to the people the meaning and worth of art. After passing his seventieth milestone Taft became interested in a project for the establishment of miniature art galleries in towns and villages throughout the land for the exhibition of photographs and models of the world's best in sculpture and painting. His memorial tablet for the Lincoln-Douglas debate at Quincy was dedicated shortly before his death.

Lorado Taft's heroic "Lincoln" stands in the center of a lovely greensward halfway between two streets, facing across one street the campus and the handsome building of the Urbana High School, and across the other the ornamental entrance to a public park. The original site was a triangular plot before the Urbana-Lincoln Hotel, which stands on the site of "the old Kerr Tavern," a favorite stopping place of Lincoln's while riding the circuit and near the Courthouse where he practiced his profession; dedication exercises took place there on Sunday, July 3, 1927, but soon afterward it was discovered that the hotel company could not give a clear title to the plot, and the statue was removed to its present and much more beautiful position, in the middle of a wide walk traversed daily by thousands of high school students.

Lawyer Lincoln is shown with his hands resting on the ends of the heavy stone slab at his back, on which are carved two inscriptions. At the top one reads (from the Peoria speech of 1854) : "If there is anything which it is the duty of the whole people to never intrust to any hands but their own, that thing is the preservation and perpetuity of their own liberties and institutions." Below are these words from the President's opinion of December 31, 1862, on the admission of West Virginia to the Union : "It is not the qualified voters but the qualified voters who choose to vote that constitute the political power of the state." These well-chosen citations reflect Taft's study of his subject.

The lines on the face of the pedestal on which the Taft statue stands inform the public that "through the generosity of Judge and Mrs. J. O. Cunningham, personal friends of Abraham Lincoln, this statue is given to the Urbana Park District." Following are the names of Franklin H. Boggs, George M. Bennett, and Joseph C. Blair, the three "trustees" who managed the bequest left for the statue by Joseph Oscar Cunningham, for years a leader of the Champaign County bar and for some time editor of an Urbana newspaper. Judge Boggs presided at the dedication exercises, and presented the memorial to the Park District; the unveiling was done by Mrs. Annetta Ayers Saunders, M.D., a niece of the donors. The sculptor spoke briefly on "The Younger Lincoln."

The address of the day was delivered by Dr. William E. Barton. After alluding to the crude achievements of primitive man as an artist and a sculptor, to the necessity for America to build the foundations of a material civilization before entering the field of art, and to how after Washington's death it "became the ambition of practically everybody in America who attempted to do anything with the hammer and chisel" to carve an effigy of him, Dr. Barton went on to show that "Abraham Lincoln almost immediately suggested himself as an object for sculpture." Lincoln was "the most photographed man of his time," coming "into prominence when the daguerreotype was the last word in art." Barton mentioned nearly a score of Lincoln sculptors, with a sentence or so of comment : "a new era in Lincoln sculpture began" with "the majestic Lincoln" by Saint-Gaudens, said Barton, and "the features recorded in the Volk life-mask, with variations such as each artist has chosen with respect to Lincoln's age at the time represented, and the mood sought to be portrayed, have been used by other sculptors and with varying degrees of success." Weinman produced "a notable seated statue"; Borglum gave us "the democratic 'Lincoln' "; Barnard "wrought a gaunt and ungainly 'Lincoln,' " while O'Connor did not go quite so far in that direction; Mulligan's "Lincoln" is "the muscular young giant of the forest"; Daniel Chester French has "given us two imperial 'Lincolns.' . . . None of these statues is unworthy. All of them are sincere. Not all of them are great, but these are those that most truly exalt Lincoln in our imagination."

The reference to the Volk life-mask and his cast of Lincoln's hands introduced some discussion of the physical makeup of the man. The Taft statue "has for its documentary material Volk's authentic record of Lincoln's face and hands, the actual measurements of his figure, and all are informed by the spirit of the artist. He has extended Lincoln's stature of six feet and four inches to a total height of ten feet, and made it perfect in its proportions; he has done more than to copy measurements; he has given us the artist's conception of the inner life, the strong personality of Lincoln. This statue shows Abraham Lincoln as Urbana saw him, in the days when he stood at the bar of justice in the court house yonder, or spoke at political meetings in the court house square. He stands with his hands upon the railing at his back, in the calm opening moments of his argument. He leans but lightly. He is well poised. His pose is suggestive of great reserve power, and quiet confidence in the justice of his cause. . . ."

This statue, Barton continued, "is a worthy, a noble interpretation of Lincoln, long before the time when martyrdom in a way glorified him. . . . It takes a poet to interpret a great character. You cannot recreate Abraham Lincoln by telling how many inches tall he was, nor by measuring the length of his feet, nor yet by giving accurately the circumference of his hatband. The sculptor must put a soul into his creation or it is a mere thing of stone or bronze. . . . But Lorado Taft became not only a sculptor but a prophet; not only an artist but an evangelist; not only a man who had to make a living while he indulged in his theories . . . but a man who was able also to exalt the public mind, to lift the popular appreciation of things high and fine. . . . He couldn't make a commonplace Lincoln."

And now "Abraham Lincoln comes to Urbana again, where for years he was not a stranger, where the lawyers and tavern-keepers and the people in the corner grocery knew him, and where the boys and girls on the street became familiar with his tall figure. . . . Back he comes to abide permanently in this community. . . . Here where his fame increased and his reputation grew with each visit, he comes again and comes to remain."

The speaker told the citizens and students before him what they might learn from this bronze likeness of Lincoln. In him "they are to see physical strength that wrought out strength of mind and conscience. They are to see intelligence that wrought out his education with meager materials, training a mind that had native alertness, sound judgment, becoming ever more sure of itself — an incentive always to young minds as they behold in his face qualities which the young may well aspire to have permanently wrought into their characters. Nothing mean, nothing contemptible, nothing savoring of dishonor shows in those features whose undeniable reality is before us, transfigured by his inherent kindliness. . . . They are to find the spirit of a man who fought a cruel war and never hated the men he fought — who loved his country and who loved it all, even the part that was fighting against him and misunderstood him, who believed that America needed to be large and needed to be free, and who lived and died for his country in whose ideals he had complete confidence and for whose glory he gave the utmost of his manhood, his loyalty and his prayers. Such is the citizen who comes permanently to live in Urbana."

The speech was an excellent example of Dr. Barton's style. He spoke in an intimate, almost a conversational tone, out of the fullness of knowledge. He adapted his topics to the occasion, and brought home to his listeners its higher aspects. One criticism of this Urbana statue and of others of Taft's works, rare as are his powers, is that he tends to "prettify" his creations. But in this age of strident materialism, realism is too often overplayed. The statue gives even the hurrying tourist a lingering impression of nobility. It inspires. The garb may be more elegant than Lincoln's customary dress while riding the circuit, but we see an inspiring semblance of a man approaching the climactic period of a great life. We see a Lincoln about to begin that first great speech delivered at Peoria in 1854, which became a platform on which he stood during the remaining years of his life. And we see also the man who remained always a neighbor and friend in the exalted station he came to occupy.

SOURCES: *Journal of the Illinois State Historical Society*, July, 1927; *Papers in Illinois History, 1937;* Ada Bartlett Taft, *Lorado Taft, Sculptor and Citizen*, 1946; correspondence with Lorado Taft and with Prof. Rexford Newcomb of the University of Illinois.

Haig Patigian
and His Model's Tuxedo

OF THE models for Lincoln sculptors, the man who posed for Haig Patigian, the distinguished veteran of San Francisco, was probably the most amazing. He fitted the role well and became seriously interested in the job. But back of that incidental employment was an adventurous life, some details of which were related to us by the sculptor himself.

Patigian had used various photographs and studied the Volk life-mask for the face of Lincoln, but finding a model with the proportions and physical characteristics of the President who would pose naturally baffled him for some time. Finally he hit upon the idea of going to the employment agencies and looking over the applicants for work. At the first agency, the crowd that jammed the pavement surged about the sculptor's car, asking as with a single voice if he wanted help. In the center of the throng, "towering above all the rest," stood a Dane who said not a word, but kept on rolling a "Bull Durham" cigarette. Patigian beckoned him forward. "I think you will do," he said. The man did not accept until informed that all he would be required to do would be to sit in a chair and pose for a statue. "Gee! That's soft!" exclaimed the crowd almost in unison. "I'll take it," said the giant with the "Bull Durham." The sculptor seated him in a bootblack's chair near at hand to look him over, smiling with approval.

In the workroom "Theo," as Patigian decided to call his model, proved difficult to fit satisfactorily with the available coats. At noontime he was absent more than two hours. At last the bell rang, and there stood "Theo" with a bundle under his arm. He was "sorry to be late," but he "lived a long way out" and "wanted to tell his landlady that he had found a job" — and he had "brought along a coat that would fit." To the sculptor's amazement, the bundle contained a tuxedo, almost new. It could be used to get the folds in the sleeves right. Patigian made no comment, and they proceeded to work.

After several months, the posing finished, the sculptor told "Theo" he might have his coat back. "Keep it," was the reply; "I'll never wear it again." And then the Dane astonished Patigian with its story. "I wore that coat only once," he said, "the day I bought it, and that night I killed a man when I had it on. I was working a few years ago for a mining company up in the mountains, and spent my time prospecting for the company, and let my pay accumulate for about six months. Back in town I collected to the amount of about a thousand dollars. There was a saloon in the town known as 'The Time and the Place.' Every night in that joint there was a big poker game. I liked poker and went over there with my dough. I had seen pictures of guys playing poker while dressed in tuxedos, so I went to a clothing shop and bought a suit, and when I sat in on the game I was all dolled up. It was 'freeze-out' poker. As time went on one guy after another went busted and quit. At length there were left only the town's ace gambler and me. I never had so much luck in my life; I couldn't lose. A crowd gathered to watch us. Mostly they boosted for me. They got the gambler sore by their joshing him over being licked by a kid.

"At last, he dealt the cards and shoved out all his chips for a bet. I felt sorry for the fellow, feeling somehow that he was bound to lose that wad. 'Look here,' I said, 'I don't want to break you. Take some of your chips back.' He got nasty. When the showdown came I had all his money. He took off his watch and a diamond ring. I said 'No,' and offered to give him back some of his cash. He began to call me ugly names, and declared I had been cheating him all night 'and you're not going to get away with it.' At that he pulls his gun, but before he can pull the trigger I yank my six-shooter out of my breast and drill him through the chest. The sheriff arrested me and took me to jail, but next day some of the fellows who had watched the game told the judge that I had fired in self-defense, and he let me go. That cured me of poker, and of wearing tuxedos."

Patigian had been interested in Theo from the first. He gave him regular employment as a model and man-of-all-work about the studio. The Dane proved to be a good carpenter, an excellent electrician, and an all-round mechanic; he learned to make moulds and plaster casts. His enthusiasm for the "Lincoln" increased as it neared completion; when the clay model was finished he burst into eloquence. The sculptor came to the climax of the tale with a bit of posing on Theo's part. It was a treat to sit across from Patigian and watch him roll a cigarette while he recalled:

"Theo stood before the statue, gazed at it in silence for a while, as he rolled his 'Bull Durham,' and said: 'When I was a kid in Denmark I used to stop and look at a big statue they had made of a guy that had been good to the kids. Well, I used to think that was the finest statue ever made, but this here beats that one in Denmark all to a frazzle!' He paused to light his cigarette while looking steadily up at the clay features of Lincoln, and then perorated as follows: 'No, he was not a good-looking man, but he sure had the most *profane irony of character* of any one that ever lived.'" Mr. Patigian says that the words in italics were uttered with great emphasis. Where shall we look for a more original observation about Lincoln or a Lincoln statue?

The statue was cast in bronze and placed in a commanding situation in front of the San Francisco City Hall, facing the Civic Center. The contract for its erection had been signed in 1923, as the result of the work of the Lincoln School Association, of which we have written in a previous chapter, to replace the Mezzara "Lincoln" which had been destroyed in the great fire of 1906. Local veterans joined with the Association in organizing a Lincoln Monument League, and over $25,000 was raised for the purpose. The League approved the sculptor's design, and preparations to start work on the monument were under way, when the president of the League died very unexpectedly. A prolonged discussion ensued; new ideas were brought forward, and not until 1925 was the sculptor directed to proceed in accordance with the original agreement and design.

Patigian first made a full-size portrait study of the head of Lincoln, and the Grand Army members of the committee gave it their unqualified approval as a real likeness of the man they had known. Those venerable men, impatient over the delays, worried that they might not survive for the unveiling of their statue. Their interest and compliments encouraged the sculptor, and he put all his energies into the work. The oldest member of the League came to the studio one day and said in a simply modest manner that he was ninety-two years old, a Civil War veteran, and "I may pass out at any time." There were several such touching incidents. But on dedication day, Lincoln's Birthday, 1928, that veteran sat at the base of the memorial with an aged comrade, while the sculptor told something of his idea of Lincoln: "a quiet man, a thinker, a man whose natural manner and kindly face were outgrowths of his innate strength of character and confidence of purpose."

Patigian's "Lincoln" sits in a chair of state, leaning forward, his mind busy with the duties and troubles of the war days, his eyes downcast, the right hand fingering the lapel of his coat, with the elbow on the arm of the chair, and his left hand resting on his knee. He seems about to rise, perhaps to see a waiting delegation — numbers of suggestions might be offered as to the summons he is about to answer. The body is right, not "improved" by taking liberties with the chest and shoulders. But the face is the feature of this creation. It is inscrutable, the countenance cannot be read, the mind has not yet reached an answer to his problem. That pose may have been Lincoln's a thousand times as he worked at his desk in the White House. The pondering look seems to be the key to the significance of this work; the sculptor said he wished to present "a thinker." This is not a work to read at a glance. But few who see it even for the first time will hurry on with only a glance. It belongs in the class of the better "Lincolns."

Haig Patigian himself was an impressive and picturesque figure. Born in 1876 in the city of Van, Armenia, where his parents taught in the American Mission School, he has been for many years an American citizen and a distinguished member of that cosmopolitan assemblage which is the population of San Francisco. He describes himself as self-educated in art, and as having studied in Paris with occasional criticism from Alix Marquet. Most of California and other sections of the Pacific coast have been alluded to as "his territory." He has in San Francisco statues of General Pershing and General Funston, of Governor Rolph and Senator Phelan, the Taylor Memorial in the Public Library, the Guardian Angel for a mausoleum, the memorial for the Volunteer Firemen, and various other works. In addition he has in California the McKinley Monument at Arcata, the Rowell Monument at Fresno, and the Eshleman statue for the University of California. In Washington his bust of Herbert Hoover is in the White House, and his statue of Thomas Starr King in Statuary Hall in the Capitol. Many honors have been awarded to him at expositions. He has served on many art juries. His group of figures for the Panama-Pacific Exposition of 1915, representing "Steam Power and Electric Power" and "Invention and Imagination," has been described by a severe critic as "powerful and sincere." Patigian has made many portrait busts, among them one of Helen Wills Moody of lawn-tennis fame. He has created various allegorical groups — "Vanity," "Friendship," and for the Golden Gate Exposition of 1940 heroic figures of

"Rain," "Sunshine," "Harvest," and "The Earth Dormant." A gifted man and a charming companion, he was a sculptor to know, and it was with regret that we learned of his death in the spring of 1950.

SOURCES: Lincoln Grammar School Association, *Lincoln Grammar School,* 1938; courtesy of the San Francisco Public Library; correspondence and personal conversation with Mr. Patigian.

35 ILLUSTRATED PAGE 182

A LINCOLN *for Portland, Oregon, from Paris*

GEORGE FITE WATERS, born in San Francisco in 1894, went in his early years to France, mastered the language, and became so familiar with French ways and ideas that he was often taken for a Parisian. He had studied art in Italy, in London, and with Rodin in Paris. We do not know how he came to be almost an idolatrous admirer of Abraham Lincoln, but friends who knew Waters intimately declare that he read everything — books, pamphlets, newspaper clippings — he could find about Lincoln, and dreamed of a time when he might "portray him in heroic bronze."

Among the friends of the ambitious young sculptor was Lawrence Fernsworth, an American newspaperman, born in Portland, Oregon, who served for several years on the editorial staff of the Paris edition of the *New York Herald.* In 1923 a fellow Oregonian, Dr. Henry Waldo Coe, sojourning in Paris, renewed his acquaintance with Fernsworth, and in conversation Dr. Coe casually alluded to his hope of providing the city of Portland with a statue of Lincoln. Fernsworth, of course, instantly thought of Waters, and brought the two men together.

The result was the heroic "Lincoln" which now occupies a conspicuous site in Portland, where it was unveiled in October, 1928. In Fernsworth's opinion Waters "put all his artistic temperament and feeling into that creation, and it was as much a labor of love as such a work could be." The statue was privately shown to an invited gallery of some five hundred persons, including a number of notables from outside France, on Lincoln's birthday, Saturday, February 12, 1927, and pronounced to be unsurpassed, as the *Herald* reported the critics' verdict. It was the result of two years of hard labor, plus "a lifelong appreciation and love of the great Emancipator." The artist sought to catch the President's pose just after the ending of his Gettysburg speech, "as a powerful figure, yet simple and appealing, revealing the strength and character of the man." Pains were taken for historic accuracy; the life-mask and the casts of the hands were used; and the coat, obtained in Washington and dating back to the Civil War period, is reported to have been worn at the studio "by a young English accountant in Paris, who, by a curious coincidence, possessed the identical body measurements of Abraham Lincoln."

Dr. Coe, born in Wisconsin in 1857, came to Oregon in 1891, and there he founded the Morningside Hospital for the treatment of mental and nervous diseases and served for years as its director, achieving eminence in that field of practice. He gave the city an equestrian statue of Theodore Roosevelt, a replica of an equestrian "Joan of Arc," and an original "Washington," besides the "Lincoln," whose presentation to the city of Portland he did not live to witness; and he had at least one other similar benefaction in mind at the time of his death in 1927.

Only fragmentary references have been found to the work of George Fite Waters. He was both painter and sculptor, and is said to have painted portraits of President William Cosgrove and Prime Minister Eamon de Valera of Ireland for the city of Dublin, and a portrait of Dr. Gordon Hewitt for the National Gallery in Ottawa, Canada. In sculpture he produced the John Brown memorial for the Memorial Park at Osawatomie, Kansas, a bust of General Pershing owned by the French government, and a bust of James K. Hackett for the Shakespeare Memorial Theatre at Stratford-on-Avon. There are obscure references to numerous other works.

The "Lincoln" stands ten feet in height in one of the "park blocks" of Portland, opposite the Masonic Temple. The President stands with his left foot well forward, arms drooping at his sides, and his face lowered, with sadly downcast eyes. One thinks of the face as "sicklied o'er with the pale cast of thought." There is something beguiling, oddly attractive, about the attitude and the countenance. It is not difficult to imagine that Lincoln may have stood thus for a long minute after pronouncing the memorable lines at the cemetery on the site where, a few months before, thousands of furiously fighting men had lost their lives. This is a mournful Lincoln; the face is that of a man who has poured out his heart in behalf of a great cause.

The exercises were simple. In the name of the family of Dr. Coe, the statue was presented to the city by the Rev. William Wallace Youngson, an administrative official of the Methodist Church, and accepted by Mayor George L. Baker. Grand Army Department Commander William Clemmens and Mayor Baker lowered the flags that enfolded the figure. Dr. Titus Lowe, Methodist bishop of the Portland area, made the main address, dwelling on "the extraordinary place Lincoln had come to hold in the minds of thinking men the world over." Tributes were paid to the memory of the generous citizen who had brought this memorial across the ocean.

SOURCES: Correspondence with Messrs. Wayne W. Coe, Lawrence A. Fernsworth, and C. A. Gerken; photostats from the Paris edition of the *New York Herald*.

36 ILLUSTRATED PAGE 183

Isidore Konti's "Subtle" LINCOLN

THE lives of Isidore Konti and Karl Bitter were profitably interwoven. It is pleasant to dwell upon their friendship. They were foreign-born sculptors, each of whom came in early manhood to the United States and achieved distinction in his adopted country. Both were born in Vienna — Konti in 1862, Bitter in 1867; both had to contend with family opposition to their chosen careers, and both wisely concluded to accept the destiny determined for them by Nature. Konti entered the Imperial Academy at the age of sixteen, and finished his studies as the youngest pupil at Professor Karl Kundman's famous Meisterschule. He won several scholarships, among them an award of two years of study in Rome, and came to America in 1890. Bitter enjoyed a few years of study and practice in the applied arts before migrating to the United States late in 1889 or early in 1890. We do not know just when the two men became acquainted, or even whether they first met in the Old World or in the New. Both worked with the great corps of artists assembled from many countries for the Columbian Exposition in Chicago in 1893, and in the same year became associated in New York. Both worked unstintedly on the decorations for the "extraordinary improvisation," the temporary arch in Madison Square to welcome Admiral Dewey on his return from Manila Bay. Bitter's contribution to this arch was the naval group, while Konti made the West Indies and the East and North Rivers groups. Konti established his own studio in 1900.

Bitter rose rapidly to popularity and fame, serving as director of sculpture for the Pan-American Exposition of 1901 at Buffalo, the Louisiana Purchase Exposition of 1904 at St. Louis, and the Panama-Pacific International Exposition of 1915 at San Francisco. Konti was represented at all these expositions by works of high merit. For the courthouse at Cleveland Bitter modeled a seated "Jefferson" and a "Hamilton," and Konti a bronze "Justinian" and an "Alfred the Great." And then it became Konti's duty, accepted as a melancholy privilege, to complete the Pulitzer Fountain for New York City, designed by his compatriot and friend and left unfinished at Bitter's untimely death in 1915. Konti faithfully followed the design, which has been described as "the calm and happy figure of 'Abundance.'"

It would be easy to overstate the relations between these two men, the one slender with a great beard, the other slight in figure and white-bearded, each in many ways reflecting the poetic and buoyant spirit of his native city. Each must have greatly influenced the other, although Bitter, while he lived, was probably the dominant personality.

Konti survived his friend by nearly twenty-four years; his working life in America covered a span of about forty-eight years. His own roster of his works indicates pride in his professional achievements. At the Buffalo exposition his groups for the Temple of Music won many admirers, and the notable contrast of "The Despotic Age," the large group for the Esplanade, showing a callous Caesar with three captives yoked to his chariot, revealed the range of his genius. For the fair at St. Louis he produced a score of groups for two cascade fountains, symbols of the Atlantic and Pacific oceans. The recumbent figure of Morgan Dix in Trinity Church, New York; the ornate tomb of Bishop Horatio Potter of New York in the Cathedral of St. John the Divine, Gothic in style and modeled after the tomb of Edward the Confessor in Westminster Abbey; the memorial in the National Museum in Washington to Kit Carson and Lieutenant Edward Fitzgerald Beale — two men knit together in close friendship, each of whom had saved the life of the other — are included in the extensive list of Konti's creations. The mystical and poetic strain in his nature found expression in the "Orpheus" at the Peabody Institute in Baltimore, in the "Mother and Child" in the Boston Fenway, in the "Genius of Immortality" in the Metropolitan Museum, and in the "Illusion" which was acquired by the Italian government. In Yonkers, New York, where the sculptor made his home for over thirty years, may be seen his fine memorial for the heroes of the first World War; his Spanish War memorial; his Hudson-Fulton memorial; "The Brook," a marble fountain for the estate once owned by Samuel J. Tilden; and his "Lincoln."

This "Lincoln" stands on a moderately high and simple marble pedestal in Memorial Park. The dedication took place on Columbus Day, October 12, 1929. No full account of the ceremony has been found; the program may have been somewhat shortened in order to divide the afternoon with the exercises in Columbus Park. The Gettysburg Address was read; two grandchildren of Civil War veterans unveiled the statue; and the dedication address was delivered by Justice Arthur Sidney Tompkins of the Supreme Court of New York. Due tribute was paid to the sculptor, who had long been recognized as one of the most public-spirited citizens of that suburban community.

The President is here depicted as he might have stood at the close of the Second Inaugural Address, the rolled manuscript held with his right hand against his breast. The left arm and the hand with fingers widely spread suggest the ending of a gesture. The arm is relaxing at his side, the palm open toward his auditors. The left foot is advanced; the head is slightly lowered; the face is deeply marked, and bears a benign and solemn expression. At his back a wrap is thrown over a small table, and resting on this is the high hat with which Lincoln seemed so unwilling ever to dispense. There is a subtle quality about this "Lincoln" which eludes the hurried tourist, but it holds and grows upon the patient and thoughtful observer, who is likely to go away in a pensive mood.

SOURCE: Correspondence with Mrs. Johanna Konti Deutsch.

Crunelle's LINCOLN THE SOLDIER
and LINCOLN THE DEBATER

IN AN address at the unveiling of the Lincoln statue at Dixon, Illinois, in 1930, Dr. Lorado Taft recalled an incident of thirty years before, which he described as "something which had often happened since, but never with the same results." Taft was lecturing at Decatur, and had done some modeling on the stage in his customary manner. At the close a school teacher came forward, with a bright-looking youth in tow. The boy was a coal miner in the town, she said; he had arrived there with his parents not long before from France, where he had grown up in a coal-mining community. He was "obliged to work long hours every day, this lad of seventeen or eighteen. In winter he never saw daylight except on Sunday. . . . But on Sundays he would go to his teacher's studio, and draw, and paint, and play the violin, and, said the teacher, he did them all so beautifully that she thought he ought to have a chance somewhere.

"I could not forget the fine young face," continued Dr. Taft, "and the fact that he understood my French, which was very diplomatic on his part." After a time he sent for the young man to come to Chicago, "and there he cleaned pans, carried water, made plaster, and kept his bright eyes open." After several months the boy brought Taft a package wrapped in newspapers, which contained a beautifully molded baby's head. The astonished master exclaimed, "Leonard, did you really do that?" The young man asked, "Is it good?" So it was in after years with him; he would say, "I hope it is good." "Such modesty," declared the older man, "one seldom meets in the artistic world."

Many interesting facts about the youthful artist were gleaned from him by this master, who all his life was an eager friend of promising aspirants. Leonard Crunelle's home town in France — the statues in the public gardens, the fountains, the decorations in the churches, which his mother used to point out to him — had been completely destroyed during the first World War. That peasant mother must have cherished great dreams about her sons; she named one Michael Angelo, another Raphael, a third Andrea, and for the man who sat near Dr.

Taft as he related these incidents at Dixon, that mother, "trying to bequeath the gifts she did not herself possess," had chosen as a name not "plain Leonard," but "Leonardo."

Crunelle's own statement is that he was born in a coal-mining village near Lens, with the bare additional facts that he had been a pupil of Taft and had studied in the Chicago Art Institute. In his own shy way, however, he could cite with pride a highly creditable list of works. His statue of Richard J. Oglesby stands in Lincoln Park, Chicago, and his statue of another Illinois governor, John McAuley Palmer, in Springfield. In Chicago also are his "Robert Morris," "Haym Salomon," and "Washington." He won the competition for the Washington, D.C., statue of General Artemas Ward, presented to the people of the United States by the President and Fellows of Harvard College in fulfilment of the terms of a will of a New York City resident of the same name as the Revolutionary soldier. The Mayo monument in Rochester, Minnesota, is also Crunelle's, as are many decorations in Chicago parks, numerous medals, tablets, and busts. In Taft's judgment Crunelle has fulfilled the promise of his youth by his "caressing tributes to childhood."

He has also produced two good "Lincolns," presenting him at Dixon as a soldier in the Black Hawk War and at Freeport as the debater with Douglas. It will be convenient to deal with these works not in the order of their dedication but in the chronology of Lincoln's life.

In 1930 the little city of Dixon, Illinois, set aside four September days for its centennial celebration. During the century it had accumulated a rich history. John Dixon had left his home in the East, hoping to recuperate his health in a pioneer country, and settled on the site in 1830, keeping a tavern and operating a ferry across Rock River. Dixon's portrait in relief and several scenes from his pioneering days appear on a large tablet on the base of the Lincoln statue. In 1832 the place, then known as Dixon's Ferry, played an important part in the Black Hawk War. No Indian war in our history has been more written about than this, and with no other are so many famous names associated, three future Presidents — Zachary Taylor, Abraham Lincoln, and Jefferson Davis, president of the Confederacy — having some share in that campaign. A big rock near the Lincoln statue bears a tablet recording Lincoln's service in that war.

Another of the tablets which abound in Dixon marks a spot where Lincoln is said to have stood "while delivering his great speech, September 8, 1858." We have been unable to verify Lincoln's presence in Dixon on that date, but he did speak in Dixon while campaigning for Frémont, on July 17, 1856. At that time a local newspaper described him as "about six feet high, crooked-legged, stoop-shouldered, spare-built, and anything but handsome in the face," at the same time asserting that "as a close observer and cogent reasoner, he has few equals and perhaps no superior in the world. His language is pure and respectful, he attacks no man's character or motives, but fights with arguments."

The original suggestion for marking the site on which the Lincoln statue stands came from Miss Dorothy N. Law, regent of the Dixon chapter of the Daughters of the American Revolution, in 1915. For more than a decade the agitation for a suitable memorial was carried on, but with slow progress. When Louis L. Emmerson became governor, however, the local promoters obtained his backing. A ten-member commission was entrusted with providing "a fitting memorial to commemorate the services of Abraham Lincoln in the Black Hawk War in 1832." State Senator George C. Dixon was chairman of this committee, and among its members were Henry Horner, an ardent Lincolnian, who became governor in 1933; William T. Rawleigh, who had provided Freeport with its "Lincoln" in 1929; Joseph Benjamin Oakleaf of Moline, widely known as one of the "Big Five" collectors of Lincolniana; Frank E. Stevens, historian of the Black Hawk War; and Lorado Taft. This competent group decided what the memorial should be, and chose Leonard Crunelle as sculptor. Governor Emmerson unveiled the statue on September 24, 1930, as a gift by the State of Illinois to the people.

The statue stands in the center of a square atop a pedestal about six feet in height, on the face of which is chiseled the simple title "Lincoln — 1832." The thousands crowded about the monument saw a young man, with an unbuttoned shirt open at the neck, clad in a loose coat and trousers tucked into boots reaching nearly to his knees, his right hand curled around a belt while the left loosely clasps a sword. The young soldier, twenty-three years old, stands squarely on his feet, head high, looking straight forward, with a hint of stern resolution in the set jaw and the closed lips. While we cannot be sure that Captain "Abe" Lincoln carried a sword at any time in those few months of military service, we cannot assert on the basis of any known evidence that he did not. Taft, in his address, lingered upon Crunelle's artistry in thinking out "a new and original version of Lincoln." Expressing the opinion that "this Lincoln wins your sympathy, perhaps your smiles," Taft went on to say that "Abraham Lincoln had his humor and his jests, but under it all was his great power and earnestness. There is a simplicity about that figure that is very becoming to the subject."

Mr. Stevens' historical address outlined the story of the war. Stevens told how, among a lot of papers "buried" in a trunk in a hayloft, he had come upon a precious document, a roster of Lincoln's company in his own handwriting. This, he suggested, might have been written in Dixon.

Extensive advertising by the Centennial Committee had resulted in the discovery of forty-two residents in the Rock River valley born before 1850; of seven persons, three of them residents of Dixon, who had heard one of the Lincoln-Douglas debates in 1858; and of one Dixon resident who had heard Lincoln's speech there in July, 1856. Several of these old residents sat on the platform and were duly introduced.

An hour of easy motoring covers the distance between Dixon and Freeport, where Douglas and Lincoln met for the second time in their series of joint discussions of the issues in their senatorial campaign. A large boulder, three blocks from the business center, carries a tablet informing the visitor that the debate took place "within this block." This marker was erected in 1902 by the Freeport Woman's Club, and President Theodore Roosevelt came to the city in June of the following year for its dedication.

Crunelle's statue of "Lincoln the Debater" stands among the trees in Taylor Park, on a base of roughly hewn red granite. One looks long at that striking figure. There stands the Lincoln of that famous forensic duel, in his usual stance, feet in line and firmly planted, shoulders squared, hands clasped behind his back, head erect, jaw set, eyes level. The pose is challenging, almost defiant. This is the man who does not fear even the "Little Giant," the foremost senator and the most dreaded debater of that day. Lincoln is master of himself, calm, self-possessed, ready to meet his great rival. The spirit of the most celebrated of the seven debates is definitely conveyed by this delineation of the man.

The hands behind the back hold a small roll of papers, a neat touch. The special fame of the Freeport meeting is due, in the main, to Douglas' enunciation on that day, in response to Lincoln's question, of what is known as the "Freeport doctrine." Six days before, at Ottawa, Douglas had propounded what Lincoln called "seven distinct interrogatories," and at Freeport Lincoln began by answering those questions. "In order that there may be no mistake about it," he said, "I have copied the interrogatories in writing, and also my answers." He then proceeded to read the questions one by one, following each with a crisp and definite statement of his own position; then he "propounded to the Judge" — as he invariably called Douglas during that campaign — four "interrogatories" of his own, the second of which elicited from "the Judge" the "Freeport doctrine." There is thus full justification for the little sheaf of papers which the sculptor has put into his "Lincoln's" hands. Moreover, this enables the spectator to time almost precisely the moment Crunelle portrays — Lincoln has just risen to speak, and waits for the applause to subside.

The sculptor may have clothed his Lincoln more elegantly than his accustomed garments would justify. In this statue Lincoln looks every inch a statesman, not merely a frontier politician. Douglas traveled over Illinois with all the comforts and facilities of the time, but his opponent used all sorts of vehicles, including freight cars; his wardrobe could not have been very well cared for, and the campaign had opened some time before the debates began. One Freeport citizen remembered many years afterward Lincoln's wearing "a coarse-looking coat with sleeves far too short, and baggy-looking trousers that were so short that they showed his rough boots," and that "the Douglas men laughed at him and said he would be a nice-looking object to put into the Senate."

The statue was dedicated on August 27, 1929, the seventy-first anniversary of the debate. Several of the speakers dwelt upon the meaning and importance of the "Freeport doctrine." For his historical address Frederick L. Holmes chose the title, "The Fate of the Nation Was Decided That Day at Freeport." Holmes held that the debate would "stand through time as a milestone in the history of the American nation," that from that day "the question of Negro servitude became a moral as well as a political one," and that "out of that occasion spread the fame of Abraham Lincoln's sagacity, resulting in his election to the Presidency and the consequence of civil war." It was Douglas' "Freeport doctrine" that "disrupted the Democratic party into a sectional organization." The donor of the statue, William T. Rawleigh, a Freeport businessman, who had lost his only son in the World

War, speaking with deep feeling, declared that the debate "marked a change in the destinies of this nation and in the lives of both Lincoln and Douglas."

Volumes have been written about the "Freeport doctrine." It involved the issue of the restriction of slavery within its then existing limits, as opposed to the alleged right of extending it into all the nation's territories. The decision of the Supreme Court in the Dred Scott case became a factor in the question. Only ten weeks before the debate, Lincoln had made his "House Divided" speech. Answering Lincoln's question, "Can the people of a United States Territory . . . exclude slavery from its limits prior to the formation of a State Constitution?" Douglas parried with the dictum that "no matter what the decision of the Supreme Court may be on that abstract question, still the right of the people to make a slave territory or a free territory is perfect and complete under the Nebraska bill," which, of course, was Douglas' bill. It is still debated whether Lincoln, in asking that question, looked beyond the senatorial campaign of 1858 to the presidential campaign of 1860; for Douglas' answer alienated the South and precluded the possibility of the "Little Giant's" ever occupying the White House.

The exercises of the dedication day were conducted under the auspices of the Lincoln-Douglas Society of Freeport and Stephenson County. The Wisconsin legislature sent an official delegation, accompanied by a number of citizens, including Philip F. La Follette, who had been designated "chairman of the day." After Mr. Rawleigh presented the statue to the young men and women of the city and county, his two grandsons released the shroud which covered the bronze figure. The principal speaker of the afternoon was Senator George W. Norris of Nebraska, whose glowing tribute declared the name of Abraham Lincoln to be "everywhere in civilization . . . emblematic of human freedom," and went on to discuss many of the problems of the time, with the conclusion that "the spirit of Lincoln still lives, and is sufficient to lead the people to change our fundamental law so as to abolish any form of involuntary servitude regardless of the conditions on which it is based."

More than one hundred fifty persons present at this dedication had heard the Freeport debate or some other of the series. The discovery of these surviving men and women, living in Illinois and elsewhere, was an achievement of the Lincoln-Douglas Society; for weeks a corps of employees had searched them out by correspondence. Lincoln and

Douglas books, pamphlets, and pictures were displayed. The program was worthy of the occasion, and lovely weather greeted the approximately fifteen thousand spectators.

The statue abides in beauty as a reminder of the duties and privileges of American democracy.

SOURCES: A stenographic report of the unveiling at Dixon; Paul M. Angle, *Lincoln Day by Day*, 1854–1861; Edwin Erle Sparks, ed., *The Lincoln-Douglas Debates (Illinois Historical Collections*, Volume III), 1908; *Freeport's Lincoln*, 1930; *Unveiling of the Statue of Major-General Artemas Ward at Washington, D.C.*, 1938.

38   ILLUSTRATED PAGE 186

Bachman's Composite LINCOLN

OF FEW Lincoln sculptors do we know less than we have been able to learn about Max Bachman. Indeed, one may reasonably doubt if he should be included in the list of Lincoln sculptors, for he appears never to have modeled a Lincoln statue. While the towering bronze "Lincoln," so-called, which stands on a high pedestal among the elms at the apex of the Victory Memorial Drive in Minneapolis, is commonly alluded to as Bachman's, it is a composite creation, the head having been modeled by Bachman, and the Boston firm known as "Caproni's" having copied Saint-Gaudens' standing "Lincoln" for the figure. Neither can this composite properly be, as it proudly has been, described as a "replica" of the Saint-Gaudens masterpiece; it may more justly be said that a Lincoln figure based upon the famous statue in Chicago is surmounted by a head carved by Max Bachman. Bachman was with the Caproni firm only a short time, and directories may be searched in vain for his name. But Mr. Leo Toschi, foreman at the Caproni Galleries, who has been with the firm for many years, recalls him well and shows pictures of two Lincoln busts carved by him — one with and one without a beard. Soon after making these busts Bachman went to New York, where he died in 1921.

Bachman is understood to have designed the allegorical figures of the Continents for the Pulitzer Building in New York City, and in a magazine article he is mentioned as the modeler of several busts of subjects not named. It is erroneous to speak of him as "a New England sculptor."

Several plaster duplications of this composite "Lincoln" exist. One is in the Caproni Galleries, at the foot of a cobblestone driveway where visitors cannot avoid seeing it. Another stands in a school building in Boston. Still another stands in the courthouse in the Illinois city named for Abraham Lincoln. Lincolnians there state frankly that the statue is "neither bronze, marble, nor stone," but plaster of Paris, "a composite replica of body by Saint-Gaudens and head by Max Bachman," obtained from "the Caproni Galleries, Inc., Boston." The discovery of these facts solved several questions which have puzzled Lincoln students.

The Minnesota units of the Grand Army of the Republic presented the Minneapolis statue to that city. A Lincoln Monument Association, organized in 1916, had accumulated over a period of years about $7,500 for the memorial, eight hundred dollars of which was contributed in pennies by schoolchildren. Memorial Day, 1930, was a great day for the veterans who had survived to witness the climax of their patient labors. Governor Theodore Christianson said in his dedicatory address that President Lincoln "must have had a tender regard for Minnesota," since "in 1860 Minnesota had but 172,000 people, yet it furnished more than 22,000 men to the Union armies." The governor considered it appropriate that Abraham Lincoln should stand on the Memorial Drive, "where living trees, row on row, commemorate the sons of the new day who gave their lives on foreign shores for the same cause of freedom and unity."

SOURCES: *Journal of the Illinois State Historical Society*, October, 1930; Art Department, Minneapolis Public Library.

39   ILLUSTRATED PAGE 187

Fraser's LINCOLN THE MYSTIC

THE Lincoln monument at the Boulevard entrance to Lincoln Park in Jersey City, New Jersey, was dedicated on June 14, 1930. On that occasion Howard R. Cruse, chairman of the Monument Committee, said in his presentation address: "Mr. John Hay, Lincoln's secretary, told Mr. James Earle Fraser, the sculptor, that during the early days of the Civil War, when things were new to the chief magistrate and when his problems and burdens were multiplying so rapidly, the

President formed the habit of going at sunset to an eminence over-looking the national capitol, and there, seated on a rock, in solitude and meditation, he fortified his faith that 'right makes might,' held communion with the Eternal, and found the strength to bear his burdens and the wisdom to solve his problems. He said: 'The purposes of the Almighty are perfect and must prevail. In times of trial I have felt his hand upon me and submitted to his guidance.' This conception of Lincoln, the solitary thinker, the bearer of burdens, the keeper of a deathless faith and the servant of God, stirred the soul of the artist, and he has immortalized it in bronze."

We are disposed to question the accuracy of this account in a few details. No other source is known to us as an authority for this habit. John Hay died in 1905. Several errors respecting this statue were recorded in the press while the campaign for its erection was under way. Late in 1928 a local newspaper stated that the statue represented Abraham Lincoln as he appeared when he passed through Jersey City enroute to Washington in 1861, and went on to say that "it was a smooth-shaven Lincoln who visited New Jersey and was inaugurated President," with the additional bit of misinformation that Lincoln "never wore a beard until the last three years of his life." The Lincoln of this monument is in fact beardless, yet the Lincoln who is said to have gone alone, as the paper further informed its readers, to "an eminence overlooking Washington" and there to have watched "the lights of the city" while he "pondered over the problems of the strife-ridden nation," had acquired a beard in the months immediately preceding his inauguration. It would have been extremely difficult for him, in the first year of his presidency, to have gone habitually to some hill over-looking Washington to linger alone while night fell upon the city. Only one possibility occurs to the writer: in summer, when the President rode out to the Anderson cottage in the grounds of the Soldiers' Home to spend his nights, either with an escort or at other times without a bodyguard, he might occasionally have left the road and gone alone to a convenient spot for observation and quiet. Although we are willing to accept the statement atributed to John Hay as true in part, we understand that during the first summer of the war the Lincolns remained at the White House.*

* Adeline Adams, writing of James Earle Fraser in the revised edition of Lorado Taft's *History of American Sculpture,* expresses the opinion that this "Lincoln" is intended to depict "the beginning of a great life," and shows the President "in his younger days of poetic vision, of promise rather than fulfilment."

The Jersey City Lincoln Association is rightly proud of its record as the oldest Lincoln association in the United States, and "the one association," as William Walter Phelps said at its annual dinner in 1888, "that has never failed to celebrate the birthday of Abraham Lincoln since his assassination" — a statement said to be true today. At the Association's annual dinner on February 12, 1926, Mr. Cruse offered a resolution, unanimously adopted by the 123 members present, for the initiation of the memorial enterprise. Under his chairmanship, committees were appointed to make plans and to raise $60,000. The first check sent in was for $100.00, closely followed by one for $5,000 from three brothers doing business together in the city. At the 1929 meeting of the Association it was announced that the schoolchildren had contributed $3,500 in pennies, nickels, and dimes. Ground was broken for the foundations of the monument in December, 1928; the cornerstone was laid on the following Memorial Day; and at the sixty-fifth annual dinner of the Association in 1930 the successful completion of the project was announced. In his remarks that evening Mr. Cruse informed the members that he had consulted Daniel Chester French regarding the choice of a sculptor, and that Fraser had been selected largely on French's recommendation. Before the dedication day the newspapers reported that Mr. Cruse had demonstrated his faith in the success of the movement by signing on his own responsibility contracts for $35,000 with the sculptor and for $25,000 for granite, at a time when actual collections were only $18,000.

The intention from the outset had been that the monument should be placed at the entrance to what was then called West Side Park on the Hudson Boulevard, at the point "where the Lincoln Highway swings westward for its real start for the Pacific coast." This was a county park. Upon application, the Park Commissioners consented to the plan, and changed the name to Lincoln Park. The actual overall cost of the monument was $75,000, "exclusive of the subsurface foundation" contributed by the Hudson County Park Commission, of which Mr. Cruse was a member.

The work which earned for Mr. Fraser the largest measure of his early fame stands in the Presidio at San Francisco. An Indian warrior in an attitude of mental despair and physical exhaustion bestrides a tottering horse. The heads of man and animal are bowed. The point of a long spear has fallen to the ground. A horse and rider who might once have ranged a continent have reached the insurmountable barrier of the western ocean. The work is a poem in bronze, whose tragic eloquence few could fail to understand. It portrays the ultimate defeat of a vanquished and vanishing race. Prairies had been traversed, rivers spanned, mountains crossed, but the Indian could no longer defy his destiny. The sculptor named this work "The End of the Trail." Only a gifted artist, and one who also knew the American Indian, could have produced it.

James Earle Fraser was born in Minnesota. His father, one of the engineers who directed the building of the Northern Pacific Railroad across the Dakotas, took his son along to the construction camps, where the boy came into intimate contact with the Indians. He made friends with them, and throughout his manhood years the impressions they made upon his plastic mind endured. At eighteen young Fraser entered the Chicago Art Institute; two years later he was studying in France, and in 1898 won a first prize for the best work in sculpture, offered by the American Art Association of Paris. Augustus Saint-Gaudens liked Fraser's work and invited the younger sculptor to become an assistant in the studio where Saint-Gaudens was creating his famous "Sherman." The older man remained through life a steadfast friend of the younger, who is now a trustee of the Saint-Gaudens Memorial at Cornish.

Fraser is known in the art world as a man of remarkable industry and versatility. His Ericcsson memorial, and his "Hamilton" in front of the Treasury Building, are in Washington; his John Hay memorial is in Cleveland, his "Jefferson" in Jefferson City, Missouri, and his recumbent figure of Bishop Henry Codman Potter in the Cathedral of St. John the Divine in New York. For the Bank of Montreal he made a monumental "Victory"; the beautiful work picturing the "Journey through Life" is in Rock Creek Cemetery in Washington; and a crouching figure pouring water over a wheel, representing "The Primitive Inventor of Water Power," stands before the City Hall in Niagara Falls.

Several thousand people witnessed the dedication ceremonies of the Jersey City "Lincoln" on Flag Day, 1930. Commander Frank A. Cole of Van Houten Post of the G.A.R., who had enlisted at fifteen and had "dreamed of a Lincoln Monument for more than three score years," unveiled the statue. As the flag fell, revealing the figure, Comrade Walter Tully, a cavalryman who had been a member of Lincoln's bodyguard, placed a wreath before it. Following an address by Governor

Morgan F. Larson, the presentation speech was made by Mr. Cruse. "We present this memorial to the public," he said, "sensible that for a thousand years it will tell to succeeding generations the story, and proclaim to mankind the social ideals, of the most luminous life in American history."

The oration of the day was delivered by Dr. John Wesley Hill, chancellor of Lincoln Memorial University. One by one he suggested what Lincoln's views would have been on the living problems of that day. He quoted the familiar affirmation that "all the armies of Europe, Asia and Africa combined . . . could not by force take a drink from the Ohio or make a track on the Blue Ridge in a trial of a thousand years" (the atomic age was not dreamed of in Lincoln's day). "With Lincoln progress was only another name for growth, expressed in evolution, not revolution, free from violence and destruction." Lincoln knew "the difference between progress and motion. He would not attempt to rebuild the world overnight." In international matters, Lincoln "had breathed into the soul of the world a dream of peace with justice for all mankind."

The monument thus dedicated is one of the most imposing of all the Lincoln memorials. The seated figure is ten feet in height, resting upon a boulder which stands on a circular base in the center of a sweeping semicircle of red granite fifty feet in width, which is approached by easy steps. There Lincoln sits with his thoughts, face lowered and hands folded between his knees. The sculptor once told a newspaper writer: "I particularly wanted to make a sympathetic and human study of Lincoln. There are so many 'President Lincolns,' and I hoped that I might create something that would give an idea of his outdoor personality. . . . I have learned that he did much of his thinking outdoors. . . . His many-sided genius always astonishes me, and when I remember that he accomplished all he did before he was fifty-six years of age, and consider the remarkable qualities of his writings, I am amazed."

The architectural features of the base were designed by Albert Randolph Ross. Inside the granite semicircle are chiseled the famous phrases from the Second Inaugural, "With malice toward none, with charity for all." Below the inscription a wide bench invites the visitor to linger in quiet thoughtfulness. Upon the huge blocks at the ends of this exedra are inscribed respectively the final clauses of the Gettysburg Address and the closing sentence of the Cooper Institute speech, each quotation flanked by Roman fasces. The total effect of this structure, in which artist and architect have happily collaborated, is notably enhanced by the lawn before the monument and the shrubbery at its back, with their contrasts of color.

In his oration Dr. Hill named this statue "Lincoln the Mystic," and that title has been adopted as though by referendum. It is apt and right, and should endure.

SOURCES: Letters and clippings loaned by Howard R. Cruse; information supplied by James Earle Fraser; Beatrice Gilman Proske, *Brookgreen Gardens Catalogue;* Charles E. Fairman, *Works of Art in the United States Capitol,* 1913; Margaret Leach, *Reveille in Washington,* 1941; reprint of John Wesley Hill's dedication address in the *Congressional Record* of June 14, 1930.

40

ILLUSTRATED PAGE 188

The "Sculptor of Industrial America"

LINCOLN's birthday in 1932 was also Children's Day for three thousand pupils in the public schools of Cleveland, Ohio, for their pennies had provided a major portion of the fund for the Lincoln statue by Max Kalish which was unveiled on that day. The jubilant throng of children, confronted by Harold H. Burton, acting mayor of Cleveland and later to become United States Senator and Associate Justice of the Supreme Court, presiding at the ceremonies in the Public Music Hall, were aware of the significance of the occasion. "Does America have a king?" asked Burton. A great volley of "No's" replied. "Who does in our country what kings do in other countries?" The laughing children shouted back, "The President." "And how do we get the President?" "We elect him." "Who elect him?" And the youngsters, in the loudest chorus of that antiphonal exercise, thundered back, "The People." Burton, with every eye on him and all ears alert, went on to remind those young people, representing all grades in the public schools, of the foundation principles of our democracy, and outlined for them the life of Abraham Lincoln.

For nine years a Lincoln Memorial Commission had been at work on the project. On behalf of this Commission, Rabbi A. H. Silver presented the statue to the city and to the Board of Education, and it was accepted by acting Mayor Burton for the city and by E. M. Williams, president of the Board of Education, on the Board's behalf. The principal address was made by the Rev. Joel Babcock Hayden, headmaster of Western Reserve Academy. At the conclusion of the indoor exercises the audience was dismissed to reassemble with thousands of men and women waiting before the memorial in front of the School Administration Building. Miss Helen Green of East Cleveland, a descendant of Samuel Lincoln of Hingham, Massachusetts, the Civil War President's first American ancestor, drew the cords which released the flags that had draped the statue.

The sculptor of this "Lincoln," Max Kalish, was born in Poland in 1891. His death in 1945 was lamented not only by his confrères in the art world, but also by thousands of plain laborers who knew of him as the sculptor of industrial America. His impressive portrayals of the muscular power, the skillful manipulations, and the intelligence, with which labor performs tremendous tasks, reveal his sympathetic insight and challenge the attention of patriotic Americans. He has opened the eyes of many to the grace with which a brawny workman swings his sledge, the nice balance with which he poises high in the air on the steel frame of a skyscraper, the beauty of the smile on his sweat-smeared face as he responds to the greeting of his child on arriving home after a day of toil. To turn the pages of an album picturing his works is an educative pleasure — these are photographs of men derived from many lands, Americans all, who have laid the material foundations for our way of life. The names which the sculptor gave his works suggest the quality of the man, the field in which he found his themes, and his understanding of the lives of the working masses — "The Electric Riveter," "The Telephone Linesman," "The Lumberjack," "The Iron Forger," "The Water Carrier," and other works with such titles as "Power," "Resting," "Fatigue" and "Unemployed." Kalish also did fine things in other fields; for instance, "The Angry Christ and the Traders in the Temple," and pictures of children.

The story of Lincoln would appeal to such an artist. Kalish moulded a Lincoln head, and was proud to have his heroic bronze "Lincoln at Gettysburg" set up in the city in whose public schools he had obtained his early education. He studied in the Cleveland School of Art, then in New York with Herbert Adams, Isidore Konti, and C. S. Pietro, and finally won high honors in Paris.

Of his "Lincoln" the sculptor said on dedication day: "I have tried to present Lincoln in the act of delivering his immortal address at Gettysburg. I wanted to give a glimpse of the soul of the great man as he consecrated himself to carry on the cause for which the soldiers died." The President stands with the right leg swung forward, the right arm hanging at full length and swinging a little away from the body, with the hand held palm outward. The left hand holds at his side an unfolded sheet of paper. The body is stretched to its full length, and the head is held high. Below Lincoln's feet, in three panels, is chiseled the full Gettysburg Address. Lincoln may well have looked like this portrait when he uttered the closing phrases of that speech. All we know about its delivery is that he spoke with great deliberation. We may be fairly sure that he made no sweeping gestures. He may have finished in a pose somewhat like this sculpture. And the face! Intense emotion, deep lines, eyes looking upward but seeing nothing except his dream for the future of mankind. That theme dominated Lincoln's life. He was expressing in the simplest possible terms the key to his Presidency. There is action in the statue, but not too much. The face, strained and intense, with the chiseled words below, conveys his message.

SOURCES: Correspondence with Mrs. Alice N. Kalish; courtesies by the Cleveland Public Library, Mr. Carl W. Schafer, and Mr. Lawrence Lockwood; M. Landon Lewis, *The Sculpture of Max Kalish*, 1933.

41   ILLUSTRATED PAGE 189

Manship's LINCOLN, THE HOOSIER YOUTH

IN 1905, Mr. Arthur F. Hall, founder of a now well known insurance company then about to commence business, said in explanation of the name borne by the company: "We want a name so proud that men and officers will give their lives to keep it stainless. We want a name so simple and strong that the whole world will love it. There is only one name in the world that will fill these requirements." That name was Abraham Lincoln. Robert Todd Lincoln gave the company permission to use a portrait of his father as its insignia.

The Lincoln National Life Insurance Company began, twenty-four years later, the publication of a series of weekly broadsides entitled *Lincoln Lore*, over eleven hundred of which have now been issued. These are known and welcomed by all Lincolnians and by a multitude of general readers besides. In February, 1931, the company established and endowed the Lincoln National Life Foundation "to perpetuate an active interest in the life of Abraham Lincoln, to inspire in all a keener appreciation of Lincoln's ideals, and to contribute to Lincoln lore through original study and research." This Foundation continued and expanded the work which had been carried on for several years by the company's Historical Research Foundation, under the direction of Dr. Louis A. Warren, an indefatigable and able Lincolnian, whose book on Lincoln's parentage and childhood, published in 1926, had lifted him to an enviable altitude among Lincoln authorities. Through its great Lincoln collections and in manifold other ways the Foundation has placed all Lincoln students under heavy obligations for assistance. In 1928 the company awarded Paul Manship a $75,000 commission for the creation of a Lincoln statue to be erected in front of the company's building in Fort Wayne, Indiana.

Manship's first "one-man exhibition," in 1916, was a remarkable collection of sculptures, original in conception and skillful in execution, obviously the product of "an infinitude of painstaking." One critic, in a careful study of the sculptor's work, said that this display "created a veritable sensation." *Sculpteur Américain*, a book by Paul Vitry, *Conservateur* of Medieval and Modern Sculpture in the Louvre, published in Paris ten years later, dealt *in extenso* with Manship's production up to that time, listing a surprising number of works representing an unusual variety of styles with a wide range of subjects. There were medals, statuettes, small groups, war memorials, American Revolutionary heroes in bronze, Greek heroes and deities in marble, works with such imaginative and suggestive titles as "The Flight of Night," "The Cycle of Life," "The Lyric Muse," "The Elements — Earth, Water, Fire, Air," and others on such conventional themes as "Centaur and Dryad" and "Satyr and Sleeping Nymph." A roster of Manship's works to the present time would include many more, among them the "Anadyomene Fountain" and the "Armillary Sphere" at Phillips Academy, Andover, Massachusetts; the "Prometheus Fountain" in Rockefeller Center; the War Memorial at Thiacourt, France; and a group for a mausoleum in Père Lachaise in Paris.

Paul Manship began his art studies in 1885 at the Institute in St.

Paul, Minnesota, his birthplace, and continued at the Pennsylvania Academy of Fine Arts. He won the Prix de Rôme and spent the years 1909–1912 in Italy. As a "permanent reminiscence" of his student days in Rome there stands in the center courtyard of the American Academy a fountain which fellow artists have long regarded as a beguiling and original work. Manship was therefore already a veteran of international fame when he undertook the statue of Lincoln as a Hoosier youth for the Lincoln enthusiasts in Fort Wayne.

Manship worked on this commission in studios in both Paris and New York. More than five years elapsed before the statue was ready for unveiling. The sculptor toured the Lincoln country with Dr. Warren, visiting the childhood homes in Kentucky and the boyhood home in Spencer County, Indiana; he read many books, conferred with Carl Sandburg, and talked with Ida Tarbell. The Lincoln Manship would portray had left Indiana at the age of twenty-one, having lived in the woods with an axe at hand throughout his years in Hoosierdom. An axe must, therefore, be an accessory for the monument; the sculptor copied his axe from photographs in the Oliver R. Barrett Collection of Lincolniana. The boots worn by the bronze youth have been criticized — would not moccasins have been more authentic? The artist felt that Lincoln probably wore boots, and he might have found good authority in a statement attributed to Lincoln himself that he was equipped with substantial "shoes" — which may well have been boots — on the trek to Illinois.

But, it has been asked, did Lincoln own a dog? While we do not know whose dog nuzzles at the young man's side in the memorial, we do know that there was a dog with the party of thirteen persons who crossed an icy stream in 1830 in moving to Illinois. Herndon tells how the animal was left behind at the crossing, and how "Abe," refusing to abandon it, pulled off his shoes and socks, waded the stream, "and triumphantly returned with the shivering animal" under his arm. So, when Manship crossed the ocean again to Paris, he took along a hound "from across the Ohio River from the place of Lincoln's youth, and . . . just the type" he needed, to serve as a model for his bronze dog.

Evidently the artist was taking his time and doing his work with care. He had a preliminary sketch in plastic ready for inspection in 1929; the plaster model was completed in Paris in November, 1931; the casting was done in Brussels; and the statue was dedicated on September 16, 1932.

The statue stands between the wings of the company's office building in Fort Wayne; the base divides the broad steps before the colonnaded central block, directly in front of the main entrance. The figure of Lincoln is twelve feet six inches in height, and the total height above the pavement is twenty-two feet. Each face of the square pedestal carries a heavy bronze medallion, elaborately wrought, suggesting respectively the cardinal traits attributed to Lincoln — charity, fortitude, justice, and patriotism. This pedestal rests on a granite base, designed by the sculptor and the architect of the building, Benjamin Wistar Morris, to conform in style and color with the Indiana limestone of the building itself. The statue is of light verdigris, with the same harmonization in view. The Federal Building, made of the same material and designed by the same architect, stands across the street from the insurance company's building.

Lincoln, clad in linsey-woolsey shirt and butternut trousers, rests at ease against an oak stump, axe at his side, his right hand holding a book into which the index finger is thrust to mark his page, while the left hand rests upon the head of the dog. The monograph issued by the company describing this statue declares that "Paul Manship had the difficult task of creating not only a fanciful statue but one which would represent a plausible likeness easily recognized as that of Lincoln in his youth. At first he thought the task impossible of achievement, but, happily, he finally attained a masterpiece which is satisfying not only to himself but to all those who have seen it. In it we have the earnestness and seriousness of thoughtful youth, and we also see the melancholy aspect which was characteristic of the subject throughout his lifetime, and which has been depicted by the artist with rare subtlety."

We have more than once wished for an opportunity to study the face at closer range. The study of photographs, with the aid of magnifying glasses, has proved rewarding. The book has carried the earnest youth to a distant realm, which faraway region the forces which he feels dimly within himself may enable him some day to visit. He is dreaming of the land of America's youth. The poise of that lifted head and the look in those shadowed eyes are attractive — suggestive — impressive.

Dedication day had something of the aspect of an all-Fort-Wayne day. The unveiling exercises began half an hour after noon; a Lincoln luncheon, with a series of nine short addresses, was scheduled for two o'clock; and at three the Superintendent of Schools conducted a program in the plaza about the memorial, with thousands of schoolchildren in attendance. At the unveiling exercises Dr. Joseph R. Sizoo, pastor of the New York Avenue Presbyterian Church of Washington, D.C., which President Lincoln had attended, read in connection with his address a personal message from the widow of Robert Todd Lincoln, and Senator James E. Watson of Indiana brought a message from President Hoover. President Arthur F. Hall of the company made the presentation speech.

"And now we are prepared to lift the veil," he said in conclusion. "Who shall have that honor? Lincoln, himself a man of history, as President surrounded himself with men who also made history. Among the members of his Cabinet was Hugh McCulloch, first Comptroller of the Currency. Mr. McCulloch was Secretary of the Treasury under three different Presidents. The five-year-old lad who is to lift the veil is the grandson of the speaker, the great-grandson of the chairman of our Board [Samuel M. Foster], and the great-great-grandson of Hugh McCulloch. I present to you now Arthur Fletcher Hall, the third, of a line direct from Lincoln's Cabinet, who will unveil to the world Paul Manship's masterpiece, 'Abraham Lincoln, the Hoosier Youth.'" The draperies fell, the band played, the crowd cheered, and the rifle corps fired a presidential salute.

Among the luncheon speakers were Dr. Otto L. Schmidt, president of the Illinois State Historical Society; the Honorable Logan Hay, president of the Abraham Lincoln Association of Springfield, Illinois; and Miss Ida M. Tarbell, writer of many Lincoln books and papers. The satisfaction with which Miss Tarbell's address must have been heard comes home to us as we read her remarks: "Here you have a son of the Republic, one who early dreamed its dream. Freedom for all men to be secured by the union of all men was the substance of Abraham Lincoln's faith. He put it into simple terms — the right of all men to eat the bread they earn. Coupled with that right was the responsibility to earn the bread they eat. As he saw the Republic there was no place in it either for slave or for parasite. . . .

"He was the universal friend, the universal humorist. This friendliness, this humor, were so much a part of him that no burden, no sorrow, could check their natural flow. And he had no stronger allies in the dreadful days of the Civil War. His task must be done with men — all sorts of men. He saw early that he must not ask of them what was not in them to give. He must find what each could do; he must even, as he once said, use the meanness of men for the public good. Men might fool him for a time, but never long. His insight into motives was uncanny. He sensed the contempt in which many a man held him on first sight — sensed jealousy — intrigue — treachery — and again and again outwitted them — established himself, but kept his victory to himself. These men were necessary to the country. They were great men although they might not believe in his fitness, accept his judgments. With rare and unselfish humility and understanding he endured more than once the wrath of the country for losses, failures for which he was not responsible, rather than weaken popular faith in the man responsible. . . . So he could be patient, and as the years, with their torturing sorrows, went by, he learned what was not easy for him — natural satirist and lampooner that he was — to speak no harsh or bitter word of any man, which meant he must think no harsh or bitter thought. Before the end he came to that supreme self-conquest."

Nothing that Miss Tarbell ever wrote better illustrates her own penetration than these epigrams. Her words match the message, and possibly go beyond the message, which the gifted sculptor sought to communicate through his own medium of expression.

SOURCES: Several brochures issued by the Lincoln National Life Insurance Company, particularly the quarto *Lincoln: the Hoosier Youth,* 1933; A. E. Gallatin, *Paul Manship — A Critical Essay on His Sculpture and an Iconography,* 1917; Paul Vitry, *Paul Manship: Sculpteur Américain,* Paris, 1927; correspondence with Dr. Louis A. Warren, Lincoln National Life Foundation, Fort Wayne, Indiana.

A LINCOLN
"You Can't Run By"

MEMORIAL services were held at the grave of Alexander New in Wabash, Indiana, on the day that the Lincoln statue modeled by Charles Keck and presented by Mr. New to the city was unveiled there. New was born in Wabash County, and his friends said that he "always lived in Wabash," so often did he refer to it as his "home town," though his manhood years were spent elsewhere. In New York he was called "Judge" New, a title derived from his service on the bench in Kansas City, whence he had gone East to reorganize the H. B. Claflin stores. He then began the development of a powerful business organization, the Mercantile Stores Company, of which he was president, owning twenty-three department stores. Mr. New was Jewish and proud of his race and family. He gave the Lincoln statue to Wabash in honor of his father and mother, both of whom were born in Bavaria. The services at his grave, short and simple though they were, and with a relatively small number of persons present, must have been as impressive as was the ceremony for the unveiling of the "Lincoln." A eulogy of the race to which New belonged was blended with the tribute to the man: "Alexander New was a worthy son of a noble race whose members while scattered abroad over the face of the earth, without homeland, nation or flag, have steadfastly maintained their integrity and are still able to call humbly upon God in perfect faith and confidence, and to say, with David of old, 'The Lord is my shepherd.'" The onlookers, mostly members of New's race, recited the Twenty-third Psalm, and in a reverent spirit joined in the ceremonies that day in honor of the martyred President of their adopted country.

The interview which brought about the erection of this bronze "Lincoln" in Wabash took place in Alexander New's New York office. The sculptor had been invited to discuss with New the production of an appropriate memorial for the latter's father and mother. Right at the outset, however, New posed the question which revealed quite clearly that he had made up his mind as to what the monument should be. "How would you interpret Abraham Lincoln?" he asked. That was "no easy problem to solve on a moment's notice," said Mr. Keck. The sculptor suggested that he make sketches from which a choice might be made, and when he returned he brought three designs — a standing "Lincoln," a "Lincoln" seated in a chair, and a "Lincoln" seated on a rock. Mr. New went to the studio to see the designs, bringing with him Frederick H. Meserve, the Lincolnian whose avocation for many years has been the collection and study of Lincoln photographs. They liked all three designs, but Keck suggested that the "Lincoln" seated in a chair be discarded "to eliminate all disturbing and distracting elements, leaving only the figure of Lincoln." Having developed the other two designs in larger size, Keck invited New and Meserve again to his studio. He tells us that "Mr. Meserve spoke very highly of the standing figure, and Mr. New was ready to agree with him — but Mr. Meserve asked him to wait, and when he had finished speaking of the standing figure, he turned to the other one and said, 'But this is an inspiration.' And that definitely settled the question."

There could be no doubt of Charles Keck's competence to create an outstanding "Lincoln." He was born in New York, studied at the National Academy of Design and the Art Students' League in that city and in the American Academy in Rome, having won the Prix de Rôme in 1899 in open competition at the age of twenty-four. For several years Keck was an assistant to Saint-Gaudens, and he refers gratefully to the helpful interest with which that master followed his subsequent career. Keck has done memorable work in many fields of art, producing statues, busts, tablets, medals, bas-reliefs, sarcophagi, pediment sculptures, and architectural decorations, all in bewildering profusion. His equestrian "Stonewall Jackson" and the "Lewis and Clark" group, both at Charlottesville, Virginia, have won universal applause. His equestrian "Andrew Jackson" is in Kansas City, his "Booker T. Washington" at Tuskegee, Alabama, and "John Mitchell," Keck's bronze statue of the miners' leader, stands at Scranton, Pennsylvania. For the façade of the Brooklyn Museum he made the "Mohammed" to represent the Genius of Islam; in Times Square, New York, stands his "Father Duffy."

Among Keck's symbolic figures are the "America" for the Allegheny County Soldiers' Memorial in Pittsburgh, the "Liberty" at Ticonderoga, New York, and the "Victory" in Montclair, New Jersey. In South America Mr. Keck is represented by a "Washington" in Buenos Aires, and in Rio de Janeiro by a large female figure symbolizing "Friendship," with the flags of the United States and Brazil tied together with palm and laurel. The original design for this Brazilian monument called for statues of Washington and Lincoln, and of two Brazilians, with several bas-reliefs, but conditions following the first World War interfered with raising the necessary funds; so, after the figure of "Friendship" had remained in storage for several years, it was finally erected without the other statues — first on a simple base, later on a more imposing one, not designed by Keck, the cost of which was met by American importers and citizens living in Rio de Janeiro.

The Wabash "Lincoln" was dedicated on Memorial Day, 1932, in the presence of a huge throng massed on the courthouse lawn. The usual ritual was carried out, with singing and the placing of wreaths by schoolchildren; the releasing of the covering flags by Mrs. Jeannette New Blumenthal and Mrs. Netta New Myers; brief addresses by two of the donor's business associates, and a more extended address by Frank E. Jaynes, in which he took exception to the clamor for "living memorials" instead of "useless monuments" in commemoration of those who lost their lives in the service of their country. "There are such things as faith, dreams, and ideals which are of infinite value," said Jaynes, and Mr. New had presented the city with "an imperishable gift."

In 1939, in Hingham, Massachusetts, was dedicated a replica of this statue, also the gift of a businessman. Everett E. Whitney, who died in December, 1937, directed by his will the use of a stipulated sum for its purchase, requesting that it be erected on a designated site and prescribing the inscriptions for the pedestal. His wishes were fully complied with. The monument was placed in the center of a grass plot, roughly triangular in shape, amid fine old elm trees. It was at Hingham, at the foot of Boston Harbor, be it remembered, that Samuel Lincoln, first American ancestor of Abraham, lived from 1637 until his death in 1690. Hingham's Old Ship Church contains a pew marked with a tablet informing visitors that the first of the American Lincolns worshipped in that meetinghouse from its erection in 1681. Upon the front face of the pedestal of the statue is chiseled the name LINCOLN, with the familiar phrases from the Second Inaugural, "With malice toward none, with charity for all," duplicating the inscription at Wabash. At the rear is cut the record of the origin of the monument: "This monument is presented to the citizens of Hingham by Everett E. Whitney in fond memory of his father, Jason W. Whitney, his mother,

Lydia A. Whitney, his wife, Katherine A. Whitney, his son, Jason McC. Whitney."

In his dedication address on September 23, Dr. Louis A. Warren of Fort Wayne, Indiana, presented a carefully composed and excellent survey of Abraham Lincoln's relations with New England. He recalled the important services the Lincolns had performed as citizens of Hingham, mayors of Boston, governors of Massachusetts, and members of Congress. He reviewed the circumstances under which the New England Thanksgiving festival had been nationalized by President Lincoln. "Here in the very town where his forebears first established their family circles in the New World," ended Warren, most appropriately, "and in the very front yard of Samuel Lincoln, his first American progenitor, Abraham Lincoln has come back to dwell among his kinsmen, to remind us all of those sacred institutions which have contributed so much to the spiritual uplift of the nation."

This statue has been pronounced the most beautiful of all the sculptured portraits of Abraham Lincoln. Beautiful it is, so beautiful that many have criticized the artist for having "prettified" a man who was not handsome. There is substance in both these judgments. The bronze face and figure are beguiling in their beauty; the work is smooth, the angles are rounded; beholders are charmed by its contours. This is not the Lincoln whose days of decision and nights of agony deepened the lines of his bearded face. Keck presents a contemplative Lincoln, in an hour of placid repose.

The sculptor himself has told an admirer of the ideas he sought to express. Lincoln is portrayed in a simple and meditative attitude. The right hand hanging loosely over the leg "suggests the human and compassionate character of the man"; the clenched left hand "expresses the determination to do what he considers to be right." The feet are "apart and relaxed." The intention is to center attention on the hands and face. Lincoln sits upon a rock to "indicate the great outdoors of which he was a part." The simplest possible pedestal intensifies the effect of the whole.

One observer, a thoughtful man with a background of information, having spent many minutes scanning the downcast face, sent word to a friend that "you can't run by that statue; you have to stop and listen to it." As he gazed upward into the face, the muscles seemed to relax and the eyes "to rise a wee bit," as though the "sun-flooded features were breaking into a smile" as a reward for the visitor's sympathy.

Presently the eyes "became thoughtful again, but never hard, as though the old burdens had nudged him again, and he must think of them and not of you." Many sincere observers may well envy the emotional capacity which enables some persons to see such things. Only those who are willing to tarry in the presence of a genuine work of art ever can see them, and they must develop the understanding mood.

Another "Lincoln" by Keck was unveiled by the New York City Housing Authority on February 12, 1949. This work is placed in the center of The Abraham Lincoln Houses, a low-rent housing project in Harlem which provides homes for nearly thirteen hundred families, in a "recreation area" near a large playground for Negro children whose homes are near at hand. The work is a group in bronze, showing the bearded President seated on a boulder with one arm around a young Negro boy, who looks into the face of the great man with reverence and trust. The sculptor's title for this group is simply "Lincoln and Boy."

SOURCES: Louis A. Warren, *A Lincoln Memorial to Thanksgiving*, 1939; Beatrice G. Proske, *Brookfield Gardens Catalogue of Sculpture*, 1936; correspondence with Mr. Charles Keck.

"In Austere Simplicity"

IN 1859 Abraham Lincoln definitely became a candidate for the Republican presidential nomination to be made the following year. During the lustrum beginning with 1854 Lincoln had delivered public addresses outside his own state only twice — once in Michigan in 1856, and again in Iowa in 1858. But in 1859 he spoke five times in Ohio, once in Indiana, once in Iowa, at least five times in Kansas, probably once in Missouri, and three times in Wisconsin. The Wisconsin speeches were delivered at Milwaukee on September 30, and at Beloit and Janesville on the following day. Lincoln visited the state in response to an invitation to address the Wisconsin State Agricultural Society at the Milwaukee Fair Grounds. He understood perfectly the political value of appearing in a region where the German vote would be important — four months previously he had quietly obtained control of a German newspaper published in Springfield, to assure its support of the Republican candidate and party in 1860.

Though in March and again in April of 1859 Lincoln had written Thomas J. Pickett, a Rock Island editor, that he did not consider himself fit for the presidency, and had reiterated that opinion in July in a letter to Samuel Galloway, a lawyer of Columbus, Ohio, he nevertheless virtually admitted his candidacy late in December by sending Jesse W. Fell, of Bloomington, Illinois, the famous autobiographical sketch, which Fell immediately used for promotional publicity.

The 1859 trip to Milwaukee seems to have been Lincoln's only visit to that city.* A movement "to provide the city with a suitable monument to commemorate" that visit in particular and Lincoln's life and work in general was inaugurated in 1916, but not until eighteen years afterward did the memorial become a reality in bronze. The plan adopted called for a campaign for many small gifts without large contributions, with special emphasis on schoolchildren's pennies "to stimulate their proprietary interest in the monument," and on small sums to be collected in factories and workshops, without solicitation of the city's business and professional men. Eighteen thousand dollars was obtained in that way, and the E. B. Wolcott Post of the G.A.R. raised an additional five thousand. But all money-raising efforts were abandoned with the United States' entrance into the first World War, and numerous appeals in behalf of charitable and patriotic enterprises produced a situation unfavorable for the resumption of the monument movement on the return of peace. The amount which had been raised was invested under the direction of a trust company, and by 1933 had increased to $32,000.

In that year the mayor named a committee to consider whether this amount would suffice for the erection on a suitable site of a Lincoln memorial which would be "in keeping with the pride and dignity of the community." Although there had been some shrinkage in values, and some securities were not immediately convertible into cash, the committee, with $25,000 on hand, decided to invite a sculptors' competition, to which only native-born Americans would be eligible, and to offer a first prize of $1,000. A board of five judges, after twelve hours of deliberation, awarded first place to Gaetano Cecere, and entered into a contract with him.

Mr. Cecere was born in New York City. He studied there at the Beaux Arts Institute of Design, and with Herman A. MacNeil in the

* On the day the Milwaukee statue was dedicated, one of the speakers stated that Lincoln had visited the little town in 1837 while looking about for a community in which to begin the practice of law. The evidence, however, seems insufficient to establish this as a fact.

National Academy of Design; in 1920 he won the fellowship of the American Academy in Rome, and spent nearly four years there, with intervals of travel in Greece and France. Many prizes, including the Helen Foster Barnett Prize in 1924, the Garden Club of America Prizes in 1929 and 1930, and the James McClees Prize of the Pennsylvania Academy of Fine Arts in 1930, have been awarded to Cecere. He has produced several war memorials, including one at Princeton, New Jersey; various portrait monuments and pediment sculptures; many medals, including the Soldiers' Medal for Valor for the United States Army; and several groups for the New York World's Fair of 1939.

In Montana stands his statue of John Frank Stevens, which Stevens himself had the almost unique experience of seeing dedicated on the Continental Divide in 1925. Clad in the dress with which he defied the snows and storms, Stevens gazes with unwavering eyes toward the pass which he found to provide the Great Northern Railroad "a way over and on" to the Pacific. Both the "Stevens" and the "Lincoln" are marked by Cecere's devotion to simplicity, which he holds to be the foundation of good sculpture. "The simplicity that expresses only the essential lines and masses to summon a vital emotion," says the sculptor, ". . . is the great and enduring art." He believes that the purpose of a memorial is to stimulate thought, and relentlessly suppresses whatever accessories might divert attention from the definite design.

"A portrait of Lincoln," says Cecere in a personal letter, "is a challenge to any sculptor"; and adds that in the creation of his "Lincoln" he "toiled for almost two years to attain in his figure an expression of great dignity and humility." Any competent observer is struck at first view by the utter simplicity of the Milwaukee statue. As a motorist, after passing over the concrete bridge spanning the Northwestern Railway tracks, turns left into the beautiful Lincoln Memorial Drive, he sees at his right, in a small balustraded plaza, the bronze figure, eleven feet in height, standing upon a base and pedestal of the hard red granite quarried in Wisconsin. Ferdinand Eiseman was the designer of the pedestal and base. Lincoln looks westward, with Lake Michigan at his back. The arrangement is ideal.

The dedication took place on September 16, 1934. Nearly a hundred organizations took part in the long parade. The historical remarks by William George Bruce, an eminent citizen, then seventy-eight years old, who had been from the outset a leader in the movement for a monument, must have been especially impressive.

There stands Abraham Lincoln "in austere simplicity," arms hanging at full length, feet side by side in his characteristic stance, his features stern, almost grim, with a look of introspection, as of one indifferent to his surroundings. The sculptor refused to cover the face with a beard, which, he said, "would hide the fine, mobile features." The profile is much admired. One of the inscriptions on the pedestal — it is inscribed on all four sides — carries a few lines unlike any to be found elsewhere:

"The First American" . . . . . . James Russell Lowell
"One of America's Masterful Great Men" . Richard Henry Stoddard
"A Man Inspired of God" . . . . . Henry Watterson
"The Man of the People" . . . . . Edwin Markham

SOURCES: Souvenir dedication program; correspondence with Messrs. Frederick Olson, Gilbert G. Reinmund, and Gaetano Cecere.

44 ILLUSTRATED PAGE 193

Hering's Indianapolis LINCOLN

FEW American cities can compete with the capital of Indiana in the beauty and the magnitude of their memorial monuments. Indianapolis is a checkerboard city, laid out in squares, with avenues radiating from a central circle to the corners. An imposing Soldiers' and Sailors' Monument, erected by the state and completed in 1902, stands in the center of the circle, soaring nearly three hundred feet above street level, and surmounted by a huge "Victory." Leaving the Circle, one enters the World War Memorial Plaza, occupying five blocks. The Plaza contains a cenotaph in tribute to the men lost in the first World War, and a terraced mall. In Obelisk Square one finds an obelisk one hundred feet in height, representing the aspirations of the Nation. The bronze panels at the base of this obelisk represent Religion, Science, Law, and Knowledge — the foundations of the nation's hopes — and are the work of Henry Hering.

South of this square is a Memorial Building, with a shrine room, exhibition rooms, and an auditorium. At the foot of a monumental stairway stands what is said to be the largest sculptural bronze casting ever made in America, also the work of Hering. He called the statue

"Pro Patria," and in it sought to express "all there is in humanity of aspiration, valor, renunciation, and the perpetuation of the memory of the patriot fighting for the right." The statue, depicting a youth looking upward with shining eyes, one hand lifted high and the other holding a flag, is an arresting figure.

Going on, one comes to beautiful University Square, and still farther on to the state Capitol. Our special interest is in the area generally called University Park, originally set aside by the state in 1827 as a prospective site for a university, with its fine old trees, flower beds, shrubbery, and a central fountain — for here is Henry Hering's statue of Lincoln.

The original fund for the Indianapolis "Lincoln" was $10,000, bequeathed to the city for the erection of "a bronze statue of Abraham Lincoln, to be located near the southeast corner of University Square or Park" by Henry Clay Long, a Civil War veteran who had become a prominent Indianapolis businessman. Long died in 1901, but one after another successive city administrations opposed the placing of any monument on the designated site, arguing that it would "throw the design of University Square out of balance." So more than thirty years went by, with nothing done to fulfil Long's directions, until the matter was brought to the public's attention in 1933 through newspaper publicity. The Board of Park Commissioners, through the probate court, obtained possession of the legacy, which accrued interest had by that time increased to $25,000, and forthwith contracted with Mr. Hering for the creation of the Lincoln statue. He obtained their approval of his successive sketches and of his full-size model, which he was authorized to have cast in bronze. It was dedicated on April 6, 1935, on a base provided by the Commissioners, and stands, as was said by one of the speakers on dedication day, "in the exact spot where Mr. Long wished it."

Henry Hering was born in New York City in 1874. He studied for several years at the Art Students' League, and for a year or more in Paris with Philip Martiny and others. Augustus Saint-Gaudens saw some of his work and invited him to become one of his assistants, and Hering remained with the older master until the latter's death in 1907. Saint-Gaudens was often in poor health during the seven years which Hering spent with him at Cornish, New Hampshire, and many of the models for Saint-Gaudens' important commissions of this period were executed by the younger sculptor, under the constant direction and criticism of the older. Among these were the seated "Lincoln," and the "Parnell" for Dublin. Hering gladly concedes Saint-Gaudens' great influence on him, writing of him as a great man and a fine friend.

The roll of Hering's own sculptures is long, and contains numerous important works. He produced the classic figures for the Field Museum in Chicago, decorations for Federal Reserve Banks in five cities, the figures for the bridge pylons in Cleveland, the groups depicting the defense of Fort Dearborn and the regeneration of Chicago after the great conflagration, the Civil War Memorial at Yale University, and the Robert Collyer memorial relief for the Church of the Messiah in New York City. Hering has made portrait busts of Saint-Gaudens and Bishop Ethelbert Talbott; portrait reliefs of William Cullen Bryant for Williams College, and of Dr. Andrew McCosh for the Presbyterian Hospital in New York City; portrait statues of Father Jacques Marquette, for Gary, Indiana, and of Woodrow Wilson, for Indianapolis. Numerous tablets, medals, and fountains also are of his design.

Dr. Louis A. Warren was the principal speaker at the unveiling of the "Lincoln." He developed at length Indiana's share in forming Lincoln's character. The future President lived in Spencer County from his seventh to his twenty-first year, "and when he left he was not an ignorant boy, but a well-read young man, able to cope with the best of the Illinois politicians." Lincoln's career, said Warren, constituted a "challenge to the State to aid in producing other famous citizens."

There is something peculiarly ingratiating about this "Lincoln." The bearded President sits erect in a massive chair, over the back of which a fringed shawl is flung. He looks with steady gaze diagonally downward, his right elbow resting on the arm of the chair, the forearm raised, with the hand open and the fingers spread. The pose and gesture indicate, it seems to us, not argument but exposition. Hering himself explains his purpose, saying that "after reading the life of Lincoln over again and the story of the troublesome times he went through, it occurred to me that he was getting little support, and it is at this period that I decided to depict him in an attitude of assuring the public that if they will only be calm and patient he will pull them through. This caused me to use the gesture to aid in conveying my idea. I also made the features grave, with the head bowed and serious. The shawl and the tall hat in the rear of the figure helped to make a good composition."

SOURCES: The Indianapolis Public Library; Beatrice G. Proske, *Brookfield Gardens Catalogue of Sculpture*, 1936; correspondence with Mr. Henry Hering and with Mr. J. W. Fesler of Indianapolis.

Bryant Baker's LINCOLN —
The Dreams of Youth

Good boys who to their books apply
Will all be great men by and by.

THIS rhyme is understood to have been composed by Abraham Lincoln at some time during his Indiana years. The story is that young Lincoln's penmanship "after some practice became so regular in form that it excited the admiration of other and younger boys," one of whom, Joseph C. Richardson, in later years said that "Abe was the best penman in the neighborhood." For this friend Lincoln wrote "copy" which Richardson might imitate for the improvement of his own "hand," and among the "lessons" were these lines which Herndon saw when he visited Indiana after Lincoln's death. Lincoln's law partner always insisted that the man with whom he was so intimately associated for many years was constantly forward-looking, and never indifferent to the possibilities of achievement which the future might hold for him. Herndon considered these quaint boyish lines to be in character, and said in his book that Lincoln's "ambition was a little engine that knew no rest."

When were the fires of ambition kindled in Lincoln's heart? We know how determined he was to obtain an education somehow. Several years before he attained his majority he had read, among other books, Weems' *Washington* and Grimshaw's *United States,* and had formed the habit of reading newspapers — a habit which stayed with him throughout his life. Lincoln chewed and digested what he read. His stepmother described him as "considerin' like." At eighteen he had reached his limit of physical altitude. His mental horizon must have been vastly widened by his flatboat voyage to New Orleans in the following year. It seems probable that before Lincoln left the woods of Indiana some time in his twentieth year, the spark in his breast blazed into an undying flame, which might flicker at times but was never quenched.

One Lincoln sculptor, Bryant Baker, seized upon this quickening as a theme for his artistry. His statue, in Buffalo, New York, is intended to depict an inspired moment in the life of his subject — the time when the transformation from the youthful axeman into the young man of unlimited aspirations occurred. Not that the transformation was instantaneous: the change must have been rather a process than a shock; it may have covered months during which the meditative youth began to dream, and his dreams developed into hopes, which solidified into a decision on a course of action. The words attributed to Lincoln while still a boy, "I will study and be ready; then maybe the chance will come," were the basis of the address of the principal speaker at the dedication of the statue.

Bryant Baker has described his purpose in making this statue. In the sculptor's London boyhood Emerson's essays and Lincoln's speeches and writings were foremost among Baker's books. Lincoln became his idol. The Englishman had been fascinated by the rise of the American frontiersman from log cabin to the presidency, and impressed by Lincoln's struggles against tremendous odds, and his reactions to injustice and oppression. There must have been an awakening of responsibility, Baker felt, a realization that "somebody must do something about it"; and he reasoned that the awakening came within a year or so before the Lincolns removed from Indiana to Illinois. The story of Lincoln's youth and the history of the war years interested the artist particularly; and he marveled at the contrast. "I wanted to express the vision that had come to him," says Baker, "the vision that later proved him to be above all else a great philosopher, statesman and humanitarian." On the front of the granite pedestal Baker carved Lowell's lines:

> For him her Old World moulds aside she threw,
> And choosing sweet clay from the breast
>   Of the unexhausted West,
> With stuff untainted shaped a hero new.

Bryant Baker came from a line of sculptors. His father specialized in ecclesiastical sculpture and symbolism. Baker carved simple things in his father's shop at the age of nine; left school at fifteen, served as an apprentice, studied in evening art schools, and at twenty-two was put in charge of the architectural sculpture for the Victoria and Albert Museum. Four years of full-time study in the Royal Academy Schools followed. In 1912 Baker made a marble bust of the late King Edward VII, which Queen Alexandra chose as the best sculptural portrait of the monarch, and also a heroic statue of the former king, which

King George V unveiled at Huddersfield. Baker came to the United States in January, 1916. Among his American works are busts made from life of Presidents Taft, Coolidge, and Hoover, and of more than a score of other eminent public men; heroic bronze statues of Chief Justice Edward D. White and Presidents Cleveland and Fillmore, and marble statues of Caesar Rodney and John M. Clayton for the Capitol in Washington. The recumbent marble statue of Bishop James E. Freeman, in the cathedral which he promoted in Washington, was also done by Baker. Perhaps the best known of the sculptor's American works is the colossal "Pioneer Woman," unveiled in 1930 in the Cherokee Strip in Oklahoma.

The Lincoln statue was the result of a bequest by Mrs. Julia Spitzmiller for a memorial of herself and her husband, Louis M. Spitzmiller, who had died in 1934, a year before Mrs. Spitzmiller's own death. At the dedication on October 19, 1935, the master of ceremonies was Frank M. Spitzmiller, a cousin and one of the three trustees of the twenty-five-thousand-dollar bequest, and his son and the sculptor unveiled the statue. Richard Harkness Templeton, a former United States District Attorney, in his formal address reviewed the highlights of Lincoln's life, quoted from his celebrated presidential addresses and from his speech in Buffalo, where he stayed over Sunday en route to Washington in 1861.

The bronze statue is mounted on a simple pedestal near the entrance to Delaware Park, only a short distance from the Albright Art Gallery. Baker states that the statue "shows Lincoln seated on an oak log, symbolic of strength, with an axe of the rail-splitting type at his feet, a book on his knee, and the vision of his destiny in his eyes." The sculptor had to struggle with the problem of Lincoln's looks as a young man; Lincoln was thirty-seven years of age when he sat for his first photograph, a daguerreotype made in Springfield in 1846. Baker had spent four years in the study of anatomy, and had served in the United States Army Medical Corps at Washington in 1918–1919; and for his portrait of the youthful Lincoln he worked back from the Volk life-mask, using the knowledge thus acquired and every hint concerning the appearance of Lincoln as a youth which he could find in any authentic source, thus producing a portrait that is readily recognized. The sculptor expressed his "eternal gratitude" to the Buffalo committee for allowing him to attempt something new in regard to Lincoln.

The total effect of the work is arresting. A stalwart youth is in the woods with an axe — and a book. He is fingering the leaves; something he has just read has gripped his mind. The pose is not graceful; a pretty pose would have ruined the work. The left leg is buckled back with the foot cramped against the log; young "Abe" is utterly unconscious of his surroundings. Perhaps the chest is a trifle wide for the lanky youth; the boots may not quite qualify as faithful copies of his footgear in those Indiana years; he may not have worn a belt. But the whole effect arrests the serious observer and makes him forget all minor details. Most impressive of all are the eyes; they see nothing that is in sight. The set of the mouth indicates an affirmation; the young man is making up his mind that the vision he sees shall not have been glimpsed in vain. The statue, which is a quarter more than life size, is wisely placed on a low pedestal, within the range of children's eyes.

SOURCES: Beatrice G. Proske, *Brookfield Gardens Catalogue of Sculpture,* 1939; correspondence with, and material supplied by, Mr. Baker.

46   ILLUSTRATED PAGE 195

The Pleasant Story
of Cashwan's LINCOLN

IN THE autumn of 1936 Sylvester Jerry and Samuel Cashwan, in the course of an inspection tour for the Michigan Works Progress Administraton, visited the Lincoln Consolidated Training School at Ypsilanti. This school plant is in the open country, six miles south of the city. About eight hundred pupils are normally in attendance, coming and going day by day in buses. The immediate reason for the visit of Mr. Cashwan, who was well known over the state as a sculptor, was to see a series of mural paintings that had lately been completed in one of the buildings of the school. Representatives of the student body and faculty suggested to Cashwan that the school should have a memorial of the man for whom it was named, and he agreed to consider the idea.

The students regarded the statue project as "an all-student enterprise," and rallied to its support with enthusiasm. Mr. Cashwan, a native of Kiev, Russia, who had been brought to America in his boyhood, undertook an extended study of Lincoln's life and character, and in a few months his own enthusiasm fairly matched the ardor of the boys and girls. Cashwan made the statue and chose a site for it on

309

the school grounds. The junior-high boys dug the excavation for the base; the "senior-highs" poured the concrete; all hands joined in the sodding and decorative planting. Competition became so keen that each boy was limited to a working period of fifteen minutes. On May 4, 1938, the seventy-third anniversary of the President's burial in Springfield, the statue was dedicated in the presence of a thousand visitors besides the faculty and student body. The statue was unveiled by the sculptor, assisted by the youngest child in the kindergarten classes, Virginia Robbins.

This is a charming story. The schoolboys and girls think of "their Lincoln" with intelligent reverence. The foreign-born artist is today an eager Lincolnian. When some difference of views arose at first as to whether the statue should depict a young Lincoln — favored by the students — or the mature man, Cashwan went to Springfield, talked with numerous Lincoln scholars, and read many books in his search for an interpretation of his subject. The result, cheerfully accepted by students and graduates, was a bearded Lincoln, with a shawl over his shoulders, executed in buff limestone.

The artist states that he sought "to avoid pose and pompousness, theatrical gesture and exaggerated sentimentality, without stressing any ungainliness of person," and to focus on the head, "for the drama was all there." The plaster model of the head has been many times reproduced for schools and libraries, and for the Michigan Institution for the Blind.

Mr. Cashwan had his training in New York City and in Paris, where he was a pupil of Antoine Bourdelle. He has done sculptural work for the State College and the State Normal School, and has served as an instructor in architectural sculpture in the Arts and Crafts School in Detroit.

It was eminently appropriate for the students to have a major share in the dedication ceremonies. The Michigan State Normal band furnished music. The president-elect of the student council made the presentation address. The State Superintendent of Public Instruction dwelt on Lincoln's struggle for an education, the idioms of his speech as a boy, and his lifelong interest in educational matters — did he not send his own son to Harvard, and as President appreciatively sign the Land-Grant College bill?

SOURCES: Correspondence with Etheldred Abbot, Ryerson Library, Chicago; Thomas I. Starr, Detroit; B. H. Van den Bilt, Superintendent of the Lincoln Consolidated Training School; and Samuel Cashwan.

Miss Walker's LINCOLN —
Led by the "Spirit of Destiny"

THOMAS LINCOLN and his caravan, on the way to a new home in Illinois, arrived at Vincennes, Indiana, on March 5, 1830. He had begun his fifty-third year in January; his second wife, Sarah Bush Johnston, whom he had married in 1819, was eleven years younger. The thirteen persons in the party belonged to three closely knit families. "Tom's" marriage to the widow Johnston had added her three children to his family. One of her daughters, Elizabeth, had married Dennis Hanks in 1821; with their four children they constituted a second family group. Another daughter, Matilda Johnston, had married Levi (commonly called "Squire") Hall in 1826, and they and their son made a third family unit. Also in the caravan were John D. Johnston, born in 1810, grown son of the widow Johnston, and Abraham Lincoln, born in 1809, son of Thomas Lincoln and Nancy Hanks.

Their equipage was distinctly primitive: oxen dragged one or two covered wagons, in which the household wares were stowed, and in which the women and children rode and slept at times. The usual count is two wagons and four oxen, but Harriet Hanks Chapman, daughter of Dennis Hanks, "remembered" in later years "three wagons, two drawn by two yoke of oxen each and one by two teams of horses." The destination of the caravan was Macon County, Illinois, where relatives of Nancy Hanks had settled and sent back word of the extreme fertility of the soil. The distance between the old home and the new is variously estimated as 225 or 250 miles, depending on the route taken. When they arrived at Vincennes they were seventy-five miles on the way.

"Abe" Lincoln plodded along with this pioneering clan, driving a yoke of oxen. His father had sold his land in Spencer County, Indiana, and a few other possessions, and was "moving on." Whatever may have been the reactions of the son, who had just attained his majority and was already a giant in stature, to his father's final migration, he never forgot his fourteen years in Indiana. We think he made a final visit to the grave on the wooded knoll where his mother was resting, and that he went also to the little cemetery of the Pigeon Creek Church where his sister was buried.

Some writers have stated that the party stopped for about three days at Vincennes. This may be so, though satisfactory evidence has not been brought forward. That "Abe" would look about a bit if opportunity offered goes without saying, and Vincennes was worth seeing: he might have seen there several historic buildings, including the mansion William Henry Harrison had completed in 1806 — known today as one of the most important relics in Indiana — and several Catholic institutions of note. How much young Lincoln may have known about the exploit of George Rogers Clark in his capture of Vincennes can only be a matter of speculation. We doubt that the claim that "Abe" at this time first saw a printing press in operation, in the little plant of the first newspaper established in the state, can be substantiated. In 1828 he had made a flatboat trip to New Orleans and spent at least a few days in that cosmopolitan metropolis. With five newspapers published in the city by 1820, it would have been natural for a young man of "Abe's" interests to visit the plant of at least one of them during the time he undoubtedly spent in exploring the town.

Across the river from Vincennes lay Illinois. The Wabash was flooded by the spring rains. The Lincoln clan crossed by ferry, at a historic crossing — once a ford where buffaloes and Indians had worn a path, later used by explorers and missionaries — and fared on over the dismal prairies, which at that season they saw at their worst. Today a handsome bridge named for Abraham Lincoln spans the river at this crossing. On the Vincennes side motorists stop to examine the stately George Rogers Clark Memorial by the bridge entrance, with its series of murals by Ezra Winter and the Clark statue by Herman A. MacNeil. Crossing the bridge, we find beside the highway the memorial expressing Illinois' welcome for the coming of its greatest citizen. "In the late spring of 1830," we read, "a few weeks after his twenty-first birthday, Abraham Lincoln passed this way with his father's family, entering the State of Illinois for the first time."

We raise our eyes, and there is "Abe" trudging, goad in hand, his pace moderated by the oxen he drives. Upon a wide and heavy granite foundation, about six feet in height, is erected a limestone panel, twenty-six feet in length and more than nine feet high, on which are shown, in four-inch relief, a pair of oxen and a covered wagon, with a man leading the way, another man steadying a wheel, with a woman beside the wagon, followed by a little girl and a sturdy boy. "Abe" walks by the flank of an ox, an outstanding figure in bronze, a statue in the round. Floating in the air above, with an arm extended forward, is a woman's figure in long draperies. All the faces, except perhaps that of the little girl, are serious; that trek was no easy jaunt. The bodies are big, the eyes watchful. It is a fitting welcome. The monument harmonizes with the facts as we know them. The floating figure has been explained on post cards as "the hovering spirit of Lincoln's dead mother"; for the sculptress, however, the figure is "the Spirit of Destiny leading on."

This memorial was the production of Nellie Verne Walker, a member of the National Sculpture Society, who was trained at the Chicago Art Institute, studied abroad, and for several years served as assistant instructor in modeling, under Lorado Taft, at the Institute. Born in Iowa, as a child Miss Walker evinced the "entertaining faculty of putting herself into other environments in her imagination," a faculty enabling artists to see what once was, and what ought to be. Her principal works have been of a monumental character, but she has done many portraits, reliefs, and sculptural decorations for important public buildings, as well as fountains and several large ideal groups. Her statue of Keokuk, the Indian chief, for the city named for him, was erected in 1913, and the Stephenson monument in Marietta, Wisconsin, in 1922. Hers are the statue of Senator James Harlan in Washington, the Decker family monument in Battle Creek, Michigan, and a long series of portrait busts of public men.

Lincoln for many years has been one of the sculptress' dream themes. A Lincoln head modeled by her when a very young girl was exhibited at the Columbian Exposition in 1893. She "lived with the Lincoln family" for a long while before starting work on the monument at the Wabash River bridge, and she has dreamed of other Lincoln subjects and of New Salem as a site for a suitable memorial. She may well be called "a Lincolnian."

The monument "in Lawrence County, Illinois, at the Illinois end of the Lincoln Memorial Bridge, opposite Vincennes" — to quote the official script — was dedicated and presented to the state on June 14, 1938. Invitations for the occasion were issued in the name of Mrs. Jacob Fredrich Zimmerman, Illinois State Regent of the National Society Daughters of the American Revolution, and of that society's Illinois Organization. The campaign for the memorial was begun by an earlier Regent, Mrs. Julian Goodhue, and completed during the term of her successor, Mrs. Samuel James Campbell. The address was made by Dr. Louis A. Warren, and State Historian Paul M. Angle accepted the monument in the name of the State of Illinois. On that Flag Day a flagpole across the highway from the memorial and its thirty-two-acre Memorial Park was also dedicated with suitable ceremonies.

SOURCES: Official documents and program; guides to historic Vincennes; correspondence with Miss Nellie V. Walker and Dr. Louis A. Warren.

48   ILLUSTRATED PAGE 197

The LINCOLN *on* *the Ripon College Campus*

THE city of Ripon, situated sixty miles north of Madison, the capital of Wisconsin, and its twenty-five thousand people are proud of the college bearing the city's name, of the little white schoolhouse on the college campus in which "the Republican Party was born," and of the bronze "Lincoln" unveiled on the campus on July 12, 1939.

There is merit in all these claims for distinction. The college was founded in 1851. The community had then fewer than five hundred inhabitants, derived from New England, New York, and Pennsylvania. Those pioneers, of a high level of intelligence, were keenly interested in the problems of the nation in that turbulent decade. Alvan E. Bovay, a lawyer, born in New York and an outstanding resident of Ripon, became convinced in 1852 that a new political party must be formed "on the basis of the exclusion of slavery from the territories," and in a personal interview with Horace Greeley proposed that its name should be "Republican." While the Kansas-Nebraska Bill was under debate in Congress, Bovay, a Whig, with two other men — a Democrat and a Free-Soiler — called a meeting in the Congregational Church on February 28, 1854. This meeting adopted a resolution that, if the bill should become a law, its passage "will be a call to arms of a great Northern Party." The bill passed the Senate on March 4.

Another meeting was called for March 20, in the district schoolhouse. Many years later Mr. Bovay wrote: "We went into the little meeting . . . Whigs, Free Soilers, and Democrats. We came out of it Republicans, and we were the first Republicans in the Union." The "call" was backed by fifty-four men out of not more than a hundred Ripon voters; a few representatives from neighboring areas may also have been in attendance. The school building accommodated hardly more than fifty persons, but many times that number claimed in later years to have "been there."

Ripon does not hold that the village actually started the new party movement; it does claim that the "first recorded expression in the nation" of the fast-spreading revolt against the Kansas-Nebraska policy was recorded in its schoolhouse, and "the first suggestion" of "uniting under one banner under the name Republican." These claims were made anew at the Diamond Jubilee Celebration in 1929. The claim of Jackson, Michigan, to have initiated the national organization at the meeting "under the oaks" on July 6, 1854, is recognized in Ripon.

The college has operated for a century as a liberal-arts school of high ideals. It has many buildings and a splendid Student Union. Its enrollment is limited to five hundred, though this limit is sometimes exceeded.

Recognition by the town and the college of the desirability of a Lincoln memorial on the campus came from this historic background. Clarence Addison Shaler, a businessman, abandoning the manufacture of several of his own inventions, decided in 1928, at the age of sixty-eight, to devote his entire time to sculpture, and provided a bronze statue of heroic size to satisfy that need. Shaler, who described himself as a "sculptor and philanthropist," was born in Wisconsin, and had his "schooling" at Ripon from 1873 to 1879. He became one of the state's leading industrialists. His home was at Waupun, twenty miles south of Ripon; his sculptures may be seen in both cities, as well as elsewhere in Wisconsin, in Miami, Florida, in Pasadena, California, and in other cities. His loyalty to Ripon College was expressed in gifts for endowment and other purposes. He died in December, 1941. Shaler's poetic imagination is indicated by his names for some of his sculptures — "The Dawn of Day," "By the Roadway of Life," "Inspiration," "Tomorrow is Today's Dream."

Shaler's "Lincoln" is placed at a commanding spot on the college campus below the largest of the recitation buildings, where no student can miss seeing it day by day. An original feature is that "the young Lincoln" stands on the spreading roots of a tree trunk broken off at the height of his shoulders. The face is mature, the clothing seems modern; the idea would seem to be that Lincoln is no longer to be a woodsman. We are told by a plaque at the foot of the figure that "this statue . . . represents the man Lincoln at the outset of his public career. His character, formed by his early hardships in the wilderness, partakes of the strength of the oak, tempered by the warmth of his human sympathies. He is leaving that early environment in pursuit of an unknown destiny, untouched as yet by tragedy, betrayal, and disillusionment, a man at the noon of his powers, which his high resolve has already dedicated to the good of his country and of mankind."

Slightly different in a few particulars is what might be termed an "official" description of the work by a representative of the college: "It represents the great Emancipator in his youth — gaunt, awkward, rugged, kindly. He wears rough, homespun clothes, a shirt open at the neck, with sleeves carelessly rolled above the elbows. Heavy, clumsy shoes are on his feet. He stands with one long, ungainly arm stretched full length down his left side. His right hand is clenched, his left foot slightly forward. Character and strength are etched in his face. His eyes, somber and tender, gaze into the future with thoughtful and quiet intensity."

The most active participant in the simple unveiling program was Albert H. Griffith, veteran Lincolnian and Ripon alumnus, who delivered a brief address on the occasion.

SOURCES: Correspondence with Ripon College authorities and with Albert H. Griffith; address by S. M. Pedrick at the Ninetieth Republican Anniversary, 1944; William Starr Myers, *The Republican Party, a History*, 1928; Henry Wilson, *The Rise and Fall of the Slave Power*, 1874.

The Ugly Story of
Slobodkin's LINCOLN

IN AN open court in the vast building occupied by the Department of the Interior in Washington stands Louis Slobodkin's bronze statue of "Abraham Lincoln, the Rail Fence Builder." It is different, original, striking; Slobodkin copied nobody. There is no unanimity of opinion as to its value as a work of art or as a portrait of young "Abe." No other "Lincoln" has had so curious a history.

Slobodkin won the competition for a statue for the Federal Building at the New York World's Fair of 1939. The prescribed subject was the symbolization of "Unity." About five hundred artists were invited to submit designs; the successful competitor was to receive a commission for a huge plaster relief to be suspended on the façade of the building. The winning sculptor's statement is that his sketch was adjudged the best, but that the jury awarded the commission to another sculptor, since "they preferred to have me execute my piece in the round and have it exhibited at the building." Later in that year (1938) Slobodkin was commissioned to model a seven-and-one-half-foot enlargement of the three-foot sketch submitted by him for the competition. He received payment for both the sketch and the enlargement. A site for the erection of the final work was selected in the center of the pool in the Garden Court of the building. The government commissioned an "enlarger" to double the size of the armature of the working model by the mechanical methods usually employed for such exhibitions, but the sculptor himself moulded the clay for the final figure.

While the casting in plaster was under way, Slobodkin obtained permission from the Federal authorities to display his half-size model at the Outdoors Show of the Sculptors' Guild on Park Avenue. It was given the place of honor and was praised by many critics.

Slobodkin also designed the cement block on which the huge fifteen-foot statue was to be anchored in the Garden Pool, and saw it set up. But when he took Mrs. Slobodkin to the Court to see his "Lincoln," on Sunday, April 30, 1939, the guard at the entrance told them, "It ain't there any more." And, in fact, it was not: it had disappeared.

The mildest of the sculptor's expressions was that "this was a bit of a shock." The public soon heard of the vanishing of the statue, and there was excitement continuing for several weeks. Letters, telegrams, and personal contacts brought the sculptor neither comfort nor information. Artists denounced the "outrage."

In time it developed — and the newspapers told the story in detail — that the order to remove the statue before the opening day of the Fair had been issued by the Executive Assistant to the Federal Commissioner for the Exposition. This official charged that the work was "not right architecturally," that it was "too big and too high," that "pre-view visitors had scoffed at it," and added that "we can't take that sort of criticism from people representing John Q. Public. . . . I don't care what those artist fellows think, it should never have been placed there at all." After a few days the Chief of the Section of Fine Arts of the Procurement Division of the United States Treasury Department came to New York to participate in the opening ceremonies of the Museum of Modern Art. During his stay he visited the Guild's Outdoor Show, and while he inspected the half-size "Fence Builder" told a reporter definitely that the order of removal had come from the United States Commissioner to the Fair, who had instructed his assistant to "take the rap," to "say nothing," with "emphatic warnings of what might happen if he talked." The Procurement Division Chief, for himself, "did not think the Washington authorities would approve of a government official destroying a piece of government property." It did seem that the statue must have been destroyed; newspapers charged that it had been smashed with sledgehammers.

The official position seems to have been that the sculptor had been paid for his work, and the government could do what it pleased with the product. Slobodkin argued that prestige is a major asset of any artist, and that it had been a serious blow to his prospects to have the story of the destruction of his work publicized all over the nation. Told that the statue had been temporarily stored in a cellar, he said: "I knew that the Federal Building and the other Fair buildings were built on mud flats, and there could be no cellar there to hold my 'Lincoln.' I telephoned the man who had cast the model to find out if he had been called to help dismember the big piece. It had been cast in two sections. These were plastered together, and the whole anchored deep in the center of the Pool. Only by consulting with the man who did the casting could they have found the connecting irons without chipping the work to pieces."

The plaster caster had not been consulted; the statue remained "lost." The names of the parties — Edward J. Flynn, Federal Commissioner; Theodore T. Hayes, his assistant; and Edward Bruce, Procurement Division Chief — appeared day after day in the public prints. Slobodkin, with protests and sympathetic messages coming to him in every mail from individuals and organizations, consulted a lawyer. He worried over the sort of publicity he was getting, and felt that such a controversy might destroy his future. But George Grey Barnard had benefited from the tremendous ruction over his "Lincoln," and opinions might vary on that point.

The sculptor's lawyer, reminding him that they must know where the statue was before beginning a suit, brought a "show cause" order before a Supreme Court judge, asking that Commissioner Flynn be required to explain why no definite answer had ever been made as to what had been done with the statue. The judge decided that sufficient evidence existed to warrant a suit. Now the Federal Government was taking notice of the situation, and "parties came on from the Capital," according to Slobodkin, "to find out what I 'really wanted to settle the case' before it reached the court, and all I wanted was to have my statue put back — or to have a new enlargement made and set up at the Fair."

Money to decorate the courts of the new Interior Building had been appropriated, and Slobodkin was commissioned to cast the working model, which he had displayed on Park Avenue, in bronze and to erect it in one of the courts on a base of his design. He rejected the first cast for inaccuracies; the second was exhibited at the Corcoran Gallery in November, 1939, and a few months later the bronze "Fence Builder" was installed in an Interior Building court upon a block of serpentine granite, and due payment was made.

The story is worth telling in some detail as an illustration of the difficulties too often encountered even by artists of the highest standing. Regardless of one's opinion of this work, no artist should be subjected to such an indignity as was inflicted on Slobodkin. But what shall we say of the statue? The sculptor refers to it as "my Young Abe." He shows Lincoln not splitting rails, but joining them — thereby meeting the condition of the competition by forecasting Lincoln's future duty as President in unifying the sections of the nation. Only after he had completed his design did Slobodkin learn that he had rightly divined the way rail fences are built; the split rails must be joined in order to support each other.

No exact representation of the young Lincoln is intended. There are several misconceptions in the work; the shoulders are too bulky, the hair is wrong. But young "Abe" was powerful, and the effect, of a brawny frontiersman intent upon his toil, is right. We wish, however, that the statue might stand in a clearing in a forest, easy of access, with no token of a "settlement" near at hand.

The original small model — the "sketch" — for this "Lincoln" is now at the District of Columbia National Training School for Boys, on Bladensburg Road; it was damaged, however, in transit.

SOURCES: The *New York Times* and *New York Herald-Tribune;* information supplied by Mr. Louis Slobodkin and by Lieutenant Bert Sheldon of Washington.

50 ILLUSTRATED PAGE 199

Clyde Du Vernet Hunt's
THE SPIRIT OF AMERICA

THE sculptor Clyde Du Vernet Hunt is not known ever to have named his statue of Abraham Lincoln, but there is ample evidence that the name it now bears, "The Spirit of America," is "fitting and right." Letters exist in which his friends congratulated him for his expression in sculpture of "Lincoln's dominant characteristic" — "his great humanity," and at least one art critic in Paris, writing of the "Lincoln" when it was standing at the right of the main entrance of the Grand Palais, declared that the work revealed "the humanity and universal charity which were Lincoln's outstanding characteristics." This "Lincoln" is not a single statue but a group of three figures. The bearded President stands erect with an overcoat thrown over his shoulders leaving his arms free. His eyes look outward from under his high hat. At his feet sits a woman with face upturned and eyes closed. Before him stands a boy, sturdy and nude, looking trustfully at the great man. The man is not unmindful of the boy and half-kneeling woman; his left hand with fingers spread rests upon the boy's head, and the fingers of the right, visible under his cloak, touch the woman's forehead. Paris accepted the boy as hopeful young America, while the feminine figure represented Faith, and Lincoln stood for Charity, in the Biblical sense of the word. The group was on view in Paris in 1928, and in that year pictures of it were shown in American newspapers and periodicals. When the sculptor returned from France in 1938, he brought the group with him in plaster, and American interpreters set to work to fathom the sculptor's meaning. One conclusion was that he intended to portray Lincoln "as he understood him," and again "to create a symbol of the Spirit of America." For Clyde Hunt "faith, hope and charity, the primal Christian virtues," were the elements that combined to constitute "the spiritual compound we call the American spirit." His interpretation is widely held today, and doubtless the resulting name will endure. The statue presents Lincoln as "both the symbol and the interpreter of the American spirit."

Cast in bronze and placed on display in front of the Illinois State Building at the New York World's Fair in 1939, the group was permanently located in the courtyard of the Historical Museum and Art Gallery of Bennington, Vermont, following Hunt's death in 1941, when his heirs presented the statue "as a memorial to both Abraham Lincoln and the Vermont patriot and artist who held the martyred President in great and beautiful reverence."

Clyde Du Vernet Hunt was born in Glasgow of American parents in May, 1861. Many years of his long life were spent in Paris, but he always considered himself an American and a son of Vermont, where his parents had their home. His Americanism was the foundation of his character. He made no secret of his devotion to the United States, and his eloquence in the exposition of his principles in France cost him not a whit of his popularity. He came of a proud Vermont ancestry. From his great-grandfather down, his forebears served their home state of Vermont in important positions, and fought in the Revolution, in the War of 1812, and in the Civil War. Clyde Hunt himself performed valuable service in Cuba and the Philippines before returning to Paris to give his time almost exclusively to sculptor. He maintained until the end of his life a home in Vermont. His uncle William Morris Hunt, the artist, taught him charcoal drawing, and he studied under well-known masters abroad. Sculpture became his principal medium. Among his better known works are a bronze tribute to France which he named "Fils de France," and a marble "Nirvana" depicting the faith of a religious devotee.

SOURCES: The Metropolitan Museum of Art; John Spargo, *The Spirit of America; Story and Interpretation of the Statue*, Historical Museum and Art Gallery, Bennington, Vermont.

The President
and the First Lady

ON THE face of the pedestal upon which a group carved in granite is mounted in a park in Racine, Wisconsin, is inscribed: "The first monument to be erected to a President of the United States and his wife, and the first statue to Mary Todd Lincoln." Any such work is bound to excite discussion, and Mrs. Lincoln's figure will be studied more attentively than that of her husband who has been so often represented. It used to be said that trousers constituted a problem with which many artists had grappled in vain; but what shall be said of the voluminous skirts, widely spread and sweeping the ground, which were worn by the ladies of the 1860's?

The sculptor's intention is to portray the Lincolns as they appeared when they took possession of the White House in 1861, before the President's face became seamed and furrowed in the struggle to save the Union, and while Mrs. Lincoln's future was unclouded. The disparity in stature of this strangely mated couple may account for their failure to be photographed together; perhaps they thought it would never do for them to stand together on a pedestal, the bearded and relatively slender giant and the short and plump woman.

In this statue the President is seated in a heavy chair, with Mrs. Lincoln standing beside him. They are dressed for "an occasion": the new First Lady wears a party gown, with shoulders bare, with beads, earrings, and bracelets, and long gloves held loosely in one hand while the other rests on the back of her husband's hand. "Mr. Lincoln," as his wife usually called him, sits in an almost subdued attitude, quite as though he had been admonished to "sit up straight and look nice"; his hair is not tousled, nor is his tie askew.

In spite of all the remarks we have heard directed against this group, we admit our liking for it. We look with favor on any work, literary or artistic, that may help to win a respectful hearing for probably the most tragic figure in the history of American womanhood. We are glad to have the public reminded of the important role Mrs. Lincoln played in the life of the man who rode the storm in the greatest crisis in our history. We remind ourselves, besides, that any sculptor, however gifted, would need to call upon all his powers to achieve success with such a theme; and Mr. Hibbard has not scored a failure.

Why is this monument placed in Racine? Because, in the days when the shadows were gathering ever more darkly about Mrs. Lincoln in her lonely widowhood, she spent a portion of one summer in that city. After her husband's funeral she came to Chicago late in May, 1865, and remained there until July, 1867. In mid-September she went to New York for a month and then returned to Chicago. She spent the summer months of 1868 among the Pennsylvania mountains at Cresson, and in the late autumn made her first voyage to Europe, remaining there until she returned to Chicago in March, 1871. The summer of 1874 was spent at Waukesha, Wisconsin, and the winter in Florida. There followed the insanity trial, her relatively short stay in an Illinois sanatorium, her release after a second trial, and her second Atlantic crossing. She arrived again in America in October, 1880; she went to Springfield in 1881, and there died in July, 1882, in the home where she had been married. The recital of these drab facts in those years of the life of a bewildered, fearful, mourning, mentally afflicted, almost friendless woman is appropriate before we return to look at her standing proudly in all her finery beside her husband in 1861.

There may be a mistake as to the year of Mrs. Lincoln's stay in Racine. Letters written by her at Racine to a Mrs. Atwood bear dates in the summer of 1869. These letters contain convincing details concerning her habits, her visits to "the college," her relations with Senator and Mrs. Doolittle, and her son "Tad." She speaks of walking a couple of miles a day; those walks were recalled years later by a local businessman. But other letters must also be considered. From Cresson, in July, 1868, Mrs. Lincoln wrote to a friend, "We sail from Baltimore the first of August," and in another letter to the same lady a month later, "it will be the first of October before I sail." One careful biographer definitely dates her voyage "late in the autumn of 1868." Her application for a pension, read in the United States Senate on February 16, 1869, had been written at Frankfurt, Germany, and letters from Germany exist which she wrote in the last three months of 1869. Did she make a short visit to America in the summer and return to Europe? Some scholars prefer 1867 as the more probable year of her sojourn in Racine.

The Racine memorial was the gift of Miss Lena Rosewall, a pioneer resident of that city, whose entire estate, twenty thousand dollars, was left for the monument at her death in 1935. Her study of the lives of the Lincolns had convinced her that Mary Todd had done much for the development of her husband's character and the direction of his career. Miss Rosewall's will was contested, but was upheld by the Supreme Court in 1937. The executors, to whom Miss Rosewall had left the selection of a sculptor, the choice of material, the selection of a site, and other details, with definite instructions that the figures should be in the round and of heroic proportions, did not deem the time favorable for the liquidation of the estate, and postponed for a few years the fulfilment of her directions.

For this difficult commission the executors chose Frederick C. Hibbard, a Missouri-born artist of high reputation, whose works are distributed over many states. His "Mark Twain" and "Tom Sawyer and Huck Finn" are in the famous humorist's home town of Hannibal, Missouri, and Hibbard is also represented in his home state by statues of James Shields, who once challenged Lincoln to a duel, Champ Clark, Alexander Doniphan, and Henry T. Rainey. In Fort Wayne, Indiana, are his "Colonel David N. Foster" and "General Henry W. Lawton." There are Hibbard statues of Jefferson Davis in the Kentucky Capitol and in the original Capitol of the Confederacy in Alabama. For the Daughters of the Confederacy Hibbard made the beautiful memorial in Shiloh National Park, and for the Vicksburg Park an equestrian "General Grant." The list of his works includes several fountain groups, seven soldiers' memorials in as many states, and many other portrait statues.

November 4, 1942, the centenary of the marriage of Mary Todd and Abraham Lincoln, was the original date set for unveiling the Racine group, but a postponement until July 4, 1943, became necessary. The ceremonies were held "under ideal conditions" and "in the presence of a great throng." In his dedicatory address Dr. Louis A. Warren dwelt on the contrast between the self-taught prairie lawyer and the handsome, highly educated woman who had been reared in that "Athens of the West," Lexington, Kentucky. Dr. Warren was sure that if Lincoln were alive he "would ask that a good word be said for Mary," who, in the speaker's judgment, "had done much to prepare Abe for the Presidency." William H. Smith, one of the executors of Miss Rosewall's will, presented the monument to the city, and Mayor Francis H.

Wendt made the acceptance address. Dr. Clarence Seidenspinner, paying tribute to the millions of young men and women in the armed forces of the nation on that Independence Day, pictured Lincoln as a "brooding figure," to whom the casualty lists of war "were not unintelligible figures," since "each stood for a young man who had left his home to give his all for his country." Never again must the youth of the land be "sold down the river" as "was the case with those who had died in vain in the first World War." Emil Wiegand, one of the state's best known Lincolnians, assisted by a group of Boy Scouts, removed the wraps from the monument.

The work stands in East Park on a base of Minnesota pink granite five feet in height. The figures are chiseled from Elberton gray granite from Georgia. Mrs. Lincoln's standing figure is seven feet high. All four sides of the base are inscribed.

SOURCES: The official program and contemporary accounts of the dedication; correspondence with Messrs. Frederick C. Hibbard, Louis A. Warren, F. R. Starbuck, and Emil Wiegand.

52 ILLUSTRATED PAGE 201

A Kansas Schoolteacher's Gift to Hawaii

ON THE campus of a school near Honolulu, on the island of Oahu and not far from Pearl Harbor, a statue of Abraham Lincoln was unveiled on his birthday in 1944. The plaster model was in a foundry in the East when the Japanese made the raid which precipitated war in December, 1941. The casting in bronze was done on the eve of the government's limitation on the use of copper for non-war purposes, and this statue by Professor Avard Fairbanks of the University of Michigan was probably the last large order executed in bronze before the imposing of the restriction.

The story of the Kansas "schoolmarm" who mothered this statue is inspiring. Mrs. Katherine McIntosh Burke, born in Leavenworth just before Lincoln's first inauguration, was educated at Emporia College for Teachers and the University of California. She taught school in Kansas, Arizona, and Nevada, then in Alaska, and finally in Hawaii, first on the island of Kauai and then on Oahu. The Territorial Department of Public Instruction granted her a pension in 1929, and she survived in retirement to within five months of the age of seventy-seven.

Mrs. Burke was a remarkable woman. Reared on the frontier, she possessed a superabundance of that blend of self-reliance, "gumption," and enterprise aptly termed the frontier spirit. She moved from new communities to others newer still. Her first teaching job was in an elementary school in a Kansas town proudly bearing the suggestive name of Oskaloosa. When Alaska began to fill up with settlers, she moved on to Wrangell. Hawaii, with its mixture of races and its long historical background, was different, but she voyaged there for the same reasons which had kept her on the move on the continent. She returned to the mainland to die at the Mayo Clinic in Rochester, Minnesota.

We do not know how early in her long life Mrs. Burke conceived her admiration for Lincoln. She had taught United States history, and must have known of the multiplication of Lincoln memorials over the land. Why not a Lincoln monument in Hawaii? A thrifty woman, Mrs. Burke decided that the most profitable use for her savings would be a memorial of this great American hero among the schoolchildren of this American territory with whom she had labored as teacher and friend.

Sculptor Avard Fairbanks had visited the Hawaiian Islands four times; he had married in Honolulu in 1918. In the summer of 1939, a few months after the death of Katherine Burke, Fairbanks was teaching painting and sculpture at the University of Hawaii. Quite naturally the trustees of Mrs. Burke's estate invited Fairbanks to model a "Lincoln" for their consideration. The chairman of the trustees' committee saw the final model at Ann Arbor in 1941, and on his recommendation and from the evidence of photographs it was accepted by the board.

The sculptor had had an interesting career. Born in Provo, Utah, in 1897, he accompanied his father and brother on camping trips during his childhood, thus acquiring acquaintance with wild animals and with the adventurous life of pioneers and Indians. He modeled an "Indian Scout" and a "Pony Express" horse and rider when he was only fourteen, and was called the "Boy Wonder." From 1910 through 1912 he studied art at the Students' League in New York City, winning scholarships for his animal groups "Fighting Pumas" and "Fighting Panthers," which he composed on a modeling stand beside the cages in the Zoological Park, unmindful of the crowds about him. The drawing has been described as "crude" and the composition "defective," but his beasts were "alive" and "full of action."

In 1913 and 1914 Fairbanks studied in Paris, where one critic declared he could "hear the clatter of the hoofs" of his "Pony Express." He was an exhibitor at the Panama-Pacific Exposition in 1915, and in 1920 began teaching sculpture, which became his lifetime profession. Until 1927 he was assistant professor of art at the University of Oregon, and in 1929 became associate professor of sculpture in the Institute of Fine Arts at the University of Michigan, having spent the intervening year in Italy on a Guggenheim fellowship. His list of works is extensive, including medals, bas-reliefs, statues, and numerous memorials. Among his most talked-of creations are the "Doughboy," a state memorial in Idaho; "The Blessing of Joseph" and the fountain honoring "Hawaiian Motherhood," at Laie on the island of Oahu; the memorial to "Pioneer Mothers" in Vancouver, Washington; and his "Nebula" for the New York World's Fair.

After the completion of his Lincoln model, the sculptor told a radio audience how he decided on his design. He lingered on the idea of a frock-coated President; a Lincoln with a shawl would never do for Hawaii with its semi-tropical climate. Then, back in the West for his father's funeral, the sculptor sought relaxation in a field of stumps with an axe. Why not "Abraham Lincoln, the Frontiersman," axe in hand? That idea stayed with him. Back in Ann Arbor, with Lincoln books and photographs, and copies of the life-mask and hand casts, he worked out his theme, first in a twelve-inch model, then one of thirty inches, and finally a full-sized model for a statue nine feet in height. The bronze figure was sent to Honolulu in 1943, and several months later a block of rainbow granite for a five-foot pedestal arrived.

The statue's destination was the grounds of a "plantation school" — the Hawaiian equivalent of our "country school" — located at Ewa, where Katherine Burke had invested much of her life. The unveiling was witnessed by a large gathering of schoolchildren with their families and friends. Oren E. Long, Superintendent of Public Instruction, spoke on "Lincoln, the Man," and Governor Ingram M. Stainback of the Territory delivered the unveiling address. A large group of children recited the Gettysburg Address in chorus, and as they delivered the final phrase the draperies fell and the "Frontiersman" stood revealed.

The bronze "Lincoln," in a brief moment of inaction as he looks up from his wood-chopping, stands with right knee bent and right foot well advanced and resting on a log. His left foot is on the ground behind another log. The axe, which the sculptor explains is modeled on a rail-splitter's axe of Lincoln's time, is held diagonally across the body, supported by the right leg and steadied by the right hand. This young Lincoln is a brawny fellow, wide of chest and shoulders. The face has marks of mature manhood. The neck, rightly, is long; the face is strong; the whole effect is that of a strong personality. One critic has said that "the listless, gawky, sleepy-eyed Lincoln" is gone, and we have instead a Lincoln "powerful, alert, aggressive," with "eyes through which only Lincoln could visualize far ahead of time itself the great benefits to be enjoyed through a free and united nation."

SOURCES: Thomas I. Starr, "The Will of Katherine Burke Has Been Probated," *Lincoln Herald*, June, 1944; Avard Fairbanks, "Engineering in Sculpture," *The Michigan Technic*, February, 1942; *The Michigan Alumnus*, August 15, 1942; correspondence with Thomas I. Starr and Avard Fairbanks.

53 ILLUSTRATED PAGE 202

Lovet-Lorski's *Realistic* LINCOLN

THE latest, but probably by no means the last, controversial and realistic "Lincoln" to be erected in this country was unveiled on September 8, 1946, at Decatur, Illinois. It is fitting that the city should possess such a memorial. The Lincoln family's trek from southern Indiana in 1830 ended on March 14, when they camped in the village square of Decatur, which at that time contained fewer than "a dozen log houses, set in a grove of oaks." Within a few years Abraham Lincoln was making annual visits to the growing town as he rode the Eighth Judicial Circuit, attending the sessions of court in June and October with fair regularity. When Decatur was removed from the Eighth Circuit, Lincoln still tried occasional cases there, and from time to time went there on political errands.

Lincoln was probably present at a Whig mass meeting in Decatur in October, 1844. On February 22, 1856, the day that the Republican

Party was establishing a national organization at Pittsburgh, Lincoln attended the convention of anti-Nebraska editors which marked the real beginning of the party in Illinois, at Decatur. He had something to say about the platform, but deprecated the suggestion that he become the party's candidate for governor, holding that the nomination of an anti-Nebraska Democrat would be wiser than that of an old-line Whig like himself. The best-known Decatur incident in Lincoln's political career was the Illinois state Republican convention, held there on May 9, 1860, only nine days before Lincoln's nomination in Chicago. What a whoop there was when John Hanks came marching in with two ancient fence rails over his shoulder! That made "Abe" the "Rail Splitter" candidate, and the convention duly instructed the Illinois delegates to stand for him and to stay by him.

The bronze "Lincoln," eight feet high, which now stands in the middle of the wide walk leading to the main entrance of the Macon County Building, was the gift of Mr. and Mrs. Roy M. Dawson, who, with Mr. S. R. C. Scherer, chairman of an assisting committee, chose for its creation the Russian-born sculptor, Boris Lovet-Lorski. During his boyhood in Russia the sculptor had learned to revere Lincoln, and, as he said a few years ago, "throughout his twenty-six years as a citizen of the United States he had always wanted to do a 'Lincoln.'" Mr. and Mrs. Dawson were pleased by "the poetic idealism" of Lovet-Lorski's work, notably in his portrait busts, and most impressively by the "Feodor Chaliapin" in the Metropolitan Museum. The sculptor began work on the "Lincoln" at his Long Island studio in January, 1946, and, thanks to his many years of musing over the man, the statue arrived in Decatur in the following August. The unveiling ceremonies were of the usual order. Among the speakers was Dudley Crafts Watson of the Chicago Art Institute, whose theme was "Lincoln in Art."

It was said at the time that there would doubtless be "a good deal of controversy" over this statue. Unanimity is hardly to be looked for with respect to a realistic statue, and of course opinions vary. At first sight, many were offended by Lovet-Lorski's work — it wasn't "pretty"; all the awkwardness of the tall, lanky young Lincoln was unrestrainedly portrayed. That aspect was overplayed, the critics said; the hands projecting from the short coat sleeves were "too big," and so were the feet; the garments were ill-fitting.

The effect does differ from that of the ordinary portrayal; but many who can claim to speak with authority commend the sculptor's work.

Dr. Watson called it "the livest Lincoln ever to be put into bronze." The sculptor himself has written, "I made him as a young lawyer. . . . He is pleading in front of a jury." We see a Lincoln erect, solidly planted on his feet — which *were* big — with a rolled paper in the left hand, and the right hand extended forward in a quiet gesture. His hands, while big, were not so large as many suppose them to have been. The head is lifted, the mouth is set, all the features are rugged. The idea was to show Lincoln as Decatur had seen him a century before — a frontier lawyer, not aroused to the heights of fervor, offering an expository argument. One may wonder how this statue will wear. It is no work for a snap judgment.

SOURCES: Correspondence with Mr. Boris Lovet-Lorski and the Decatur, Illinois, Chamber of Commerce.

54

54   ILLUSTRATED PAGE 203

The Axe or the Book?

TWO years after the dedication of the Lovet-Lorski "Lincoln," another Lincoln statue was erected in Decatur. This memorial was provided by legislative action as a gift from the State of Illinois to Macon County, of which Decatur, a city of sixty thousand people, is the county seat. The movement for a "Macon memorial" was based on the fact that, as Lincoln wrote in his autobiographical sketch for Jesse Fell, "at twenty-one I came to Illinois and passed the first year in Macon County." Decatur, though only nine months old when the Lincolns arrived and camped in "the public square," where Lincoln is said to have indicated the exact spot to Henry C. Whitney in 1856, had already been designated as the seat of justice for the newly-established Macon County; a log courthouse was under construction in the "dimly outlined" square, and only a week before "Abe's" arrival a post office had been opened in a log cabin home.

Lincoln's year in Macon County was not spent in Decatur; the day after the Lincolns' arrival they moved on to a "location" suggested by John Hanks, about eight miles from Decatur but in the same county. There, "on a bluff overlooking the Sangamon River," was built the log cabin which became Abraham Lincoln's first Illinois home. Thomas Lincoln and his son also built a smokehouse and barn, and split rails to fence their land. In the ensuing winter Abraham and John Hanks split some three thousand rails for Major William Warnick, sheriff of the county, and in another connection Abraham shared in splitting another thousand. That winter was hard; for years it was remembered as the "winter of the deep snow." In the spring Abraham made his second trip to New Orleans and on his return settled in New Salem. Thomas Lincoln removed to Coles County, then adjacent to Macon.

State Architect Charles Herrick Hammond chose as the sculptor of this memorial Fred M. Torrey, who had worked with Hammond on other commissions. Torrey's name is familiar to Lincolnians as the creator of the statuettes of "Lincoln, the Ranger" and "Lincoln, the Circuit Rider," in the corridors of the Lincoln Monument at Springfield. A West Virginian by birth, Torrey studied for four years at the Chicago Art Institute, and was for several years an assistant to Lorado Taft. He has specialized to some extent in architectural sculpture, and his work may be seen on numerous important buildings and at universities in Chicago and other cities; but he has worked in nearly all sculptural fields. Among his works are four panels for the Louisiana Capitol at Baton Rouge, the decorations for the State Medical School in New Orleans, the "Stephen A. Douglas" at Winchester, Illinois, and the notable Mann Memorial in Topeka, Kansas. Torrey's wife, well known as Mabel Landrum, is also a sculptor, working especially on figurines of children. The husband and the wife use the same studio, but work independently. One of Torrey's "Lincolns" which we hope in good time may reach the public is "Lincoln Walks at Midnight," derived from the famous poem by Vachel Lindsay.

The three citizens of Decatur appointed by Governor Dwight H. Green as Hammond's associates on the memorial commission had as one of their first problems the selection of an appropriate site. A knoll on the Lincoln farm was contemplated, but as "it was undeveloped and surrounded by cornfields" and there was "no possible chance of its being made into a park," this idea was abandoned. The initial suggestion that the statue be erected on the campus of James Millikin University was made by its president, Dr. J. Walter Malone, whose argument, naturally, was that every day thousands of young men and women in their formative years would see this "Lincoln." There it is today, a seated figure eight and a half feet high, on a four-foot pedestal, in front of the University's Administration Building.

Standing at a little distance to examine the bronze figure, we see a young giant, with hair rolled back from his forehead, sleeves turned up and collar open, sitting on a stump with one foot resting on a log, in a position which looks cramped; he is lost in thought and indifferent to bodily comfort. His axe lies beside him; the left hand grips an open book. His face is grim, his jaw is set, the cheekbones are high. The eyes stare straight, but this "Lincoln" sees nothing and hears nothing. Even a hurried observer will catch the look of determination written all over that face. Has the young man reached some decision after a careful review of his personal problems? Has a line in that open page fired his ambitions anew?

The sculptor writes of a choice between the axe and the book. The look is that of a strong-willed workingman who sees a vision of what his future shall be. He will "strive on"; he "will be ready"; he is making his choice at the crossroads of life.

This "Lincoln" was dedicated on October 24, 1948. Dr. George Dinsmore Stoddard, president of the University of Illinois, made the principal address. Mrs. Celia Lincoln Sawyer, a fourth cousin of Abraham Lincoln, living near Decatur, unveiled the statue in the presence of a great throng, including the University student body.

SOURCES: Correspondence with, and material furnished by, Mr. Fred M. Torrey; Harry E. Pratt, *Lincoln 1809–1839.*

Daniel Chester French

DR. HENRY W. BELLOWS, the distinguished minister of the Church of All Souls in New York City and founder and president of the United States Sanitary Commission, in a magazine article published in January, 1870, described a Lincoln Memorial project then under discussion. The proposed structure was to be seventy feet in height, triangular in shape, "with truncated angles." At the base would be six equestrian bronze statues of great Civil War generals; at "the second story" twenty-one "colossal bronze statues of the chief statesmen and philanthropists, or civilians," of the war period; and a statue, "larger than life, of Mr. Lincoln, seated and signing the Emancipation Proclamation," at the top. Besides all this the memorial would carry several groups of allegorical figures depicting the establishment, progress, and abolition of slavery, and bas-reliefs showing the firing on Fort Sumter, Lee's surrender, and the passage by Congress of the abolition amendments to the Constitution. It is difficult to visualize the monument thus described, but not at all difficult to realize the profound regret with which later generations would have looked on the structure had it ever been erected.

Dr. Bellows wrote with becoming discretion. He did not want the enterprise defeated: a monument "ought to be built while the consciousness of the political, military and philanthropic achievements of the war is fresh and infallible, so that it shall be the honest expression of the very people who quenched the rebellion, and who know how and by what agencies and agents they did it!" The result, he continued, should be "grand and majestic, with something of the vastness and roughness of this stage of the popular taste," but it must at least be "an honest expression of American largeness of feeling and grandeur of purpose." This plan seemed to Dr. Bellows to have "more elements of success" than any other of the many memorial projects under consideration in different sections of the country. He had his doubts, however. The monument "was designed and will be erected by Clark Mills," a man who had "forced his way from the plasterer's trade up to the artist's vocation," a man of "colossal enterprise, self-confidence, and swiftness of execution." The "more learned artists" of the time deprecated Mills' works, but it was easier to laugh at them than to excel them.

A voluntary group of citizens got behind the scheme, and in the last week of March, 1867, Congress passed a bill incorporating the Lincoln Monument Association. The act constituted a corporation for "erecting a monument in Washington commemorative of the Great Charter of emancipation and universal liberty in America." Among the twenty-nine incorporators were James Harlan, senator from Iowa and prospective father-in-law of Robert Todd Lincoln, who became the president of the corporation; Senator John Conness of California, who had introduced the bill; Representative Shelby M. Cullom of Illinois, an old friend of Lincoln; and Nathaniel P. Banks of Massachusetts. The corporation was empowered to collect money by voluntary contributions, and to own property exempt from taxation. Gifts came in, mainly from the West, ranging from twenty-five cents to a hundred dollars each. In 1868 the Secretary of War was authorized to give the Association "damaged and captured cannon out of which to cast the statues of the principal figures in the Memorial," contingent upon the possession of $100,000 cash on hand by Francis E. Spinner, Treasurer of the United States and also treasurer of the Monument Association.

For some time the corporation looked like a going concern; while money came in slowly, there was no slackening in the current. But methods "not wholly delicate" were used by the "energetic agent" of the corporation in soliciting contributions: should not the friends of the men whose faces would be on display in the monument contribute to it? Dr. Bellows regarded this way of doing things as "one of the vulgarities inherent in republics." That influential clergyman was in a somewhat ambiguous position, believing that the nation must provide a suitable memorial to the martyred President, but unable to endorse the movement then under way. "We can expect little of really symbolic beauty and aesthetic perfectness in the products of the immediate participants or spectators of the great war," he wrote; it was "too early for painting, poetry, and sculpture to make the best use of the materials which the Civil War has so properly furnished for the muses of the future." As to poetry, Dr. Bellows was wrong — witness Walt Whitman and James Russell Lowell. Both with respect to architecture and sculpture, he was right.

For nearly three score years the nation waited for a truly great Lincoln Memorial in the national capital. During the period of waiting six attempts were made. A bill introduced by Senator Cullom late in 1901 was reported adversely by the Committee on the Library. In 1902 Cullom secured passage of a bill which President Roosevelt signed, but nothing beyond studies and reports resulted. In 1908 Representative Samuel W. McCall of Massachusetts could obtain only a committee report on his bill. In December of that year Senator Charles W. F. Dick's concurrent resolution died in committee. Early in 1909 a similar resolution by Senator Dick failed in the House. Even in February, 1909, the centenary month of Lincoln's birth, Representative McCall could again obtain only a favorable committee report.

At last Senator Cullom and Joseph G. Cannon of Illinois, former Speaker of the House, obtained passage of a bill for a commission to secure plans. President Taft signed this bill on Lincoln's birthday, 1911. The President was *ex officio* chairman of the commission created by this act; Cullom, Cannon, McCall, George Peabody Wetmore of Rhode Island, Hernando DeSoto Money of Mississippi, and Champ Clark of Missouri were the associate members. In the ensuing eleven years the commission held thirty-one formal meetings, filling vacancies as they occurred. Only Taft, Cannon, and McCall of the original body survived until the Memorial was dedicated in 1922. The commission chose the site for the Memorial, selected Henry Bacon to prepare the final plan, Daniel Chester French to design and construct the statue and the pedestal, and Jules Guérin to execute the decorative paintings. Many unforeseen problems had to be solved. It became clear in time that the dimensions of the statue must be greatly increased; it was decided to substitute marble for bronze; while the Memorial itself did not settle, the terrace wall around it was found to be sinking, and this fault had to be rectified.

The commission had the benefit of wise advice throughout its existence. "The Commission claims no credit," said Taft on dedication day, "except that it asked those who knew what to do, and did it." The Commission on Fine Arts studied many proposed locations for the Memorial, holding always that the structure must combine beauty and grandeur, and recommended the Potomac Park site. John Hay well stated their idea that "the monument must stand alone, remote from the common habitations of man, apart from the turmoil and business of the city, isolated, distinguished, and serene." It should stand on the axis of the Capitol and the Washington Monument, but must not compete with them in height. The vista down the line of Dome, Obelisk, and Temple is more than two miles long.

Americans recognize on sight the building which arose on this site. The colonnade around the walls is 188 feet long and 118 feet wide. The names of the thirty-six states of Lincoln's time are on the frieze, and those of the forty-eight states of today on the walls above the columns. The structure is Doric, but Ionic columns divide the interior into three chambers. The central chamber contains the statue, while the wall of one of the chambers carries a massive stone tablet on which is carved the Gettysburg Address. The Second Inaugural Address is similarly inscribed on the opposite wall. Guérin's murals are on the walls above these addresses. The beauty of the scene is enhanced by landscaping and by the reflecting pool. The cost of the Memorial proper was $2,900,000.

The work did not escape savage criticism in this land of free speech, and, while most of the attacks were founded on ignorance and incomplete information, some came from competent critics. Gutzon Borglum is reported to have said as early as 1912: "In heaven's name, in Abraham Lincoln's name, don't ask the American people even to associate a Greek temple with the first great American." The *Independent* declared the proposed building to be "a public confession of architectural insolvency," and a year later avowed that "Lincoln was more Gothic than Greek" and that his "forebears who built a log house were better architects than those who are now in control at Washington." Various resolutions of protest, one by the Illinois chapter of the American Institute of Architects, were adopted.

But there was also an abundance of spirited rebuttal. A son of John La Farge defended Bacon's design ably in the *Independent,* making the point that the temple would stand for the spirit of Lincoln and would have nothing to do with the surroundings of his early years. Ralph Adams Cram scored heavily when he wrote: "I can admit the validity of the criticisms that may be offered, and in spite of them still hold that the architect could have done nothing nobler than this, since life itself could give no impulse towards a thing more original and contemporaneous." As a thing of beauty the Memorial "stuns and stills us all by its masterliness." It does not achieve vitality, "instinct with the breath of flourishing life," for this is an age of concrete and steel frames. The demand is made for something new and indigenous as an expression of Lincoln; the demand is easy, but the driving force that alone can produce new art forms is not here. The temple does not express the externals of the man, nor his humor and manners, but "the qualities that made him great, the nobility of soul, the deep sense of honour, unselfishness and self-sacrifice, the tenderness and loving-kindness, are things that are unchangeable from generation to generation and command the same symbolical expression through the art of any time or mode." The Memorial "does fittingly show forth the inherent nobility of the man it commemorates," and it "well expresses the eternal reverence of a nation." Henry Bacon was "supremely right, to go back to the finest things we can find in some period of the past when art was an integral part of life."

A year after the dedication of the Memorial, Mr. Bacon's fellow-craftsmen rendered him a dramatic testimonial for his creation of one of the most beautiful buildings in the world. On that evening in May, 1923, the President of the United States bestowed on Bacon the highest honor within the gift of the American Institute of Architects, the Gold Medal; and the ceremony took place on the steps of the Lincoln Memorial.

Though we have no account of the method by which the commission selected Daniel Chester French to create the statue, there is no risk in assuming that the commissioners took advice, consulted records, and made comparisons. The public has endorsed their decision with enthusiastic unanimity. How splendidly the sculptor rose to that challenge!

"Dan" French, as he was called throughout his life, was born in Exeter, New Hampshire, in 1850, and spent what his wife called his "most crucial years" on a farm in the vicinity of Concord, Massachusetts. His parents noted his liking for taxidermy, but the feat which really excited the family occurred late in December, 1868. As the story is told, "Dan" "came into the house whittling away most industriously on a raw turnip." He added a few finishing touches and held it up to view, and there was applause "as the family recognized a frog dressed in man's clothing, skilfully carved out of the hard vegetable." They encouraged him to look forward to a career in art. Proper facilities for study were few in Boston at that time. Dr. William Rimmer instructed French in artistic anatomy; he spent hours at a time in the Athenaeum looking at the Greek casts; and Miss May Alcott, the artistic member of Bronson Alcott's family, who had studied abroad, provided him with sculptor's clay and modeling tools.

The town of Concord decided to erect a statue of the Minute Man on the battlefield near "the rude bridge that arched the flood" in 1775. Young French boldly submitted a sketch, first to Ralph Waldo Emerson and then to Judge E. Rockwood Hoar, in private, and the recommendation of the latter in town meeting is said to have induced his townsmen to take a chance on the ambitious young man. All the instruction "Dan" had enjoyed had been with Dr. Rimmer, plus a few weeks in the studio of J. Q. A. Ward. His models were made in a badly-lighted room in a Boston business block. Lorado Taft's careful statement is that "he had the intelligence to appreciate his subject, the imagination to conceive it vividly and simply, and the skill — or, perhaps, considering his youth, the ingenuity, to express it in adequate terms. . . . On the whole, it was, and is, a figure to be enthusiastic about. The applause which went up on the unveiling was not the usual perfunctory hurrah." That first work "was done with conviction and charged with emotion." The unveiling took place on the centenary of the day "the shot heard round the world" was fired, in the presence of the President and other dignitaries from Washington, while Lowell,

Longfellow, and Emerson marched in the procession. But it was French's father who did the unveiling: "Dan" had gone with natural eagerness to Italy in the preceding year, and never saw his work in bronze until he returned to America.

French spent two profitable years with Thomas Ball, who invited him to work in his studio in Florence. He met many influential American and British artists, musicians, and writers. There followed a couple of years in Washington and nearly a decade in Boston and Concord. In 1887 French established a studio in New York, and two years later moved to Stockbridge. There was no need for him to seek the public any longer. Among the works which came from his diligent hands, to mention only a few, are the statue of Rufus Choate in the Boston Courthouse; the bust of Emerson, of which the sage said, "That is the face that I shave"; the John Harvard in Cambridge, the Lewis Cass in the Capitol in Washington, the group of Gallaudet and his first pupil before the Columbian Institute for the Deaf, also in Washington; the groups symbolizing Asia, Africa, Europe, and America for the New York Customs House; and the celebrated memorial for Martin Milmore — "The Angel of Death and the Sculptor" — in Forest Hills Cemetery in Boston.

Our special interest is with his two "Lincolns" — the standing figure in the Nebraska city named for the President, and the seated "Lincoln" in the temple in Potomac Park. The city of Lincoln, Nebraska, is the capital of a state of rolling prairies and flat horizons. Its Memorial Capitol was designed by Bertram Grosvenor Goodhue of Boston with careful consideration of its physical setting. It is an architectural triumph. From the center of the basic square, long and only two stories in height, soars a four-hundred-foot tower, with a memorial chamber under the dome at the top, in token of the ideals and aspirations of the people. Decorations reflecting the history of the state and symbolizing the progress of mankind adorn practically every room in the building, culminating in the "Sower" at the summit of the dome. The effect is inspirational. The name of Lincoln occupies the position of honor in the governor's reception room, between those of Franklin and Marshall. In the Memorial Chamber is carved an inscription from the Second Inaugural Address.

French's "Lincoln" is erected about seventy-five feet from the west entrance to this building, facing west. Back of it, on a marble slab measuring twenty feet by twelve, is inscribed the Gettysburg Address. The nature of the dedicatory ceremonies for this monument on Labor Day, 1912, may readily be guessed: patriotic songs were sung, the Gettysburg Address was read, there were speeches by Governor Chester H. Aldrich and others, with an oratorical climax by William Jennings Bryan, whose address we have been unable to obtain. Two veterans of the Civil War unveiled the statue.

The sculptor shows the President standing, with his arms hanging straight and his hands clasped. His head is tilted forward, as if he were thinking of the address he is about to make. Mr. French is reported to have said that he "kind of felt as if Lincoln must have stood like that for a few minutes before he began his Gettysburg speech." A pleasing story tells of the posing of the figure. The Monument Association at Lincoln had commissioned Frank M. Hall to select a committee, which in turn would choose the sculptor. Someone told Mr. Hall that his mother had seen Lincoln several times on his speaking tours, and had noticed his curious way of standing before he began to speak, with hands clasped as though arranging his ideas. Hall was just ready to unbox a small model which French had sent him, and when the box was opened, to his surprise and delight, there stood Lincoln in precisely that same pose.

This work has often been compared with Saint-Gaudens' standing "Lincoln." The verdicts have been various. The basic ideas are similar; the President is about to speak to the people. The Nebraska "Lincoln" has more of an emotional quality, perhaps suggested by the gripping of the hands. The Saint-Gaudens does not depict Lincoln at any defined hour of his presidency; the address inscribed upon the stone behind the French exactly dates that bronze figure. The President is on the field at Gettysburg, surrounded by the graves of the men who fell in that terrific struggle. He has listened to the oration in which Edward Everett portrayed those three days of carnage. It is a solemn hour; he is deeply moved. The fortunes of the nation are still uncertainly balanced. The "Lincoln" at the Nebraska Capitol is the heavily burdened man who is oath-bound to preserve the Union. His mind is flooded with the exalted concept of the future of America which he is about to put before a somewhat tired and impatient throng. He is intensely anxious that his message shall be understood, containing as it does the central idea of his life. In that sad face we read his thoughts. With many currents of feeling surging in his heart, he will presently lift his head and speak.

It was two years and three months after the dedication of the Nebraska statue that the Lincoln Memorial Commission named Mr. French to create the statue for which the temple in Washington was intended. For this central feature of the building French designed a seated "Lincoln," probably the largest marble statue ever made. The figure is nineteen feet in height; standing, it would tower twenty-eight feet. It is composed of twenty-eight blocks of Georgia white marble, which were cut separately and assembled only on the pedestal in the Memorial. They fitted, we are told, as perfectly as if carved from one block and sawn apart. The width of the work, including the drapery over the chair, is nineteen feet. The pedestal of Tennessee marble is ten feet high.

Memorial Day, May 30, 1922, was appointed for the presentation of the building and the statue to the government of the United States. In every respect it was a great occasion. A complaisant weatherman provided a perfect day. Among the thirty-five hundred invited guests were representatives of all departments of the government, and diplomatic corps, numerous patriotic organizations, and many distinguished citizens. The vast multitude for whom no special provision could be made covered acres of ground, from the reserved section to and around the reflecting pool. Amplifiers carried the speeches throughout the grounds. Applause greeted arriving dignitaries; the ovation of the day was bestowed on Robert Todd Lincoln as he walked to his seat on the platform. Chairman William Howard Taft of the Commission, then Chief Justice of the United States, served as presiding officer. The invocation was offered by Dr. Wallace Radcliffe, pastor emeritus of the New York Avenue Presbyterian Church, which Lincoln had attended. Bishop Samuel W. Fallows of the Reformed Episcopal Church, Chaplain-in-Chief of the Grand Army of the Republic, offered the prayer of dedication.

All the addresses were excellent; any sensitive person reading them today will be moved, not by any purple passages, but by their simplicity and lofty tone. The principal of Tuskegee Institute, Dr. Robert R. Moton, must have been an impressive figure, as he stood at the feet of Abraham Lincoln and spoke as the representative of his race. Contrasting the pioneers of freedom and the pioneers of bondage, he traced the "development of the two forces that were to shape the destiny of the nation." There are, said Dr. Moton, "in all our vast country none more reverent than those twelve million black Americans who, with their fellow-countrymen of every race, pay devout homage to him who was for them, more truly than for any other group, the author of their freedom." The speaker dwelt on the Negro's obligation to justify the price paid for his freedom. The poignant significance of one passage is even more evident today than when the words were spoken: "No one is more sensible than the Negro himself of his incongruous position in the great American republic. . . . Today black men and white in increasing numbers are working together in the spirit of Abraham Lincoln to establish in fact what his death established in principle — that a nation conceived in liberty and dedicated to the proposition that all men are created equal can endure and prosper and serve mankind."

Edwin Markham arose to read what he described as a "revised version" of his Lincoln poem. What a picturesque figure he was! In "the Whirlwind Hour" darkening upon the nation, he said, the "Norn Mother" made "a Man to match the mountains and the sea." Lincoln had "the rectitude and patience of the cliff" and "the good-will of the rain that loves all leaves." His was "the pity of the snow that hides all scars" and "the tolerance and equity of light." His soul was stilled "by the hush of spacious prairies"; his words "were oaks in acorns"; his thoughts were "roots that firmly gript the granite earth." "Up from the log cabin to the Capitol, he came," and

> He held his place —
> Held the long purpose like a growing tree —
> Held on through blame and faltered not at praise,
> And when he fell in whirlwind, he went down
> As when a lordly cedar, green with boughs,
> Goes down with a great shout upon the hills,
> And leaves a lonesome place against the sky.

Mr. Taft's presentation address, which followed, was studded with epigrammatic sentences containing indefinitely expansible ideas. "The years have faded the figures of Lincoln's contemporaries and he stands grandly alone. . . . We feel a closer touch with him than with living men. . . . The harmony of his message with every popular aspiration for freedom proves his universality." The Chief Justice briefly reviewed the progress of American art, and outlined the work of the Memorial Commission. It was "well that half a century should pass before his people's national tribute to him takes form in marble, that it should wait until a generation instinct with the growing and deepening perception of the real Lincoln has had time to develop an art adequate to the expression of his grandeur." Taft called the Memorial the "culmination of the highest art of which America is capable, and therefore fit to commemorate a people's love for the Nation's savior and its greatest leader." It stands of right on the banks of the Potomac — "visible in its distant beauty from the Capitol whose great dome typifies the Union which he saved, seen in all its grandeur from Arlington, where lie the Nation's honored dead who fell in the conflict, Union and Confederate alike. It marks the restoration of the brotherly love of the two sections in this Memorial of one who is as dear to the hearts of the South as to those of the North. . . . Here is a shrine at which all can worship." Turning to President Warren G. Harding, Taft concluded: "Mr. President, in the name of the Commission I have the honor to deliver this Lincoln Memorial into your keeping."

In his response President Harding reviewed a few of the questions which had confronted Lincoln in the days when "passion was aflame." In the Constitution there was "an ambiguity which only a baptism in blood could efface." In his struggle for unity Lincoln had proved himself "incomparably the greatest of our Presidents." At the end of this, the longest address of the day, the President said: "Fifty-seven years ago this people gave him from their ranks, sprung from their own fiber, this plain man, holding their common ideals. They gave him first to the service of the Nation in the hour of peril, then to their Pantheon of fame. With them and by them he is enshrined and exalted forever. Today, American gratitude, love, and appreciation, give to Abraham Lincoln this lone white temple, a pantheon for him alone."

Of the statue in the chamber behind the speakers, Mr. Taft had said in his address: "The colossal figure of the Beloved, . . . the work of . . . one of our greatest sculptors, fills the memorial hall with an overwhelming sense of Lincoln's presence." For a full understanding of the masterpiece wrought by Daniel Chester French in the seventh decade of his life, we must linger long in its presence. For the comprehension of its meaning many factors must be taken into account. Lord Charnwood, studying the work from photographs, seized upon "the delicate minuteness" with which the hands had been treated. In a long letter to the sculptor, Lincoln's English biographer expressed his warm admiration for the work. Writing in a singularly objective manner, he dwelt on many items that American observers might easily overlook. Into that statue, said Charnwood, the artist "must have put much of his heart's blood."

The Civil War President sits in a massive chair of state, the sides of which end at the front in flat-faced pillars. On these are carved Roman fasces, symbolic of the power and indivisibility of the American Union. Atop these pillars, as on the arms of a chair, rest Lincoln's hands. There is only a slight indication of tension in the fingers; they seem almost to caress the thonged rods below them; but these are powerful hands, moulded for action. The pose of the figure conveys the same suggestion. The primary impression is of rest; the muscles are relaxed; but this is not the man who sprawled for comfort in the office back in Springfield. The President is calm, his head high, his torso erect; the body is instinct with life, ready on the instant for action.

When the statue was first shown, "Lincoln Triumphant" was suggested as a title for it. That was not a happy proposal. Assuming that the sculptor's intention was to represent for all the people and for all time the man who had saved the Union, there was nothing of the exaltation and pride, of the arrogance with which a Roman general displayed his trophies, in Lincoln's heart with the ending of the war. He rejoiced that the war had ended with victory for his cause, but the man who made the unforgettable visit to Richmond and whose mind was filled with plans for reconstruction without penalty was never more gentle and unassuming than in the early days of April, 1865. He was weary, and sad over the wreckage which the whirlwind had caused. In the Second Inaugural Lincoln told what was in his heart, and that same story is told in the statue in the Memorial Temple. The furrows in that face — the sorrow in those eyes — the solemnity with which in reverie he looks back upon the wonder of the four years of his presidency; he had not willed the war, but the war had come, and in the sight of the nation and of the watching world he had sworn to "preserve, protect and defend the Constitution of the United States." He had not controlled events, he had been controlled by them; and events had made necessary the raising of armies, the sacrifice of thousands of lives and of millions of treasure, and a proclamation for the liberation of the slaves. Amid derision and obloquy, and the selfish demands of lower-minded men, Lincoln, in the faith that "right makes might," had dared to do his duty as he understood it.

There he sits, a majestic figure, with the marks of a mighty struggle stamped on his face, and rests a little while. He looks out at the towering obelisk which expresses the veneration of the people for the Father of their Country. Beyond, he sees the great dome of the Capitol — the dome which had been completed during the years of war. He had studied maps on which lines had been drawn between the North and South; now, that dome stands for an undivided country. He gazes beyond the obelisk and the dome into the future, thinking of his hopes and plans for the uniting of hearts and hands that should follow upon the passing of the "mighty scourge of war." Did not both sections "read the same Bible and pray to the same God?" No longer must each "invoke His aid against the other." So much remained for him to do; he must "strive on. . . ."

What the genius of the artist has produced in enduring marble must be supplemented by the vision and the imagination of the observer. We look up and read the lines, written by Royal Cortissoz, inscribed upon the wall above the head of the statue:

IN THIS TEMPLE
AS IN THE HEARTS OF THE PEOPLE
FOR WHOM HE SAVED THE UNION
THE MEMORY OF ABRAHAM LINCOLN
IS ENSHRINED FOREVER

SOURCES: Adeline Adams, *Daniel Chester French, Sculptor,* 1932; Josephine Latham Swayne, ed., *The Story of Concord Writers,* 1906; Edward F. Concklin, *The Lincoln Memorial,* Washington, 1927; H. P. Caemmerer, *Washington, the National Capital,* 1932; Mrs. Daniel Chester French, *Memories of a Sculptor's Wife,* 1928; Johnson Brigham, *James Harlan,* 1913; Leonard R. Nelson, *Nebraska's Memorial Capitol,* 1931; the *Congressional Globe* and *Congressional Record;* numerous magazine articles, articles in art and architectural periodicals, and newspaper clippings.

The article by Dr. Bellows appeared in *Old and New,* January, 1870.

Addendum: The Story of
Henry J. Ellicott's LINCOLN

IN 1941 Mr. Stefan Lorant published an attractive volume covering the life of Lincoln in photographs. Informed Lincolnians noted at once a remarkable picture showing a coffin, surrounded by a guard of honor, under the dome of the Capitol in Washington. The scene purports to be the martyred President lying in state in 1865. On a high pedestal facing the coffin stands a statue, seemingly carved in marble, of the man whose body the coffin is assumed to contain. A plate on the front of the pedestal carries the name "Henry J. Ellicott."

Most Lincoln students were sure there was something wrong about the picture. They noticed variations in certain details from the known facts. The present writer published the result of his own investigation, with facts from others who also went on the trail, in the *Lincoln Herald* of February, 1947. Bert S. Sheldon, captain of police at the Capitol, searched widely for facts in Washington. Just who made the final score may be open to question. We claimed in our magazine article to have initiated the search and to have offered a reasonable explanation of the problems involved. Mr. Lorant most courteously gave us all the information he possessed — the original negative bore a certain number in the National Archives, and the caption was correct: "Lincoln's Remains Lying in State at the Capitol."

Our first task was to find the facts about Ellicott. Born in August, 1847, of an eminent Maryland family, he studied with famous teachers at the National Academy of Design. His gifts were early recognized. Many "works," including the equestrian "General Hancock" in Washington for which Congress appropriated $50,000, are attributed to him. He lived in Washington, and served as chief modeler for ethnology groups shown at the National Historical Museum. But no information concerning a Lincoln statue was discovered.

There *was* a "Lincoln," however, and young as he was, Ellicott was its maker. We noted that contemporary prints referred to it as of marble, while the *New York Times* and the *Boston Journal* said it was of plaster. That was a discovery. But the big discovery followed: in

Harper's Weekly of August 29, 1868, a picture was found showing Ellicott's statue in the Capitol at the lying in state of — Thaddeus Stevens! And the *New York Times* had the statement that Stevens' casket was placed "immediately in front of the plaster statue of Mr. Lincoln." The statue was a sculptor's model, not a finished work, although it looked like marble. And the Archives' data were incorrect.

At the time of "Thad" Stevens' death, the members of the two houses of Congress were not in Washington, nor were the officers of the House. The duty of arranging for the funeral fell therefore to the Sergeant-at-Arms of the Senate, and the Superintendent of Public Buildings "issued the formal orders." The body was removed to the Capitol, the rotunda was kept open, a Negro company of Zouaves was chosen as a guard of honor. *Harper's Weekly* stated that about six thousand persons, white and black, viewed the body. In that period of bitter strife the Radicals decided to "capitalize the passing of the greatest radical of them all for purposes not altogether magnanimous."

As to the origin of Ellicott's plaster model, we offer one suggestion — Lot Flannery's marble "Lincoln" was dedicated, as we have seen, on April 15, 1868. There had been a lively competition for the award. "A great many models in clay" had been submitted to the committee, we are told. Flannery's was their unanimous choice. We think it very probable that Ellicott's model was entered for the competition. We do not know what may have been its ultimate disposition. Ellicott died on February 11, 1901.

In our magazine article above referred to, we indicated our wish that any authentic additional facts for the story of Ellicott's "Lincoln" would be welcome. None has been received. The contemporary photograph reproduced here is from the files of The Lincoln National Life Foundation, Fort Wayne, Indiana.

Index

351